PASSPORT to
ADVENTURE

Cover design by Gerald Monks
Cover design resources from iStockphoto.com
Inside design by Aaron Troia

The author assumes full responsibility for the accuracy of all facts and quotations as cited in this book.

You can obtain additional copies of this book by calling toll-free 1-800-765-6955 or by visiting http://www.adventistbookcenter.com.

Library of Congress Cataloging-in-Publication Data

Names: Aguilera, Rich, author.
Title: Passport to adventure : daily devotions for juniors / Rich Aguilera.
Description: Nampa : Pacific Press Publishing, 2016.
Identifiers: LCCN 2016027917 | ISBN 9780816361892 (pbk.)
Subjects: LCSH: Junior high school students—Prayers and devotions. |
   Travel—Religious aspects—Christianity—Prayers and devotions—Juvenile literature. |
   General Conference of Seventh-Day Adventists—Prayers and devotions—Juvenile literature.
Classification: LCC BV4850 .A38 2016 | DDC 242/.62—dc23 LC record available at
https://lccn.loc.gov/2016027917

July 2016

PASSPORT to ADVENTURE

Daily Devotions for Juniors

with *Rich Aguilera* "THE MUD GUY"

Pacific Press®
Publishing Association

Nampa, Idaho | Oshawa, Ontario, Canada
www.pacificpress.com

The Real Celebration

For the Lord himself will come down from heaven with a commanding shout, with the voice of the archangel, and with the trumpet call of God. First, the believers who have died will rise from their graves. Then, together with them, we who are still alive and remain on the earth will be caught up in the clouds to meet the Lord in the air. Then we will be with the Lord forever.
1 THESSALONIANS 4:16, 17, NLT

Three buddies and I were traveling through Europe when I was in college. We were on our two-week Christmas break. During the days leading up to the New Year, the guys in my travel group and I were trying to decide where we should spend New Year's Eve. London, Rome, and Barcelona were ideas, but in the end we decided on Paris. By December of that school year, we had been living and studying in France for almost four months. Most of us had picked up the language pretty well by then, so we liked the idea of being somewhere that we could communicate with people.

We arrived in Paris at 8:00 A.M. on December 31 and found a place to stay that night. Twelve hours later, by 8:00 P.M., the main street in Pairs, Champs-Élysées, was filled with tens of thousands of people. By 9:00 P.M., all the cars on that street had been gridlocked in traffic and did not move again till after midnight. It became a mile-long parking lot, ten lanes of cars across. Over the next hour, more and more people poured into the street. Fireworks were going off and people were singing and celebrating in the streets. The celebration peaked at midnight and continued into the night. By 12:30 A.M., we were trying to get to the metro station to get back to our room. Thousands of others had the same idea. If you do not like crowded places, this would have been a nightmare for you. So many people were smashed into our metro train that a young woman a few feet away passed out. We finally made it back to our room at 3:00 A.M. after fighting to get through thousands of people celebrating the New Year.

At the Second Coming, there will actually be two big celebrations. First, believers who died will rise from their graves. That's going to be a pretty unusual reunion, since we might be meeting people who died thousands of years ago! Next, God's people who are alive and those who have been resurrected will together be taken up into the clouds for an even bigger reunion with Jesus. Wow! I can't wait for all that to happen!

Uncertainty on the Beach

"Keep this Book of the Law always on your lips; meditate on it day and night, so that you may be careful to do everything written in it. Then you will be prosperous and successful."
JOSHUA 1:8, NIV

I recently went to Fort Myers Beach, Florida, for spring break with my family. I was sitting in a chair enjoying the sun as it began to set. Since it was late in the day, there was only a group of three guys in the water in front of me about chest deep. Everyone else was playing on the beach. Suddenly, the three guys started running toward the shore yelling, "Shark! Shark!" A few feet behind them, I immediately noticed a fin sticking out of the water. You'll never guess what I did. I jumped up out of my chair and started running into the ocean, passing the three guys who were rushing out of the water as fast as they could. You must think I'm crazy, but I'm not. When I saw the fin, it only took me a split second to recognize that the fin actually belonged to a dolphin. My younger son was nearby, and I told him to follow me in.

A lone dolphin had wandered onto our beach and was swimming north along the beach about fifty feet out. My son and I followed him as long as we could, at one point getting to within about twenty feet of the dolphin. You see, the day before, we had spent part of a day with some friends on their boat. As we cruised on the boat, we spotted a bunch of dolphins swimming around. In one instance, we had stopped the boat because a pod of five dolphins spent about ten minutes swimming around our boat, playing, spinning, and splashing a foot or two away from the hull. We were thrilled with the little free show they gave us, and that time we spent with those dolphins is the reason why I instantly knew how to tell the difference between a shark and dolphin fin.

When we spend time with God, we learn more about Him. That's how it works. The same is true for friends—the more time you spend with them, the more you know them. Make time each day to spend with God praying and reading the Bible. Those are the best ways to get closer to God.

The Getaway

"But when you pray, go into your room, close the door and pray to your Father, who is unseen. Then your Father, who sees what is done in secret, will reward you."
MATTHEW 6:6, NIV

Every once in a while I get the privilege of visiting an incredibly unique and rare place. Several years ago, my wife and I were traveling in Greece, and one of the places on our list to visit was the remote town of Meteora, five hours north of Athens on the road toward Albania. You're probably wondering what would drive us to want to go visit such an out-of-the-way location. I have a reason, and it's a little embarrassing to admit. I once saw a movie with some scenes that were filmed there. I didn't want to visit the place because of the movie, but it was the movie that made me aware that this place existed. After a five-hour train ride from Athens to a town called Kalambaka, we exited the train station. We next needed to find a way to get to the place we were going, up in the mountains outside of the city.

The word *meteora* literally means "suspended in the air," and it is the location where six monasteries were built starting in the 1500s, high atop a bunch of natural rock pillars, some that stood more than twelve hundred feet tall! Originally there were more, but these were the ones that were left. Imagine standing at the bottom of a cliff looking a thousand feet straight up a cliff, and at the top there was a large monastery complex. Keep in mind, there were no stairs to get up there. Access to the monasteries was difficult, and it was that way on purpose, because the monks there clearly wanted to live in solitude. To get up there, it required either long ladders that were lashed together, or large nets and baskets that were used to haul up people and supplies.

Sometimes it's necessary to just get away, especially when you spend time with God in prayer. Our verse today reminds us that some of the best quality prayer time you will experience happens when you hide out in your room and secretly pray to your Father in heaven. Find time today and every day to retreat to a quiet place to spend time with God.

A Time of War

*"You will hear of wars and rumors of wars, but see to it that you are
not alarmed. Such things must happen, but the end is still to come."*
MATTHEW 24:6, NIV

For many years my wife's parents lived in Atlanta, Georgia. We would drive
down from Michigan to visit them at least four or five times a year for the
weekend. If we stayed Sunday, we'd look for interesting things to do together
around Atlanta. One time we decided to visit Stone Mountain, just north
of Atlanta. We drove up into the beautiful wooded countryside until we
reached this natural landmark. It was quite impressive; it's a huge piece of
granite rock towering almost nine hundred feet above the surrounding area.
We found out that there is a steep hiking trail to the top that is almost three
miles round trip. We huffed and puffed our way up and enjoyed an awesome
view of the surrounding area along with a lovely breeze to cool us off.

Later that evening, we went to the side of the rock face where that evening
there was going to be the Stone Mountain Laser Show Spectacular. We went
around and found this big outdoor grassy theater area with enough space
to seat thousands of people. The rock face had a huge carving of three Civil
War leaders carved into the rock, and it is said to be the largest bas-relief,
or shallow carving, in the world, about the size of two football fields! Once
it was dark, a laser show about the history of Georgia was projected on the
surface of the granite along with narration and music. Major battles took
place in Georgia during the Civil War.

Battles between good and evil have been around for millennia. Long ago,
war arose in heaven when Satan rebelled against God. As the end of time
on earth nears, the Bible says there will be more wars and rumors of wars
here on earth. Prophecy says these are signs of things to come before the
end. Have you looked around recently? As of this writing, there are currently
about a dozen armed conflicts going on right now in the world, in which
more than one thousand people die each year in each one. The end is near.
God is coming soon. Our call is to live each moment as if it's the last.

A Two-Wheel Adventure

"Because he loves me," says the LORD, "I will rescue him; I will protect him, for he acknowledges my name. He will call on me, and I will answer him; I will be with him in trouble, I will deliver him and honor him. With long life I will satisfy him and show him my salvation."
PSALM 91:14–16, NIV

Martha's Vineyard is an island that is part of the state of Massachusetts. It's about twenty miles at its longest and about ten miles at its widest. When I was a kid growing up in Massachusetts, my father decided to take my sister and me biking on a Sunday day trip to Martha's Vineyard. We drove to Woods Hole and boarded the ferry. Our goal was to try to circle the island using a neat bike trail. We passed cute towns and beaches and beautiful colonial homes, and eventually we found a nice place and stopped for lunch. We needed to keep an eye on the clock in order to get back to catch the ferry to take us back home.

Suddenly, about five miles from the port, my bicycle got a flat tire! None of us had any kind of equipment to fix a flat bicycle tire, and we were far from any town in which we could find help. I had a kid's bike, and it was way too small for my dad to ride. And if we walked the last five miles back, we would never make it in time to catch the ferry. We prayed, and then my father looked at me and told me that it would be hard, but that I needed to ride my bicycle with the flat tire all the way back to the ferry. He was right; it was hard. What surprised me was that my dad rode way ahead of me those last five miles. I thought he was leaving me behind, although he was never out of sight. The farther he seemed, the harder I worked to keep up with him.

Years later as a parent, I finally understood that he had gone ahead because it would make me work harder to keep up the pace so we could make it to the ferry before it left. Some would call it "tough love," but it helped me understand that sometimes God allows hard things to happen because He knows what's best for us in the long run. When things get hard, trust God; He wants the best for your whole life, not just the next minute of your life.

A Journey of Biblical Proportions

Your word is a lamp for my feet, a light on my path.
PSALM 119:105, NIV

I was working in the country of Jordan one summer. Each weekend I had the option of taking a trip to explore the surrounding areas. We were in Jordan digging at an archeological site, and considering that we were in lands where biblical events took place, we were always anxious for the weekend to come so we could borrow the staff car and go exploring. One weekend a group of us decided to take the car to the northern border of Jordan. The western border of Jordan touches the country of Israel, but on this day we would be traveling north to a spot where Jordan borders Israel as well as the Golan Heights and Syria. You're probably wondering why we wanted to travel toward that area, and I will tell you in a moment.

Once we had finalized our plans, we eagerly awaited the weekend to come. The time finally came and we packed up the car, got our map, and four of us guys headed out. After a couple of hours of driving, we started to climb higher up a mountain because we were heading up toward a high lookout point right on the border. We finally arrived at the lookout and pulled off the road. We got out and walked to the edge of the overlook spot. Down below us, we could clearly see what we had come there for. Before us we could see the entire Sea of Galilee. This is where the storm thrashed the disciples' boat while Jesus slept. It's where the disciples went out on their boats to fish. This is where Jesus walked on water and where many other miracles were performed. On the northern shore was Capernaum, where Jesus lived.

We are so blessed to have the Bible. People have died trying to obtain this Book. It's filled with amazing stories that God has revealed, which give us an understanding of the history of our universe and how much you as an individual are loved by God. Don't take your Bible for granted; make a habit of reading from it every day and letting God guide your path.

The Border Crossing

The woman said, "I know that Messiah" (called Christ) "is coming.
When he comes, he will explain everything to us." Then Jesus
declared, "I, the one speaking to you—I am he."
JOHN 4:25, 26, NIV

While living in Jordan I decided to take a trip west into the neighboring country of Israel. No one else was able to join me, so this was to be a trip I would have to take all by myself. By then I was quite comfortable finding my way around Jordan, so when the time came, I took a bus from the capital, Amman, down to the border between Jordan and Israel, well below sea level. At the border, the bus crossed over the Jordan River, and a few moments later it stopped at the border crossing point in Israel. The military presence there was noticeably increased. I, along with all the other passengers on the bus, got off and went into a building where, for the next hour or so, I went through a rigorous check of all my papers and possessions. I had a camera with me. The inspector instructed me to take my camera out and remove the lens cap. I did as he said. Next he asked me to show him the camera. I did. After that he asked me something I didn't expect at all. He asked me to take a picture of the ceiling. I didn't quite understand what all this was about, so I proceeded to ask him if I could take a picture of him instead. Bad idea. He had a fit and insisted that I follow his orders and take a picture of the ceiling. So I did. This finally satisfied him that the camera was actually a camera and not a dangerous device.

I finally finished going through all the inspections and questions and was allowed to officially enter the country of Israel! Being there made me think that one of the saddest stories of the Bible is the story of the Jews rejecting their own Messiah. After spending hundreds, even thousands of years awaiting and anticipating His arrival, most Jews didn't recognize Him. They had become so focused on the law that they didn't see that He was the Lawgiver and had precisely fulfilled the prophecy of the coming Messiah. I'm so glad that He is my personal Savior. Make a point of accepting Him as your Savior every day!

Walking in Jesus' Footsteps

"For God did not send his Son into the world to condemn the world, but in order that the world might be saved through him."
JOHN 3:17, ESV

After crossing the border from Jordan to Israel, I found a bus stop right there by the Jordan River. I remember thinking to myself that the Jordan River sure looked small at that location. I went out to the bus stop and purchased my ticket to Jerusalem. Soon a bus came and took us back up the hilly terrain toward Jerusalem. Our first stop was at a city you may have heard of before, Jericho. Although today Jericho is a modern city, the ruins of the old city are still there for anyone to see. I think it's super cool visiting places mentioned in the Bible because it only helps to build my faith.

The bus continued up and to the west until I finally saw the old walls of Jerusalem. The first thing I did when I got off the bus was to pull out my map and the information I had collected before my trip about where I would stay. My plan was to stay at the local Adventist church there. There are not many Adventists in Israel, but I was happy that the local church allowed me to stay there a couple of nights while I visited the area. As I walked along the outer wall of the old city, every once in a while I would hear what sounded like a boom in the sky. I soon discovered that those were sonic booms from Israeli jet fighter planes flying overhead and traveling at the speed of sound.

Once I made it to the inside of the walled city, my goal was to find the Via Dolorosa, the route Jesus took on His way to Calvary when He died to save us from our sins. Soon I was able to find it, and I began to slowly walk along the path. I was brought to tears as I followed the path, knowing that two thousand years ago in that very spot, Jesus carried His cross to His own execution. It hit me that day that the Son of the Creator of the universe, who made me, loves me so much that He was willing to take my punishment on my behalf. Thank God today for His gift of salvation!

The Truth About Gold

Jesus answered: "Watch out that no one deceives you."
MATTHEW 24:4, NIV

My favorite mountain range in the world is the Alps. I was driving though Austria with my wife several years ago, and I found the most amazing small, winding road that went through the Alps. I found myself stopping constantly to take pictures at every pass and turn. Innsbruck is one of those cities with intense Olympic history. The winter Olympics were held in Innsbruck not once but twice, in 1964 and 1976. As you walk around the city, you can still feel the Olympic pride and presence in the streets.

As we walked around the old town that day, we came to what I was told is the most famous square in the city. At one end of it is a building called the Goldenes Dachl, which means "golden roof." As you can imagine from the name, the building has a big gold roof that covers a balcony, where, in the 1500s, the emperor would come out with his wife to observe the festivals in the square below. We were amazed and dazzled by the amount of gold just sitting there out in the open. Since I tend to be curious sometimes, I set out to learn the value of that roof. It was amazing to think so much gold would just be sitting around only about twenty-five feet off the ground. As I learned about that famous gold roof, I soon discovered that the roof was made up of 2,738 fire-gilded copper tiles. Wait a second: copper? What happened to the gold? I had been so gold-struck with the roof that when I found out it was really copper, I felt deceived.

Have you ever felt deceived? Satan is good at that. I think one of his most famous deceptions is getting people to believe in evolution. Remember, Satan is trying to convince people that God isn't real, which means he has to fool people into believing that things suddenly came to life all by themselves, and that our immense, complex universe created itself, plus many other ideas that go against logic, science, and of course, the Bible. Jesus warns us in the Bible not be deceived and to always be ready to share the truth with anyone.

The Jet of Geneva

"I will make them and the places surrounding my hill a blessing. I will send down showers in season; there will be showers of blessing."
EZEKIEL 34:26, NIV

Geneva is the one European city that I am most familiar with. The school I attended for a year in France was just across the border from Geneva, Switzerland, so whenever we students had to go buy something or catch a train, we usually crossed the border into Geneva. During the course of the year, the international border crossing guards became familiar with us and eventually rarely even asked to see our passports as we crossed back and forth almost on a daily basis. We found Geneva to be a wonderful city, clean and modern with many historical areas to enjoy as well.

There is one landmark in Geneva that is above the rest, though. And I literally mean "above the rest." It's called the Jet d'Eau, which means "jet of water." It's basically a fountain but much more powerful than your regular run-of-the-mill fountain because of how high the water is sprayed up into the air. The jet of water is visible throughout the city, and you can even see the jet of water when you fly overhead in an airplane at 33,000 feet! The pumps shoot water straight up into the air more than 450 feet, and at any given moment there are more than 1,800 gallons of water in the air! It's impressive to get close to see where the water is being shot up into the air by such a strong machine. As you know, with gravity, everything that goes up must come down. Visitors often walk out on the stone jetty to get a close look at the fountain. As you walk out, you try to determine how close you can get without getting hosed by the water coming back down. It's not that simple. People forget that when there is any slight change in the wind direction, they can be completely drenched. Can you imagine one thousand eight hundred gallons of water raining down on you all of a sudden?

The book of Ezekiel has a phrase that you may have heard before: "showers of blessing." Seeing the jet of water in Geneva was like a daily reminder that God wants to shower us with blessings every day. Ask God to shower you with blessings today!

The Wet Italian Day

Therefore my heart is glad, and my whole being
rejoices; my flesh also dwells secure.
Psalm 16:9, ESV

Ah, Venice! What a unique city. During my year living in France, I couldn't resist Venice, Italy, and I found myself traveling to Venice four times that year. Every time I went it was a wonderful experience, and I got to explore different areas of the city. Even after my year in Europe, I've returned to Venice at least two more times to visit. If you're not very familiar with Venice, it is a city in northeastern Italy that is located on a group of 118 small islands separated by canals and linked by bridges. There is a lot of wonderful art and architecture to appreciate there. Every time I went, I had a wonderful time, except the last time I went something was different: the tide was high. The Italians call it *acqua alta,* which literally means "high water."

Venice is prepared to absorb about a three-foot increase of sea level, but any more than that and the city starts to flood. If the water goes up another twenty inches, it would cause almost half of Venice to be under water! When we arrived the last time I went, I took the boat taxi around the city, and we were amazed to see that many of the homes were flooded on the first floor. The famous San Marcos Plaza, which is usually filled with thousands of tourists, was deserted because it had become one giant lake. Instead of enjoying Venice as I had gotten used to, we spent the entire time looking at how different Venice was during *acqua alta.* In addition to the high tide, it was raining that day, and as you can imagine, we got pretty soaked that day in Venice.

It would have been really easy to have a grumpy attitude that day. After all, I had spent a lot of money getting my family there, and now our day was ruined. What many people don't realize is that we get to choose if we're going to have a bad attitude or not. A lot of people think they are forced, but it's really a choice. Choose to have a glad heart today and every day. It's what God wants for you.

Bus-Size Fish

The LORD is my light and my salvation—whom shall I fear?
The LORD is the stronghold of my life—of whom shall I be afraid?
PSALM 27:1, NIV

My family and I boarded a small boat I had chartered on Isla de Mujeres in Mexico. Soon we were heading twenty miles out into the Caribbean Sea to find whale sharks, which were supposed to be migrating that time of year. Seeing whale sharks in their habitat sounded very exciting and scary all at the same time, since an adult whale shark is about the length of a school bus. When a creature is migrating, that means it's on the move, so for the next two hours our captain followed a grid pattern in search of the sharks. Since they often swim along the surface, they were supposed to be pretty easy to spot. Suddenly, the captain and his first mate started to cheer and point: whale sharks off the port bow! I was traveling with my family, so my two sons and I quickly put our snorkeling gear on. That's right; we were going to jump in and swim with them! When you stop and realize that you are about to jump in the water with creatures the size of a bus, it can be a little intimidating; but, knowing they are filter feeders, we knew they were looking for plankton to eat, not people.

The captain maneuvered us into the path of the oncoming shark and told us to jump in. By the time the bubbles cleared, we were staring at a four-foot mouth just a few feet in front of us! The shark changed course to miss us, so we turned to swim alongside this enormous creature. We were only able to keep up with it for a few minutes. Our captain then picked us up, and we did this over and over again without any fear.

We all have fears in life. By getting to know God better, we discover that He can help us overcome any fear we may have. Share your fears in private with God, and then ask Him to help you overcome your fears. He won't let you down!

An Evening in Rome

And we urge you, brothers and sisters, warn those who are idle and disruptive, encourage the disheartened, help the weak, be patient with everyone.
1 THESSALONIANS 5:14, NIV

I recently traveled to Rome with my family. Our hotel was right in the old part of the city, so after checking into our room we decided to go for a walk. Rome at night becomes a different kind of city. During the day, everyone is rushing around working or studying, the shops and markets are busy, and people are dressed in their professional attire. In the evening, everything changes and there are even more people on the streets, but now everyone has come out just to hang around with their friends and families. The cafés on the sidewalks are full of people sitting back, chatting, and enjoying each other's company. The plazas are filled with friends or couples walking around enjoying the evening. Restaurants are full of people eating together, and it seems like you can always hear music somewhere in the background.

Soon we entered a large plaza called the Piazza di Spagna, which was filled with hundreds of people. In the middle there was a long set of steps going up a hill toward a church. These steps are probably the most famous place to just sit around in the entire city. They've been around for hundreds of years, and they are called the Spanish Steps. My kids were curious how many steps there were from top to bottom, so while my wife and I sat down to enjoy the atmosphere, we watched the boys carefully count the steps all the way up. They counted 135 steps. While we were there, we also bought some gelato and ate it while sitting on the steps. Gelato is a delicious Italian ice cream that is made in a ton of wonderful flavors. There are so many neat places in Rome. It's no wonder someone invented the phrase "Rome wasn't built in a day." It means that good things take time and require patience.

Do you have enough patience? Let me give you one simple piece of advice: you will live a happier life if you can learn to be a patient person. It's not easy, but it's definitely better to have a lot of patience than not enough patience in life. Ask God today for patience.

Twenty-Four Hours of Pain

Do not be yoked together with unbelievers. For what do righteousness and wickedness have in common? Or what fellowship can light have with darkness?
2 CORINTHIANS 6:14, NIV

After getting married, my wife and I sat down and made a list of places we wanted to visit so we could plan and save up money. We were married in the month of March, so we made plans and took our first trip four months later to Cancun, Mexico. Our trip went, well, interestingly. First of all, if you ever consider going to Cancun, you may want to go during the winter months, because if you go in July as we did, you will boil. Since we live in Michigan, we're not used to one-hundred-degree weather, and that is exactly what we got when we stepped off the plane—one hundred degrees and one-hundred-percent humidity. It hit us like a wall when we stepped off the plane. Since we were young and on a tight budget, I found us a little cheap motel in the city center. Apparently, we got our money's worth. The room wasn't very nice at all, and there was no air conditioning either. To make matters worse, the first day there I drank some of the tap water and got a nasty stomach sickness. I spent the entire second day in bed, boiling to death in our non-air-conditioned room and waiting for my stomach sickness to pass. It was not fun. Fortunately, it was only a twenty-four hour thing, and the third day we were able to continue with our adventure.

I'm grateful that my wife didn't make a big stink about our crazy first trip together. She stuck by me that day till I felt better. Someday you might get married. I know it's weird to talk about this now, but I need to tell you that who you marry is probably one of the most important decisions you'll ever make. God has some advice for you, though, and I'd like to mention it now so you can keep it in the back of your brain. It's in our verse today, and it's pretty simple. Don't marry someone who doesn't love God. Some people get married thinking they can convince their spouse to change and love God. Sometimes it happens, but most of the time it doesn't. Decide today to some-day marry someone who loves God.

Blemished or Unblemished

So we have come to know and to believe the love that God has for us. God is love, and whoever abides in love abides in God, and God abides in him.
1 JOHN 4:16, ESV

Yesterday I shared with you a story about one of the first trips my wife and I took after we got married, which was to Cancun, Mexico. At the end of our first year married, we went on our second trip together. We had been furiously saving up so that for our first anniversary we could go on a trip abroad. After discussing possible locations to visit, the destination on the top of our list was Spain. We made our plans, got time off from work, and purchased our tickets. Soon we arrived in Madrid, rented a car, and set off to do a drive around the country.

At the time when we took our trip, my wife was a huge fan of these porcelain figurines called *Lladros* that were made near Valencia, Spain. Unfortunately, these little collectable figurines were incredibly expensive, so she never thought she'd ever get to own one. When we were planning our trip to Spain, one day someone told my wife, "Did you know that if you go to the place that they make Lladros, there is a small, unknown side shop where you can buy figurines that have minor blemishes for cheap?" My wife was very excited about the possibility of owning her own Lladro! Maybe she could find one with a minor blemish that she could afford. Sure enough, when we traveled to Spain we made a point of finding the shop in Valencia, where she was able to get a figurine for around twenty dollars! The one we bought was beautiful. As we stood there in the shop, we looked and looked all over the figurine to see if we could find a blemish, but we couldn't see one. To us it was perfect! Let's fast-forward twenty years. Today I looked up the value of the same unblemished version of the Lladro we bought and was shocked to see that it was selling for $850!

Even though we are sinners and have fallen to Satan's temptations, to God we are priceless. We're each blemished with sin, but when we ask God to forgive us, we're cleansed! Thank God today for His unconditional love and forgiveness!

Toledo Steel

For physical training is of some value, but godliness has value for all
things, holding promise for both the present life and the life to come.
1 TIMOTHY 4:8, NIV

Heading south out of Madrid, Spain, the first larger city we approached was a city called Toledo. As we approached, we could tell right away that this was a city rich in history. We first drove through the ancient city walls and into a labyrinth of narrow streets. We got lost immediately because we soon discovered that the streets there were nothing like many of the streets in North America, which are often parallel and perpendicular and quite predictable. It seemed as though at every intersection the other streets went off in different directions.

On this trip I was traveling with some friends, and as we drove into Toledo, one of my friends suddenly said something that took us by surprise. He simply said, "I want to buy a sword here." We were surprised by this very random comment, but he went on to tell us that Toledo has been a very traditional sword-making, steel-working center for the last twenty-five hundred years! As we explored the narrow streets of Toledo, we finally found a store that had a sword my friend liked. He talked to the owner, and they settled on a price. As we waited, we learned quite a bit about how they made the swords and how Toledo steel had become the standard source of weaponry for the Roman legions. The swords were indeed very impressive, very solid, and incredibly detailed. The construction of these swords requires a very select choice of raw materials and a very hot forging temperature of 1,454 degrees Fahrenheit. I found it interesting that putting a sword through fire is what makes it stronger.

Since we are living beings, doing exercise is what makes our bodies stronger. After exercising a new muscle group, I feel like my muscles are on fire, but that is what is making them grow stronger. God has given each of us amazing and complex bodies that need exercise and good food in order to operate properly. Make a plan to keep your body in good shape. By the way, as our verse today reminds us, exercise is good, but don't overdo it either; nothing is more important than having a strong and growing connection with God!

The Unusual Encounter

*Live as people who are free, not using your freedom
as a cover-up for evil, but living as servants of God.*
1 PETER 2:16, ESV

When we arrived in Seville, Spain, there was pretty much one place I was looking forward to seeing more than anything else—the Seville Cathedral. It's one of the three largest churches on the planet. As is the case with many bigger European cities, finding parking was a challenge, and we found ourselves driving in circles for at least thirty minutes. We finally found a spot, even though it was quite a ways from the cathedral. As we walked toward the cathedral, we soon saw the huge bell tower in the skyline. It was the cathedral! As we approached the massive church, I couldn't help but be amazed at the sheer size of the building's footprint. Inside there was lots to see as well. I was surprised to find Christopher Columbus's tomb in the cathedral. We finally decided to climb up the 343-foot tall bell tower to get a great view of the city.

As we stood there watching from the tower, three college-age girls arrived and hung a huge banner out the window of the tower and then handcuffed themselves to the tower and the banner! They seemed determined to be there for a while, and they clearly believed in something. There was almost no one else up there, so I walked over to them and asked them what they were protesting and what the banner said, since we couldn't see it from inside the tower. She said the sign said, *"Fuera Rusos de Lituania!"* which means, "Russians: Leave Lithuania!" If you are a history buff, you might recognize that this was the year 1990, when Lithuania declared independence from Russia. If there's one common thing about history, it is the desire for independence. People want to be free to do their own thing, make their own decisions, and run their own country.

Since God loves us so much, He also gave us independence and freedom to make our own choices in life. If God forced us to do something, we would be slaves, but by giving us freedom of choice, He proved to the universe how much He loves us. We can show our love in return by freely choosing to serve God.

The Other Famous Wall

*I appeal to you, brothers and sisters, in the name of our Lord Jesus Christ, that
all of you agree with one another in what you say and that there be no divisions
among you, but that you be perfectly united in mind and thought.*

1 Corinthians 1:10, NIV

My wife and I had rented a car in London and were driving all over the United Kingdom. On the way to Scotland, there was one very important landmark where we absolutely had to stop and visit—Hadrian's Wall. Usually when I think of the British Isles, I don't think of the Romans, but the Romans used to govern what is today known as England, back in the second century A.D. That's when Emperor Hadrian ordered a wall to be built there, which was the northern border of the Roman Empire. We drove through the wonderful rolling countryside as we followed our map to a part of the wall we could visit. Even though the wall had been built around eighteen hundred years ago, a great portion of the wall still remains today.

The original wall ran for about seventy-three miles east to west through England, about ten miles south of the border with Scotland. We were able to find a nice secluded part of the wall and parked our car. We were very excited to see that there was a trail that tourists could take alongside the wall, so we decided to hike a portion of the trail. The portion we hiked was extremely hilly, which gave us great views of the wall disappearing in the horizon. The Romans built sixteen forts along the length of the wall, and the remains of those can also be visited. It turns out that walking along the trail is very popular and people from all over come to hike the entire wall, a hike that takes about six days.

The Romans built lots of walls all over Europe. In China, the Great Wall is also a famous wall that was built. Unfortunately, all these walls were built for the same reason, to create a division between people. Satan would like nothing more than to create division between God's people. Because we're all sinners, there are often disagreements, hurt feelings, and misunderstandings between members of the church. That is why we must all commit to being forgiving, loving, and to serve each other in order to stay united in Christ. Will you make that commitment today?

Use Them or Lose Them

"To one he gave five talents, to another two, to another one, to each according to his ability. Then he went away."
Matthew 25:15, ESV

As my wife and I continued driving north through the United Kingdom, we soon left England behind and entered into Scotland. The lush rolling hills finally led us to the city of Glasgow, a rich cultural center and the largest city in the country. After a short visit, we continued driving east to the capital, Edinburgh. Edinburgh has a wonderful old, historic feel to it. It's not a huge city, and towering over the entire old city center is a castle perched up on a hill.

We walked around the city and then up to an overlook that looked over the entire city. Edinburgh is a wonderful city, but there's one thing that really made it stand out—the Fringe. What is a Fringe? Well, it's the largest arts festival in the world. Every summer Edinburgh hosts this arts festival that lasts almost a month. More than twenty thousand performers from about fifty different countries come to this city to showcase their talents in many different categories, such as comedy, theater, circus, and music. About three hundred different venues are used to feature more than three thousand shows during the festival. I was amazed thinking about how much talent is in this city each summer during the festival!

Everyone has talents, and that includes you. Do you know what your talents are? It's your job to know or to figure it out. Assuming that you know some of the things that you are good at doing, the next question is, What are you doing with those talents? Usually, it comes down to two choices; you are either using those talents for your own glory, or you are using them for God's glory. Since God is the One who gives out talents in the first place, He has asked us to be responsible with the way we use them. If you use them to bring glory to God, then you are using your talents to witness to others! My favorite thing about all this is that if you use your talents, God will bless you with more. Jesus' parable of the talents specifically talks about this!

The Road Hole

"Stop judging by mere appearances, but instead judge correctly."
JOHN 7:24, NIV

Golf is an interesting sport. I remember when I was little and I used to flip through the four channels that existed on TV in the 1970s, and once in a while on Sunday there would be a golf tournament showing. I couldn't believe that people would actually play this sport because to me it looked like the most boring thing in the world. Everyone had to be quiet while people hit a little ball around a big grassy course. To me it seemed like being in an outside library and people were being shushed—because a person had to concentrate to hit their little golf ball the best they could. I remember thinking to myself, *I'll never play that sport!* Maybe you already know that I ended up trying golf when I was an adult and I really enjoyed playing it.

When I was around thirty years old, I had the opportunity to travel to Scotland, where the sport of golf was started. During our time there, I made a point of stopping by to see one of the most famous golf courses in the world, regarded as the "home of golf." We arrived in the city of St. Andrews and found the course. The name alone seemed to be rich in history; it was called the Royal and Ancient Golf Club of St. Andrews. When I got there I wanted to see the course, but I specifically wanted to see if they would allow me to walk the seventeenth hole. You see, the seventeenth hole has one of the most infamous sand hazards in the world called "the Road Hole," which is essentially a huge deep sandy hole that seems to swallow up golf balls. Somehow, to me, the game of golf went from being a boring-looking sport to an enjoyable way to spend a few hours with some friends.

We often judge things by appearances, and we usually end up misjudging things and creating problems. A wise person will not rush to judge something quickly. Pray to God for wisdom today.

The Short Golf Game

"I have told you these things, so that in me you may have peace. In this world you will have trouble. But take heart! I have overcome the world."
JOHN 16:33, NIV

As I mentioned yesterday, when I grew up I learned that I was judging the sport of golf by its outer appearance, which wasn't very fair. When I became an adult, I was offered a chance to go golfing for the first time. I'm not talking about mini-golf; I'm talking about real golf, complete with a bag of golf clubs. A friend had won a free "golf-for-four" package from a local radio station, so we set out to give the game a try. I don't remember too much except that we set off to do eighteen holes that day but we had to quit after about fifteen holes because we ran out of golf balls. I had bought about twenty-five used golf balls that day for us to use because I figured we'd probably lose some in the woods or in the ponds they put throughout the course to challenge us. Somehow we managed to lose all of them before finishing, so we had to leave. The funny thing is that I totally enjoyed myself that day.

Golf is not an easy sport to play. Sometimes there are sand hazards, where it's hard to hit the ball out, and the most challenging are the water hazards. Those are little ponds and streams that seem to attract golf balls to fly into. And to make things even more challenging the course is designed to make it harder for you by putting woods on either side of the course, or areas with tall grass.

Satan works pretty hard to put challenges in our path every single day too. Sometimes he causes problems between friends or family members, or problems at school. If you ever listen to the news, you can see how he creates problems between cultures, countries, and religions as well. He wants to make us struggle, and he wants us to give up. He is our number-one enemy. We mustn't let him ever have his destructive way in our life. Because it's a sinful world, we will have challenges, so anticipate them and confront them with God on your side.

A Strange Market

No temptation has overtaken you that is not common to man. God is faithful, and he will not let you be tempted beyond your ability, but with the temptation he will also provide the way of escape, that you may be able to endure it.
1 CORINTHIANS 10:13, ESV

Hong Kong is a unique city. My wife and I had a little time to explore the city, so I had prepared a list of places we could visit. One of them was pretty interesting and unlike anything I had ever seen before. We followed some directions and arrived at the Hong Kong Bird Market in Kowloon. I figured this would be a street with a few bird shops, but I was very wrong. There were dozens of stores and shops selling birds! Just try to imagine for a moment what that street sounded like! There were tiny birds, large birds, white birds, colorful birds, quiet birds, noisy birds, birds that were pretty peaceful, and birds that constantly fluttered around. Each shop was jam packed from floor to ceiling with cage after cage, each one with a bird in it. There were so many birds there! The Chinese traditionally liked to keep birds as pets, and many people still do.

What I found interesting was that nearby there is a park where the old folks come with their birds in their cages and where they come to take their birds for a "walk," much like you would take your dog for a walk in the park. Obviously, you can't put a leash on a bird, and it's too risky to take the birds out of their cages in order to really stretch out their wings because they'd probably fly away. Many of those birds have lived in captivity their entire lives, so they don't even know that they're captive.

Satan wants us to live as captives too. He's also hoping we don't realize it. He wants to tempt us to get hooked on sin. He figures if he can get us to try something, maybe we'll get hooked and addicted. Drugs, smoking, and alcohol are a few examples of things that are destructive and addicting. Don't fall for Satan's traps; otherwise, you might end up trapped in his cage hooked on destructive habits. If you already know that something is destructive, don't even take a chance, saying you'll try it. Ask God to help you stay far away!

Remember Calvary

May the God of hope fill you with all joy and peace as you trust in him,
so that you may overflow with hope by the power of the Holy Spirit.
ROMANS 15:13, NIV

Every five years the church selects a city to hold meetings to discuss church matters. In 2015, the meetings were held in the city of San Antonio, Texas. Maybe you were there! Although I had several responsibilities during the event, I still made time to visit the city and the area around it. One day we went to a place nearby called Natural Bridge Cavern and took a tour of the cave there. Another day we visited the Alamo, which was originally a church mission but later the location of a battle between Mexico and the Texans. The Texans wanted to be independent of Mexico. The battle that took place there was lopsided because about 180 soldiers tried to defend against some four thousand attacking soldiers. You may already know that although they bravely fought their best, the courageous soldiers of the Alamo were overrun by the Mexican army and most of them died. Interestingly, this did not discourage the Texans; it actually helped them have more courage, because they regrouped and returned to defeat the Mexican army only a few days later. Historians say that their rallying cry for the Americans was, "Remember the Alamo!" Because of the sacrifice of those soldiers in the first battle, the American army was motivated to come back and win.

There is also a battle that has already been fought for us that we should never forget, and our rallying cry should be "Remember Calvary!" Because of Jesus' sacrifice, the rest of us can now have eternal salvation. There is no doubt that we will all go through struggles during our lives here on earth, so we need to encourage each other during the battles. Every day we need to be reminded that God has already won this battle for us and that by staying close to Him we can be assured to be on the winning side! If you see someone down and discouraged today, bring hope to that person. Remember Calvary!

Rocky Loaves of Bread

When one of those who reclined at table with him heard these things, he said to him, "Blessed is everyone who will eat bread in the kingdom of God!"
LUKE 14:15, ESV

We landed in Havana on the island nation of Cuba. I was pretty excited to spend the next three weeks getting to know the island better. My mother is Cuban, as well as my wife, and even though I had been to Cuba before, I was thrilled to be on a complete east-to-west tour of the island with the church. Our tour started by driving to the western-most large city, Pinar del Rio, where we then started a slow seven-hundred-mile trek across Cuba to the last city on our tour, the eastern city of Guantanamo. After our first event in Pinar del Rio, we headed east but decided to take a short stop in one of the neatest natural features in Cuba, the Viñales Valley. The valley is about seven miles long by three miles wide, and, while the valley floor is flat and lush with palms and plantations, these amazing towering limestone outcrops known locally as *mogotes* shoot straight up hundreds of feet off the valley floor. They look kind of like round half-loaves of bread that dot the valley in this part of Cuba.

During our visit at that time in Cuba, restaurants were extremely uncommon, so if you needed to eat while traveling, the most common option was to pull over in a town and ask for the nearest *paladar*. These aren't quite restaurants; they're the homes of people who have set aside a part of their patio or dining room to cook a meal for guests on the spot. As we drove through the middle of the valley surrounded by these towering cliffs, we found a *paladar* in which to stop and eat. The cost was very reasonable, and since it was purely home-cooked food, it was fantastic. Since we were in the home of this woman, she treated us like family and served us a huge banquet!

Some day in heaven, we will also be sitting around a table, surrounded by a wonderful natural environment, being served a huge banquet feast. I can't wait for that day! Can you?

The Old Box

Each of you should use whatever gift you have received to serve others, as faithful stewards of God's grace in its various forms.
1 PETER 4:10, NIV

While in Havana, Cuba, my family was approached by a man carrying an old box covered with cardboard, rags, and tape. The box looked really old. In Spanish, he said, "Hey, friend, for a dollar, I'll take your picture with a hundred-year-old camera." I was interested in seeing how this camera worked, so a dollar was well worth it. Over the next few minutes, he proceeded to open the camera and pull out a plate where he mounted something on it, put it back in, and covered it with a dark fabric. He positioned us in front of the camera, and then using his hand he quickly opened and closed a small hole on the side of the box facing us. He next put his hands under the dark fabric and reached into the box and spent a few minutes doing something. Soon he pulled out a piece of paper with a "backward" image of our picture—that's when white is black and black is white. I was completely intrigued. He next proceeded to set the whole thing up again, and this time he put the negative picture in front of the hole in the box and again he quickly opened and closed the hole with his hand, basically taking a picture of the negative. Again he reached under the fabric with his hands and developed the new negative that had now turned black back to black and white back to white. He then handed me the small photo, which was maybe two inches by two inches. I was amazed, and I immediately paid him the dollar for this unique souvenir.

Today we take for granted how easy it is to take pictures. We do it without even thinking with a variety of devices at our disposal. Is there anything today you are taking for granted? I want to invite you to quickly make a mental list of some of the things you are blessed with that you might be taking for granted. Don't forget to also thank the people who have provided them for you. Lastly, honor God by using those things to bless others!

The Unexpected Trade

He has told you, O man, what is good; and what does the LORD require of you
but to do justice, and to love kindness, and to walk humbly with your God?
MICAH 6:8, ESV

My family was spending the next three weeks touring across the island of Cuba. Each night we'd go to a different church that would be filled up with children and adults. I would set up my screen and all my special effects and I would give them a special presentation. Part of my presentation involved using 3-D glasses. I had brought about one thousand pairs of glasses, so every night the kids were in awe as they put on 3-D glasses for the first time in their lives and watched the images jump off my giant screen.

Driving across Cuba was not easy. Sometimes gasoline was not even available and we'd have to find someone in the black market to buy or trade with. One time we traded a box of fruit for a five-gallon jug of gasoline. Another time we traded a spare car part we had in the trunk for gas. One of the things my two boys did during this trip was to give out chewing gum to all the kids they encountered. Every day they gave out hundreds of pieces of gum, which was a rare treat for the kids. One day we had pulled over in a town and we were trying to arrange for some more gasoline. On the other side of the quiet dirt road, a small boy and his mother were walking by. My older son jumped out of the car and ran over to them. He reached into his pocket and pulled out a pack of gum and gave it to the boy. What happened next totally surprised me. As my son was turning to leave, the boy stopped him and reached into his bag, pulled out a mango, and handed it my son. I'm not sure what they said to each other at that point, but I was moved to see that two people could be kind and generous to each other with no strings attached.

Jesus did those types of random acts of kindness all the time. He was always thinking of others before Himself. I asked my son how he felt being kind to the boy and receiving kindness in return. He said it brought him great joy.

Memory-Lane Brain

But our citizenship is in heaven. And we eagerly await a Savior
from there, the Lord Jesus Christ, who, by the power that enables
him to bring everything under his control, will transform our
lowly bodies so that they will be like his glorious body.
PHILIPPIANS 3:20, 21, NIV

The city of Santiago, Cuba, is the second largest city on the island. It is a super hilly city, and it happens to also be the city my wife lived in for several years during her childhood. During our time there, we wanted to make sure we made this a "trip down memory lane," so we did a little bit of additional exploring there. As you can guess, the first place she wanted to visit was the building she lived in during her childhood. It was right on the corner of a hilly street. We were fortunate to be able to go inside the house and see her old room, the kitchen, bathroom, and other areas of the house she hadn't seen in more than thirty-five years. There are very few building supplies available to buy in Cuba, so we were even surprised to see that the paint in her room was still the same too! It was a pretty neat experience watching her walk from room to room remembering the past and her childhood days in Cuba. From there we went outside and started walking up the street to see if we could visit the school she had attended, which was only a couple of blocks away. The administrators welcomed us in, and we strolled around the school as she pointed out areas she distinctly remembered. Her dad had served as a pastor in this city at a couple of churches, so during our time there we made sure to visit both of them as well.

The recurring theme to her comments was that everything seemed so small now. The church seemed small, her room seemed small, and the school playground seemed small. Did they shrink? Of course not, but the way our brain remembers places changes over time. Some experts say we only use about 10 percent of our brains. When it's time to take tests at school, we sure wish the other 90 percent was being used! I can't wait to get to heaven because God has promised to re-create us with perfect minds and bodies. That is the way He originally made us before we messed up and fell into sin. What a wonderful day that will be!

The Young Witness

What you have learned and received and heard and seen in me—
practice these things, and the God of peace will be with you.
PHILIPPIANS 4:9, ESV

My son wanted to buy a souvenir from Santiago, Cuba, since my wife had lived there when she was a child. The problem was that we couldn't find a store that sold souvenirs. The next day we were going to be leaving, and he still hadn't found a souvenir from Santiago. That morning our driver took us to the old castle and fortress on the coast overlooking the ocean just outside of Santiago. The fortress walls are huge, and a deep dry moat surrounds the castle. As we were leaving, way off in the distance we saw what we had been looking for—a man was selling souvenirs! This was the only chance for my son to get something to remind him of this unique city.

In Cuba, it is expected that one negotiates for almost everything you sell or buy, but what surprised me was that my son asked if he could go alone to negotiate with the man. We gave him a few dollars, and he went over to the man while we waited a few yards away. My son was only about ten or eleven years old at the time, so I was surprised, but for some reason he wanted to do the negotiating alone. I'm not sure what all they said to each other, but in the end, my son got a souvenir for half price, which is about normal and expected. That's when it occurred to me that for the last couple of weeks in Cuba, my son had been watching me closely. Every day as we stopped to buy bread or fruit or gasoline, we would have to negotiate for the price. Now he wanted to try negotiating on his own for his own souvenir.

Even though you might be young, there are other people watching you too. Maybe some kids in the grades below you are watching you. Perhaps the woman who lives next door sees how you play with the neighborhood kids. Part of our job as Christians is to be a witness to others, and I would say that one of the easiest ways to witness to others is by simply letting them see how you live your life as a follower and imitator of Christ.

Misunderstood

Those who consider themselves religious and yet do not keep a tight rein on their tongues deceive themselves, and their religion is worthless.
JAMES 1:26, NIV

Several years ago, we took my father-in-law with us to Spain for a couple of weeks. Several days into the trip, we drove to the city of Córdoba in the south of Spain. Many historians believe that Córdoba was the most populous city in the world in the tenth century. When we arrived, we first went to see the famous Córdoba Cathedral, since it is widely considered to be one of the most accomplished monuments of Moorish architecture in the world.

After the tour, we sat down in front of the cathedral to soak in the environment and relax a little. That's when a large group of people came around the corner making a bunch of noise. They were protesters. They had drums and were chanting and clapping their hands. We watched as they went by across the front of the cathedral and around the block again. We were not able to catch what exactly they were protesting, so the next time they passed by, we went up to one of them and asked. The person we spoke to was pretty excitable and we didn't quite understand what they were protesting, but the best we could tell, they were protesting against the mayor of the city of Burgos, which is a city in the northern part of Spain. Around and around they went. We were amazed that they would be so upset with the mayor, so we tried to approach one of them again to get more information. This time we spoke to someone who spoke a little clearer. We were embarrassed to discover that we had completely misunderstood the first person because the truth was that they were protesting against a company building a Burger King in front of the cathedral! We were shocked by how much we had completely misunderstood the truth!

This is why gossip is very dangerous. When you repeat something, especially something negative, nothing good is going to come out of that, plus it's very likely the information you are repeating may not even be accurate. As Christians we need to resist gossip. The Bible speaks very plainly and strongly about people who can't control their tongues. Don't be one of them!

Anxious and Impatient

But now you must also rid yourselves of all such things as these:
anger, rage, malice, slander, and filthy language from your lips.
COLOSSIANS 3:8, NIV

I was very excited as my wife and I drove from the Red Centre of Australia toward the city of Sydney, the last stop in our tour through Australia. Before leaving Sydney, we would first spend a couple of days exploring the city. Since I had studied architecture in school, the reason I was very excited to arrive in Sydney was to see the most famous architectural landmark in the entire country—the Sydney Opera House. As you probably can guess from the name, it is a performing arts center, and it was built extending out into the harbor so it could be surrounded by water on three sides. It's very easy to spot this building because it's made up of the huge white, shell-like sections. The building was not easy to build. It took the builders four whole years just to figure out how to build those roof shell shapes. The architect was determined to make the building resemble a modern sculpture, and most people agree it's an amazing building.

When I pulled into the city and saw the opera house in the distance, I drove straight toward it. I was ready to park and explore! I was so excited! Unfortunately, after driving around for fifteen minutes we weren't able to find any parking spaces. We drove a little farther away and still didn't find any parking. We drove even farther! We ended up finally finding a space almost two miles away! I was pretty frustrated at this point, because I was so anxious to just get there, but there was nothing I could do. At that point should I have screamed and lost my temper? That never helps.

I'm sure at some point you have also felt frustration about something. Our sinful reaction is often to explode and lose control. Others even use curse words. None of these reactions help, and usually they make matters worse. God wants us to be in control of our temper and in control of our language. Satan would like to see the worst possible reaction from you when you're frustrated. Ask God today to help you keep control when you feel like you're going to lose your temper.

The Rickshaw Ride

"For where two or three are gathered in my name, there am I among them."
MATTHEW 18:20, ESV

When my wife and I landed in Hong Kong, we had a long list of things we wanted to see and do, but we only had a few days to do them. One thing we definitely wanted to do was to take a day trip to Macau. Macau is a city that can be reached by ferry from Hong Kong. This is no ordinary city, though. Macau, which is completely surrounded by China, was a Portuguese colony from the mid-1500s until 1999. When our ferry arrived in Macau, we got off and stood in amazement at this modern city before us. Moments later, an elderly Asian man approached us and asked us if we wanted to get a tour of the city by rickshaw. Rickshaws are three-wheeled bicycles that have a seat behind the driver for a couple of passengers to sit in. In many Asian cities, they're very popular. I didn't recall ever having ridden in one before, so we accepted his offer. We climbed on and headed into Macau. This turned out to be the perfect way to see the city.

Macau is not a huge city; it's only about twelve square miles. Try to imagine an area that's about three miles wide and four miles long. The thing is that it ranks number one in the world of the most densely populated sovereign states on the planet! More than six hundred thousand people were living in those twelve square miles!

Soon our rickshaw driver stopped at the bottom of a hill. In front of us at the top of the hill was the most recognizable landmark in the city—the ruins of St. Paul's, a church that burned down in 1835. The only thing that remained was the front of the church, which was left as a reminder of what was there before. Behind that front façade was nothing. To me, this served as a reminder that God's church is not a building; it's people like you and me. In some parts of the world, people meet for church under a tree or in homes. Don't wait to just meet at church. I encourage you to organize gatherings in various places with your family or friends. God will be there!

The Mountain in the Way

He replied, "Because you have so little faith. Truly I tell you, if you have faith as small as a mustard seed, you can say to this mountain, 'Move from here to there,' and it will move. Nothing will be impossible for you."
MATTHEW 17:20, NIV

A couple of weeks after arriving to study in France for a year, I decided that one Sunday I would hitchhike somewhere for the day. I had heard hitchhiking in Europe was common and safe, so I ventured out to find out for myself. I decided that I would go toward the city of Chamonix in the middle of the Alps, right on the border of Italy. Chamonix is about a sixty-mile trek. The only thing separating Chamonix and Italy is the tallest mountain in all of Europe, Mont Blanc.

The hitchhiking went pretty well. Almost immediately I got picked up and started making my way toward Chamonix. Sometimes I'd get picked up and go five to ten miles, sometimes more. Little by little I made the voyage till I arrived in Chamonix by early afternoon. I felt like I could go a little farther, so I continued hitchhiking to see if I could make it to Italy. In order to do that, I would have to hitch a ride with someone going in that direction through a tunnel under Mont Blanc. It took about half an hour, but finally someone picked me up and took me through the seven-mile tunnel under the mountain. I had never gone through such a long tunnel before; it just kept going and going. I tried to imagine how much work it took to drill it, and I was sure it was saving tons of time and gasoline, because any other route between Italy and France would be much longer if they had to build a road all the way around a huge mountain range. Wouldn't it be cool if the people who built the tunnel could just say, "Mountain, move out of the way!" Instead they spent years and millions of dollars building it.

In the Bible, Jesus is quoted as telling His disciples that having faith is a very big deal. He told His disciples that even if they only had a little bit of faith, they would be able to do great things. The Bible says that even with a tiny amount of faith, we could command mountains to move! Ask God today to increase your faith.

The Ultimate Fort

The LORD is good, a refuge in times of trouble. He cares for those who trust in him.
NAHUM 1:7, NIV

When I was little, my dad loved to pile us in the car and take summer road trips. Every year we'd take a long trip, but sometimes we'd take shorter ones for a long weekend. From where I grew up in Massachusetts, we once decided that our road trip would be to head north to Canada. My dad was always hunting for a new place to explore, and on this particular trip we decided to head to Halifax, Nova Scotia. As we left the United States behind, we first entered New Brunswick and drove through the beautiful countryside. Then we entered Nova Scotia and made our way toward Halifax. We spent a couple of days in the area, but what I remember the most was visiting Fort George on Citadel Hill. Right in Halifax there is a hill that overlooks the entire city. As a young boy, I was quite thrilled when I got the chance to visit a real fort.

When we went inside, there was much more to see. Every hour there was a neat ceremony for the changing of the sentry guard. The music of bagpipes was playing in the background while sentry guards wearing their traditional regiments marched around. I remember admiring their tall, fuzzy hats as they also performed several military maneuvers and fired their guns as part of the exhibition. My favorite part was when they rolled out a cannon and proceeded to load it. I wondered to myself, *Will they fire the cannon*? Sure enough, they fired it with a big boom. As a kid, I would daydream of having a fort and defending it against attackers.

The Bible teaches that God is our fortress in time of trouble. Sometimes we think we can just solve all our problems on our own, but God invites us into His fortress to take refuge with Him! Why face the enemy alone when you can have God on your side? Ask Him today to surround you with His fortress of protection and love! The Bible says He cares for those who trust Him.

One Master, One Castle

"No one can serve two masters. Either you will hate the one and love the other, or you will be devoted to the one and despise the other. You cannot serve both God and money."
MATTHEW 6:24, NIV

Scotland is a wonderful country to drive through. The terrain can be rocky and mountainous one moment, then green and lush the next. One of the stops we wanted to take while driving through Scotland was a visit to Balmoral Castle. While British royalty are entitled to many castles and palaces, Balmoral Estate is one of the few that is not the property of the Crown, since it was purchased privately by Queen Victoria's husband as a retreat in 1852. When he bought it, he concluded that it was too small, so he built this new castle and tore down the old one. Let's pause here a moment. I need to mention that most of us have a hard time understanding the need to tear down a castle in order to build a new, bigger one, but that was the case here.

When we visited the castle, our tour only allowed us to go into the large ballroom, because the rest of the castle was being used regularly as part of the royal family's private retreat. We got to walk around the gardens and the stables as well. I have to say it was impressive to see how some people live, especially considering this was only one of their small country homes.

I once saw a bumper sticker on an expensive car that said something like, "He who dies with the most toys wins." This quote is talking about owning lots of material possessions. It's not a sin to be wealthy, but unfortunately much of the time people who are wealthy make that the number-one thing in their lives.

The Bible warns us to not love money. Loving and craving material things is an easy distraction from being close with God, and the Bible makes an excellent and truthful point that we can't have two masters. It's one or the other. If you are blessed with wealth, that's OK, but ask God to help you to not let it become your master. Instead, pray that God may help you use it to honor Him.

The Blocked Path

An intelligent heart acquires knowledge,
and the ear of the wise seeks knowledge.
PROVERBS 18:15, ESV

Victoria Falls is on the border between Zimbabwe and Zambia, in Africa. We had just spent the day viewing the waterfalls from the Zimbabwe side, but I had read that there were some unique views from the Zambian side as well. The first thing we had to do was to go to the Victoria Falls Bridge that spans the gorge that the water falls into. The bridge crosses the gorge a mere 420 feet above the water! The bridge itself is unique because it was built in England, then transported to Zimbabwe and assembled in 1905. Halfway across the bridge we saw something very interesting—bungee jumpers! We stopped and watched them jump and fall 230 feet toward the river down below, only to bounce back up and down a few times.

After crossing the bridge we were met with the Zambian border crossing and passport control. The Zambian side had a steep, narrow trail that you could follow all the way to the bottom of the gorge, but what happened next caught us by surprise. About twenty feet ahead on the trail was a huge troop of baboons just sitting on the trail. There must have been ten or twelve of them, both adults and babies. We stopped a moment to see what would happen next. Nothing happened. They just sat around as if we didn't exist. Getting off the path wasn't an option because there was dense jungle on either side, so my wife and I looked at each other, knowing we had to make a decision. Continue or go back? We decided to continue, so we simply walked through the middle of the troop, passing within inches of several baboons! They just watched us pass as though we were other random jungle creatures.

Every day we make dozens of decisions. Some are important; some are trivial. How do we make good decisions? Be wise by listening to advice from people with experience. Become informed about all the possible outcomes. Most important, ask God to give you wisdom to make the best decision.

Blessed With Work

Whatever you do, work at it with all your heart,
as working for the Lord, not for human masters.
COLOSSIANS 3:23, NIV

During the year I studied in France, I carefully used the little money I had taken in order to be sure not to spend it foolishly. My number-one priority was to use it to travel. Unfortunately, I soon discovered that traveling in Europe is very expensive. By the time I returned from my Christmas break travel adventure, I was almost out of money. The next school break would be in about six weeks, so I started thinking of what I could do to make a little money.

As students, we were already required to work on campus, so I concluded that I needed to find an additional job that I could do off campus. I went down to the nearby city of Geneva, and I went to the office of the newspaper and asked if I could place a small ad offering my services to do odd jobs. I was surprised to get a call a day or two later from a woman in Geneva who needed temporary help for about a month or so. Her daughter had been in an accident, and she wanted to focus her time on doing everything possible to help her recover: take her to the doctor, take her to do physical therapy, and so on. She needed someone to take care of all the housekeeping duties during this period. For more than a month, every day after school, I took the bus to her house in Geneva and worked for several hours each day, cleaning her house, doing laundry, ironing, washing dishes, and driving her and her kids around to her various doctors' appointments. God blessed me greatly because I was able to find this job. The job lasted almost exactly until the next school break, and I was able to make enough money to travel the rest of the school year!

As you get older you will soon get a job. I want to encourage you to be an excellent worker, even if you are doing a simple job. When you do excellent work, even if it's flipping burgers, cutting grass, or sweeping, your excellent work is a way to give God the glory. People will notice something special about you—that Jesus is in your life.

The Mosquito Sacrifice

By this we know love, that he laid down his life for us,
and we ought to lay down our lives for the brothers.
1 JOHN 3:16, ESV

Have you ever been to summer camp? I love summer camp. In my conference we go to Camp Au Sable every summer. It's probably my most favorite week of the year. Every year the leaders recruit a group of wonderful staff for the summer. The chefs make delicious food for us three times a day. There are fun worships and meaningful spiritual encounters. I don't even need to mention the endless activities designed to keep us busy and active all day long, such as horseback riding, wakeboarding, working on model rockets, zip-lining, riding go carts, fishing, and much more. The friends you meet at camp are the kinds of friends you make for a lifetime.

Toward the end of the week the last time we were there, a canoe trip was organized. I decided to take a canoe with my two sons for an expedition that would last a couple of hours. First we crossed the lake and then entered a stream that eventually joined with a river. After leaving the lake and starting to make our way down the stream, we were suddenly overcome by mosquitos. Not one or two mosquitos—a horrible swarm of them! We had to do this combination of paddling and waving our arms to keep them away. For some reason, my older son was a big target—perhaps his blood is extra sweet! He was really struggling to keep it together, because they were all around his head and he has a mild allergic reaction to mosquito bites. There was nothing we could do to get away from these mosquitos; all we could do was try to survive and paddle fast. I did come up with one thing to help him. I took off my shirt and hat and gave it to him. He put the hat on over his head and wrapped my shirt around his legs. You can probably imagine how many times I was bitten, but I joyfully gave my son my hat and shirt in order to protect him.

Love does that. God demonstrated amazing love when He allowed His Son Jesus to be sacrificed in order to save us. Today, I invite you to decide to love God back as much as He loves you!

Where Is Everyone?

And let us consider how we may spur one another on toward love and good deeds, not giving up meeting together, as some are in the habit of doing, but encouraging one another—and all the more as you see the Day approaching.
HEBREWS 10:24, 25, NIV

There's a little island on the Caribbean Sea that belongs to Mexico called Cozumel. The island is about twelve miles off the coast of Mexico, and it's about thirty miles long and about ten miles wide. My wife and I landed on Cozumel, and we took a taxi to our hotel. We had heard Cozumel was a quiet island, and we wanted to just relax for a few days. After a couple of days of relaxing, we finally decided to venture out to explore the rest of the island.

About thirty miles of Cozumel faces the coast of Mexico, while the other side of the island has another thirty miles that faces the Caribbean Sea. We were staying on the side that faced Mexico, but we were curious about seeing the rest of the island. We rented a scooter and ventured out. We drove south to the bottom point of the island and followed the road around to the side that faces the Caribbean Sea. What we saw completely surprised us. Actually, what we *didn't* see is what surprised us. There was nothing there except a small dirt road. We drove mile after mile up the coast. There was absolutely nothing. No hotels, no stores, no shops, no houses, nothing. We couldn't even find signs that there was electricity on this side of the island! The small road was literally the only developed thing on that side of the island for miles. Of course, we enjoyed stopping at some of the secluded beaches and walking around some rocky coves, but we were still impressed at how deserted this side of the island was. While it was fun to go for a short while, it would seem hard to be completely alone and isolated for a long time.

God created us that way. He created us to be part of a social group of people to interact with, to comfort, and to help each other. Your church family is meant to be part of that group as well. Sometimes we spend time serving our community. That's great, but don't forget to also love and do good deeds for your brothers and sisters in Christ.

The Most Important Flight

After that, we who are still alive and are left will be caught up
together with them in the clouds to meet the Lord in the air.
And so we will be with the Lord forever.
1 THESSALONIANS 4:17, NIV

A few years ago I was invited to go down to Colombia in South America to speak at a few events. Since I'd be flying down all the way from the United States, they wanted to plan their long weekend in such a way that they could arrange to have me speak at a few different places. That sounded very logical to me. I wasn't sure when I'd have the opportunity to go back to Colombia again, so I told them to go ahead and plan the long weekend however they thought would work best. What happened over the next couple of days was impressive.

I flew from Chicago to Houston, then from Houston to Bogotá, then Bogotá to Medellín. I made my way out of the terminal and I was met by my host for the weekend. She took me directly to the college in Medellín, where I would be presenting that very same night. I set up and got ready, and before I knew it, there were about five hundred kids that had filled up an auditorium.

I had a great time at the event, but when the event was over, I quickly packed up and went to bed. I was awakened early the next morning and taken to the airport, where I took a quick flight to the town of Barranquilla. After my presentation there, I went straight back to the airport and flew to Bogotá and then was on another flight to Cúcuta the next morning. I did my presentation there in the morning, packed up, and headed straight back to the airport, where I took a flight back to Bogotá, then another flight up to Bucaramanga. I did my presentation that evening for the fourth and final time. The following morning, I flew back to Bogotá, then on to Houston, and finally Chicago.

Did you get all that? I ended up taking eleven flights in about three days! I did a lot of flying. But the real flying I'm looking forward to someday will be at Jesus' second coming. The Bible says we will fly up to meet Jesus in the air! That's going to be awesome! I can't wait for that day. How about you?

Your Eyes Have Been Opened

*"And now why do you wait? Rise and be baptized
and wash away your sins, calling on his name."*
Acts 22:16, ESV

I love to go snorkeling. No matter where I go, I'm always looking for the best snorkeling spots to visit. When I was in Hawaii a few years ago, I did a little bit of research and found that on the island of Oahu there is a pretty good snorkeling spot at Hanauma Bay, which is actually a volcanic crater. We drove a little ways from Honolulu till we reached the crater and parked up by the rim. The bay had been formed within the crater, and probably a full one-fourth of it was open to the ocean, while the rest of it was protected. Since our boys were little at the time, this was a big advantage. We walked down into the crater to the beachfront and found a nice spot. I got my snorkeling gear out and headed into the water. Fortunately, at the time of year we went, there were not many people, so I think the fish were not scared off, because I saw hundreds and hundreds of fish of all colors and sizes. I even spotted a green sea turtle.

My boys were about five and two years old at the time. During the whole time that I was snorkeling, they were having fun splashing around in the water right at the shore. After snorkeling for a little while, I went to shore and convinced my older son to see what I was doing. I put my mask and snorkel on his head and I showed him how he could use the mask to put his head underwater to see what was there. He was shocked to see how many fish had been swimming around him all that time! When he came back up, he had a completely new perspective of the place.

When we go under the baptismal waters, we also come up as a new person with a new outlook on life. Our sins are washed away, and we now live with hope and joy that can only come from the Father. If you have not been baptized yet, I invite you to accept God's gift and sacrifice so you can experience true joy and happiness!

Nature on Parade

On the glorious splendor of your majesty, and
on your wondrous works, I will meditate.
PSALM 145:5, ESV

While studying at Andrews University, I always traveled home to Southern California to see my parents and family for Christmas. It was a nice break from the winter weather. I had several other relatives living in the area, so one year one of them suggested that we try something new during the holiday; they suggested we go and see the Rose Parade in person on New Year's Day. We discussed the idea and researched a little about what was involved to go see the parade. Distance wasn't a problem; Pasadena wasn't too far. The parade started pretty early, so it would have to be an early day. We liked the idea, so on New Year's Eve we packed up the car with folding chairs, made some lunches, and went to bed. Early the following morning, we drove to Pasadena to park and stake out a spot along the parade route.

The tradition of the Rose Parade started in 1890, so it is well known, and hundreds of thousands of people come from near and far each year to see this spectacle. I have to admit, it was very impressive to see float after float go by, decorated from top to bottom with colorful natural materials. That was the rule; every surface of the float framework had to be covered by things such as flowers, plants, seaweed, bark, seeds, vegetables, and nuts. In addition to the amazing floats, huge marching bands also went by, as well as equestrian teams, animals, and occasionally a convertible car would go by with a famous sports figure or celebrity on board, waving at everyone.

I've seen several parades in my life, but this one was extra special because of the rule of only using natural materials. You know who designed and made all those natural materials, right? Yes, God. Nature is all around us for us to appreciate and enjoy. As a matter of fact, next time you look at nature, remember that you are looking at God's own artwork. Also remember He didn't create it for Himself; He created it as a gift for you!

A Mountain of Solitude

And after he had dismissed the crowds, he went up on the mountain by himself to pray. When evening came, he was there alone.
MATTHEW 14:23, ESV

After we finished filming at Yellowstone National Park, the production schedule called for us to travel south to Grand Teton National Park, which has an amazing mountain range. Now let me tell you that the Rocky Mountains are amazing looking mountains. I've seen them in every state they span across, but there is something special about the Teton Range. As we drove south, we could suddenly see the range rising up off a flat valley. I think what drew me to the range was how steep and rocky the mountains are. Many other large mountain ranges are massive and often covered practically to the top with trees, but the Tetons are rocky all along the top, plus there are several glaciers up there with year-round snow cover. Sitting right in front of the range was Jackson Lake, where we decided to catch a boat ride to approach the foot of the mountain range. It turns out we were the only people on the boat besides the driver.

It was late in the day, and we were advised that this was the last boat going out, which meant we'd have to hike a couple of miles back to our car when we were done visiting. We had flashlights, so we weren't worried. The good thing about it was that there was no one where we were going. We hiked a while up a trail till we reached our destination. In front of us was a thundering waterfall crashing down and misting everything in sight. Even after we finished recording, we just sat there a little while to soak it in.

Usually, magnificent waterfalls are crowded with hundreds of people. On this day we just sat there alone looking and listening and feeling the power of water falling down to the rocks below. The water was coming from a melting glacier above. The whole experience reminded me of when Jesus got on a boat to get away from the crowds for a little while, or when He went up a mountain to be alone in prayer. Make time each day to find a quiet place to be alone with God in prayer. Disconnect from all your devices and connect with God today!

Forever Faithful

"And if you faithfully obey the voice of the LORD your God, being careful to do all his commandments that I command you today, the LORD your God will set you high above all the nations of the earth. And all these blessings shall come upon you and overtake you, if you obey the voice of the LORD your God."
DEUTERONOMY 28:1, 2, ESV

Did you go to the 2014 Forever Faithful International Pathfinder Camporee in Oshkosh, Wisconsin? I'm sure everyone who went has a different adventure to share. My adventure started at home in Michigan the Sunday before Oshkosh. Compared to a lot of other travelers who came a long way, we only had about a five-hour drive. At the time, I owned an old RV, and we decided to try to see if it could make it to Oshkosh. We bought windshield paints and wrote messages all over the side windows, such as "Be Forever Faithful" and "Oshkosh Bound!"

Soon we were on our way, but after about thirty minutes I looked in the rearview mirror and noticed something flying off the roof of my RV. I pulled over and climbed up on the roof to inspect. Sure enough, my roof was flying off in pieces! I went to a store nearby and bought eight huge rolls of duct tape and taped about half of my roof down. We pressed on till we arrived.

If you were there that first day, you remember the rain and the mud as thousands of people poured onto the grounds. This was my first time to Oshkosh, so I had a lot of new experiences as the days passed. By the first day, the weather sorted itself out, and every evening we enjoyed an amazing program about the story of Daniel, video highlights of the day, and of course, Chico the Lion. During the day there were tons of activities going on, and practically everywhere you turned, someone was comparing and trading pins. It truly was impressive to be there with about fifty thousand other people from all over the world celebrating this wonderful event. In the end, we were challenged and encouraged to always be faithful to God no matter what.

Just as Daniel was challenged throughout his entire life, even to the point of death, he always stayed faithful to God. Will you do the same today in everything you do? I pray that you will be forever faithful to God in everything you do.

The Unexpected Vendor

Give thanks in all circumstances; for this is God's will for you in Christ Jesus.
1 THESSALONIANS 5:18, NIV

When my wife and I arrived in Johannesburg, South Africa, we discovered that the rental company did not have the car I had reserved for our two-week vacation. Instead, we got a different car that didn't even have air conditioning. At first, I thought this was a big deal and I was going to die. The deeper we drove into the African bush, the hotter and hotter it got.

Soon we left the city and drove toward Gaborone, Botswana. From Gaborone we would have a fourteen-hour drive north to reach Chobe National Park—our first safari adventure. There were times we didn't see a person or another car for an hour or two. It was incredibly desolate. During one of these long stretches, in the distance I saw a local man sitting on log on the side of the road. As I got closer, the man stood up, picked up a watermelon from the ground and came right to the edge of the road. Next, he hoisted the watermelon up high over his head and held it there proudly, hoping I would stop to buy the melon. We did not stop for the watermelon because we didn't have a way of cutting it or preparing it, but after we passed him I wished I had stopped to buy it. I wondered how many hours this man sat there every day in the hot sun waiting for a car to pass so that he could hopefully sell this melon in order to make a couple of dollars.

I felt bad not stopping, and I felt ashamed about being upset that I didn't get a car with air conditioning. My attitude changed that day. Do you ever get grumpy because you don't have something you want? Stop and be grateful for all the wonderful things God has given you!

Living Large

Draw near to God, and he will draw near to you. Cleanse your hands, you sinners, and purify your hearts, you double-minded.
JAMES 4:8, ESV

There are many wonderful things to see and experience while visiting Paris, France, but one of the most impressive places is located about fifteen miles outside of Paris—the Palace of Versailles. One of the most well-known kings of France lived there for many years—King Louis the 14th. He was quite the flamboyant and dramatic person who loved to celebrate even the smallest daily routine. We had to see this place, so we bought our tickets and took the official tour of the palace. The palace itself was magnificent, with around seven hundred rooms, two thousand windows, twelve-hundred and fifty chimneys and sixty-seven staircases! In room after room, we were amazed at how luxurious each room was. There were state apartments and private areas for the king and queen, chapels, galleries, ballrooms, and even a theater for opera. The palace is also famous for the gardens with expansive grassy areas, huge fountains, and long walkways.

One of the most famous parts of the palace is the Hall of Mirrors. As the title hints, it's an elegant 240-foot long hall filled with no less than 357 mirrors. Every day, King Louis walked through the Hall of Mirrors to get from his apartment to the chapel. Before electricity, the room was lit from one end to the other with about one thousand candles on chandeliers, which helped reflect the candlelight. A bunch of people would assemble to simply watch him walk down the hall. He sure liked his unusual routines!

Everyone has unusual quirks. We're each a little strange in our own ways. Some people think they've done too many bad things and that God wouldn't want them anymore. Wrong! God wants you to come to Him as you are. We're all sinners. It's not your job to get your heart cleaned up; only God can do that. You just need to come to Him every day and He will embrace you and purify your heart!

Crossing Canada

*The L*ORD *God took the man and put him in the*
garden of Eden to work it and keep it.
GENESIS 2:15, ESV

Each summer when I was a kid, my father would take a month of vacation and we would drive from the east coast of the United States to the west coast—taking a different route there and a different route back. One year my dad decided to drive north to Quebec in Canada and start west from there. We drove up to Montreal and started driving west along the Trans-Canada Highway, which connects the Atlantic and Pacific coasts.

Our first stop was Ottawa, the capital of Canada. Soon we were making our way across north of the Great Lakes to Thunder Bay on the edge of Lake Superior. We continued west out of Ontario and entered Manitoba and the central plains to Winnipeg. The plains continued on through Saskatchewan and eventually into Alberta toward Calgary. Every time we entered a new province, we'd pull over and take a picture with the sign welcoming us to that province. In Calgary we could see the Rocky Mountains off in the distance. Soon we were surrounded on all sides by a magnificent range of mountains in every direction as far as the eye could see. At this point, the divided highway we had traveled on for hundreds of miles had now become a two-lane highway as it weaved through the mountains. Soon the Rockies were behind us and we were in British Colombia, with the end of the Trans-Canada Highway in sight. Ahead, the last city before re-entering the United States was Vancouver. Our journey took us three thousand miles across the country, while along the way we took in the beauty and majesty of the landscape around us. Canada is a beautiful country!

No matter where you live, you are surrounded by nature. Since the beginning, God put us in charge of nature. He told us to work it and protect it. Let's each do our part to protect the planet God has put us in charge of managing!

Learning From a Crater

For everything that was written in the past was written to teach us, so that through the endurance taught in the Scriptures and the encouragement they provide we might have hope.
ROMANS 15:4, NIV

A few years ago while filming a video series, I had to travel to one of the many natural features in Arizona. This one is called Meteor Crater. The landmark is exactly what the name implies—a crater where a meteor hit the earth at some point in the past. When you tour the crater, you first go to the visitor center, which takes you right to the edge of the crater rim and provides a magnificent view. The crater is about 3,900 feet across and 570 feet deep. There were several paths that led us around the rim and a little ways down into the crater to telescope platforms that give visitors an opportunity to get an even closer look.

As I toured, I noticed that there were little signs here and there stating as a "fact" that the meteor impact occurred fifty thousand years ago. When you read something that states it happened hundreds of thousands or millions of years ago, a red flag should come up in your brain because, first of all, it's absolutely impossible that anyone could know for sure. That's the first big problem. In the case of Meteor Crater, I was able to observe that when the impact left a crater, one could see the various layers of earth and rock exposed beneath the surface. The Bible teaches that during the time of Noah a global flood covered the earth. The flood seems to have caused the layers on the surface of the earth to be deposited the way we see them. When the meteor hit, the impact exposed those layers, which implies that the layers were deposited first by a flood; and then, second, this meteor hit and created a hole and exposed those layers.

This simple biblical conclusion seems to clearly show us that this meteor crater was probably formed a few thousand years ago, sometime after the flood. I love that the Bible provides us a base of knowledge so that we can understand the history of our planet. I also love seeing how nature confirms the things written in the Bible. What an amazing book!

The Gold Cup Final

*Don't be jealous or proud, but be humble and
consider others more important than yourselves.*
PHILIPPIANS 2:3, CEV

In the summer of 2007, the CONCACAF Gold Cup soccer tournament was hosted in the United States. This tournament is played every two years between the best teams in North America, Central America, and the Caribbean nations. Halfway through the tournament I read that the final would be played at Soldier Field in Chicago, which is near my home. I was surprised to find that there were plenty of tickets left for the final game and that the pricing wasn't too bad. After asking around a little, I found out that the reason was that no one knew who would be playing at the finals yet, so most people were waiting to see who would play before buying tickets. I thought that attending a Gold Cup Final would be cool regardless of who played, so I bought tickets for my whole family. The weeks went by, and the tournament passed from the group stage to the quarterfinals. I was excited to see that the United States had advanced along with their biggest rival, Mexico. I started to think to myself, "Wouldn't it be amazing if the United States and Mexico played in the finals!" Soon, the tournament advanced to the semi-finals, and then the teams to play at the final were set—the United States and Mexico would play for the championship—and we already had our tickets! The game was incredibly exciting! Mexico scored first at the end of the first half, but less than twenty minutes later the United States scored and tied it. Then about ten minutes later, the United States scored again to win the game.

Winning is great, but I have to tell you that good sportsmanship is more important. How you act and what you say when you win or lose is important. Don't be loud and proud when you win. And when you lose, don't be a sore loser. Remember, it's just a game. As Christians, we have a great way to witness to others through our actions when we win or lose.

The Long Way Around

Walk in wisdom toward outsiders, making the best use of the time.
COLOSSIANS 4:5, ESV

A lot of my traveling has to do with work, but once in a while when I travel with my family it's because we have accumulated enough frequent flier miles to take a trip. One day I saw a promotion on Cathay Pacific airlines that would take us to Johannesburg, South Africa for a very low amount of miles. But getting there would not be easy; we would have to travel through Cathay Pacific's hub in Hong Kong. Normally, if you live in North America, you travel to Africa by flying east over Europe. This time we would have to travel west—the long way around the world—to get to Africa.

Our flight started in South Bend, Indiana and flew about thirty minutes to Chicago. In Chicago we changed planes and flew west to San Francisco, California—another four hours of flying. In San Francisco we changed planes again and flew to Hong Kong. This flight was almost fifteen hours long. This particular flight was very unusual because we crossed over the international dateline. That means we jumped ahead twenty-four hours in time. In other words, one moment it's Tuesday night, 8:00 P.M., and a minute later it's Wednesday, 8:01 P.M.—a full day later. We just skipped a day! The grand finale was the flight from Hong Kong to Johannesburg, which was another thirteen hours flying. Did you add it up? Our trip to Africa required us to spend thirty-three hours on a plane, not to mention hours of layovers, plus we completely skipped over a day getting there! Crossing the dateline on the way back was strange too; instead of skipping over a day, the clock goes back one full day and you relive that same day a second time!

Time is a gift we're each given. We get twenty-four hours each day. What do you do with your time? Do you waste time or are you productive with it? When you spend time doing something, do you get a benefit in return? Do you glorify God with your time? God wants us to be careful with our time. He encourages us to be wise about how we use it.

In the Sky Down Under

Kings take pleasure in honest lips;
they value the one who speaks what is right.
PROVERBS 16:13, NIV

My wife and I were in Cairns, Australia for a couple of days experiencing the Great Barrier Reef. Soon our time there would be over, and we would drive toward the center of the continent. Before leaving, we went to the outskirts of the city to visit the Skyway Rainforest Cableway. Right next to it there was an aboriginal cultural center where I enjoyed a boomerang demonstration. A man threw the boomerang, and it came right back to him! Later, in the gift shop I bought a boomerang, but I was never able to get it to come all the way back to me.

Although the northeast corner of Australia is very dry, there was a fascinating little pocket of rain forest in that area that the Skyway allowed visitors to experience. Soon we boarded a little gondola that took us up into the rain forest. Sometimes the gondola took us high above the rain forest canopy; other times it dipped down so we could get a closer look at the forest floor. There were stops along the way, too, where we could get down and explore the area a little through some trails in the rain forest. The cableway extended almost five miles into the rain forest; so, by the time we made stops we were in the middle of the forest in an area barely disturbed by humans. After walking five minutes into the rain forest on a small path, it truly felt like we were surrounded by a natural paradise!

Being there reminded me of the Garden of Eden and how Adam and Eve lost their home there because of disobedience and dishonesty. Sometimes we think we can get away with telling small lies; but, perhaps you've already discovered how one small lie can quickly grow into a huge lie that can cause a lot of damage and pain. Take pride in being known as an honest person. Having honest lips is another way we can witness to people about our love for God.

An Underground World

But grow in the grace and knowledge of our Lord and Savior Jesus Christ. To him be glory both now and forever! Amen.
2 PETER 3:18, NIV

Several years ago my wife and I went to visit some friends who lived in Toronto, Canada. They were wonderful hosts as they took us around to visit some of the main landmarks of the city. As we drove around we soon found out about one of the most famous landmarks, except we couldn't quite drive to it. That's because it was hidden under our feet! In the year 1900, the first pedestrian underground walkway was built to allow shoppers to get from one side of the street to the other without having to deal with the traffic at the street level. As the years passed, more and more tunnels were built, expanding the network of underground pedestrian passageways between office buildings, stores, gyms, food markets, doctors' offices, parks, and even apartment buildings. It's so big that now there are various subway stations connecting different parts of the passages.

Today the network of passages is called PATH. Theoretically, you could live down there for your entire life! As we walked around down there with our friends, we were impressed at how far it goes. We later found out that there are about eighteen miles of passages down there, connecting around one thousand two hundred stores into what some consider the largest mall in North America! Technically, that honor goes to West Edmonton Mall in Alberta because it's an actual mall, but we were amazed at how you could find pretty much anything you needed by walking through the Toronto tunnels. These networks have been growing and expanding for more than a hundred years. New plans include almost doubling the size of the network in the years to come!

Businesses grow, cities grow, and people also grow. You are growing too—but don't forget that growing doesn't just mean getting taller. The kind of growing that God wants to see in us is growing in wisdom and in humble service to God and others. Will you commit today to a complete growing package for God? As you grow, remember to give God the glory for all the wonderful things you do!

Chunnel Tunnel

He tends his flock like a shepherd:
He gathers the lambs in his arms
And carries them close to his heart;
he gently leads those that have young.
ISAIAH 40:11, NIV

During our most recent trip to Europe, my boys asked if we could make a quick stop to visit London in the United Kingdom. Originally, we did not plan to include London in our trip because it was a little more difficult to get to, since the U.K. is an island separate from the mainland. When I started wondering about when we would get another chance to visit Europe as a family, I decided to look at options on how to include London. There were basically three options I could think of. One, we could all fly, but that would be way too expensive. Two, we could take a ferry across the English Channel and drive to London. The third option was to take the Chunnel. You're probably wondering, what is a Chunnel? It's the nickname given to the Channel Tunnel that runs between France and the United Kingdom. It was finished in 1994, and at its deepest point under the English Channel it is about 250 feet below sea level. That's more than twenty stories down!

Near Calais, France we arrived at the French side of the tunnel. We paid for our ticket at a toll booth, and then we were signaled to join a line of cars. Soon they guided us to board special trains that would carry us through the tunnel to the United Kingdom. At first I thought the Chunnel was a tunnel that cars could drive through; instead, we boarded a train that comfortably carried our car to the other side in only thirty-five minutes.

There is something comforting about being carried to our destination. It's comforting to know that God is watching over us. When we submit ourselves to Him, He will carry us in His arms and hold us close. I love the example the Bible uses of a shepherd and his flock. We are God's lambs, and He holds us close to His heart. Ask God to be your shepherd and lovingly carry you and protect you today.

The One-Day Pass

"Have I not commanded you? Be strong and courageous. Do not be frightened, and do not be dismayed, for the LORD your God is with you wherever you go."
JOSHUA 1:9, ESV

After driving through Europe, my family and I crossed the Chunnel and arrived in London early to see how much of the city we could see. We had a family meeting to decide what important landmarks we wanted to make sure we visited. After parking in the outskirts of the city near one of the metro stations—called the Underground—we entered the station, found a machine, and bought four all-day Underground passes, figuring this would be the best way to see as much as possible.

First, we went to St. Paul's Cathedral, where Princess Diana got married and many other important historical events happened. From there we went to the Tower of London, which was built as a castle almost a thousand years ago but ended up getting used as a prison for about 850 of those years. Next, we visited the Tower Bridge, probably the most famous drawbridge in the world. Then we visited Big Ben, the famous clock tower at the Parliament building; and around the corner from that was Westminster Abbey, the church where most coronations occur as well as where royalty are buried. Our next stop was Piccadilly Circus. No, it's not a circus; it's one of the busiest commercial intersections in the city. Our final stop was Buckingham Palace, where the royal family spends most of their time. When the reigning monarch is in the palace, their "standard," or personal flag, is flown. When the monarch is not in the palace their standard is removed.

If God had a standard, it would always be flying. God is with you everywhere you go. He will never leave us, and He will never let us down. Will you call on God today and every day?

Leaning on God's Word

"Therefore everyone who hears these words of mine and puts them into practice is like a wise man who built his house on the rock."
MATTHEW 7:24, NIV

While driving through Italy we decided to stop and see one of the most famous landmarks in the world—the Leaning Tower of Pisa. We parked and walked through the city wall to the open grassy plaza where the tower is located. The leaning bell tower is actually one of three buildings in the complex. Right next to the tower is a cathedral and baptistery, but the tower is what draws millions of visitors to the town of Pisa each year. The building of the tower started in the year 1173—the tower is almost a thousand years old! The tower's tilt began during construction, and experts say it was caused by a poor foundation on ground that was too soft to support the weight of the tower. Back then, buildings like the tower took decades to build, and some cathedrals took hundreds of years to build! The tilt increased during the decades before the tower was finished; and by the time it was finished, there was nothing that could be done. It stayed like this for hundreds of years, each year tilting a tiny bit more. In recent years, major efforts and millions of dollars have been spent to stop the tilting. The interesting thing is that all of this could have been avoided if only the builders had built the tower on a solid foundation one thousand years ago.

The Bible says that people who hear God's words but don't put them into practice are like foolish people who build a house on sand instead of a solid foundation like rock. The Bible gives us hundreds of pages of wisdom from God—telling us about the past, the present, and the future! A lot of people trust in man's fallible ideas about the world, but I love knowing I have built my knowledge of the world based on God's Word.

The Big Five

"But seek first his kingdom and his righteousness, and all these things will be given to you as well."
Matthew 6:33, NIV

Have you ever heard someone talk about the "Big Five" in Africa? The Big Five refer to five animals that were considered by hunters as the most dangerous and difficult animals in Africa to track and hunt on foot—the lion, the elephant, the cape buffalo, the leopard, and the rhinoceros. Sadly, for many years hunters have traveled to Africa with the purpose of killing these increasingly rare animals for sport. When I traveled to Africa with my wife several years ago, we spent two weeks on several different safaris in three different countries. The only difference is that I didn't have a weapon; I had a camera. I bought a special telephoto lens just so I could zoom in as close as possible to photograph these wonderful animals as they roamed around their natural habitat. My goal when I went to Africa was to see how many of the Big Five I would be able to see and photograph. In the end, we were able to see four of the "Big Five" during our time there. The only one we didn't see was the most elusive one—the leopard. Seeing animals in their natural habit was one of the most unique experiences I've ever enjoyed in my adventures. Let me tell you, though, it was not easy to find all of them. Of the four we saw, the hardest one to spot was the rhino. We spotted one on the very last day, and I felt blessed and rewarded at the end of my two-week search for these animals.

Sometimes the good things in life require us to seek them out; rarely do they come and find us. In the book of Matthew we are reminded that every day the most important thing we should seek out is God's blessings. Don't just automatically assume that you will be blessed in every single thing you do. Connect with God daily. Talk to Him; share your thoughts and worries and goals with Him. God has wonderful things in store for you today. Seek Him out!

A Few Big Differences

*"For false messiahs and false prophets will appear and perform
signs and wonders to deceive, if possible, even the elect."*
MARK 13:22, NIV

When my family and I landed at the airport in Istanbul, Turkey, we exited the terminal and got into a taxi. We went to our hotel in the middle of the Old City and dropped our things off at the hotel; immediately we left, walking toward the Sultanahmet Park. The park is located between two of Istanbul's most famous landmarks— the Blue Mosque and Hagia Sophia. For a thousand years, the Hagia Sophia was the largest church on the planet. In 1453 it was converted to a mosque, a Muslim place of worship, for almost five hundred years till it was converted into a museum in 1935. On the other end of the park is the Blue Mosque, a four-hundred-year-old mosque for the people of Islam. I had never been in a mosque before, so I was glad to hear the inside could be visited. As we approached the entrance we quickly learned about the very strict dress code that must be observed by all people visiting the mosque. We were given bags and asked to take our shoes off and put them in the bags during our entire visit inside. Next, my wife was given a scarf to cover her hair, while other women who wore shorts were provided with a robe to wear. Everyone was quiet and reverent as they toured the mosque.

Sadly, there are a lot of tensions between some of the main world religions—including Christianity and Islam. Are God and Allah one and the same? Muslims do not speak of Allah as their heavenly Father. Their Quran does not refer to God as Jesus did, calling Him Father. Plus, Muslims claim Allah has no son, which is contrary to one of Christianity's central truths found in John 3:16 that God gave His only Son, Jesus, on Calvary to save us. It would seem that comparing God and Allah is a mistake and a dangerous distortion of the entire gospel of Christ. Still, I encourage you to be respectful of other religions. Our job as Christians is to share the wonderful gospel of Christ with everyone.

Stronger Than the Sea

*Then Moses stretched out his hand over the sea; and the LORD caused the
sea to go back by a strong east wind all that night, and made the sea into
dry land, and the waters were divided. So the children of Israel went into
the midst of the sea on the dry ground, and the waters were a wall to them
on their right hand and on their left.*
EXODUS 14:21, 22, NKJV

While touring Europe with my family, we entered the country of the
Netherlands, which some people refer to as Holland. I've been
asked before, "So which is the correct name of the country? Holland or
Netherlands?" The answer is Netherlands; Holland is a region on the west
coast of the Netherlands. As we entered the Netherlands our boys had one
particular thing they were anxious to see—the famous dikes, or levees, of the
Netherlands. This is actually a fascinating country because about half of the
country is below sea level!

Over the years, the Dutch have built an incredible dike and levee system to
hold back the waters of the sea through a series of canals, pumping stations,
dams, and dikes. Dikes are huge mounds of dirt that run for miles and miles
and work to keep the higher waters from flooding the land that is below sea
level. We decided to visit the largest levee in the country—the Afsluitdijk
Levee. It is so big there is a highway running along the top of it. We figured
driving across this levee would be the best way to appreciate its magnitude. It
was completed in 1932 and runs for twenty miles! The cool thing is that right
in the middle of the twenty miles there is a rest area with a lookout tower we
could climb to get a fantastic view of the entire surrounding area and see that
the water on one side was higher than on the other.

The levee immediately reminded me about the story of how God held back
the Red Sea so that the Israelites could cross. It took humans five years to
build this one levee, plus millions of dollars and thousands of workers. On
the other hand, compare that to the power of God, who simply commanded
the waters of the Red Sea to retreat so that Israelites could pass through.
Friends, we worship a powerful God!

A Trip to Corinth

*And now these three remain: faith, hope
and love. But the greatest of these is love.*
1 CORINTHIANS 13:13, NIV

When I was in school we were required to memorize all the books of the Bible. For some reason I really enjoyed this assignment, and I loved saying all the names as quickly as I could. One time as a kid I was even asked to get up in front of the church to recite the books of the Bible. Have you ever wondered about the names of some of the books? I used to be curious about names such as Galatians and Ephesians and Corinthians. It took me a while to figure out that these were letters Paul wrote to the churches in places he visited. Galatians was written for the people in Galatia in what is central Turkey today. Ephesians was for the people in Ephesus in western Turkey. Corinthians was a letter for the people of Corinth, in Greece.

A while ago I traveled to Greece with my wife, and we decided to include the ancient Bible-times ruins of Corinth in our tour. After walking around and exploring the ruins we found a spot on the ancient main street and sat down. I opened up my backpack and pulled out my Bible and turned to the books of First and Second Corinthians and began to read, imagining how the words in this letter Paul wrote were first read there in the town we were visiting. There's one chapter in 1 Corinthians that I will never forget—chapter 13. The entire chapter is about one thing: love. Paul goes on and on, saying that even if we do all sorts of wonderful things but we don't have love and show love to others, we're missing the entire point of Christianity. I encourage you to read the entire chapter today, because you will see just how big of a deal it was for Paul to make sure we and the Corinthians understood this singular point. Go out today and show love to the people around you!

Don't Miss It

If it is possible, as far as it depends on you, live at peace with everyone.
Romans 12:18, NIV

While I was living in France I planned a trip to Spain, and I tried to create a rough plan and route to follow with a handful of great locations to visit. There were several Spaniards studying at the college in France, so one day I talked with one of them in the cafeteria about my trip, and they simply said, "Be sure you don't miss Segovia. You will not be disappointed." I had never heard of Segovia before, but I trusted my friends' suggestion and included it in my travel plans. Let me tell you now that Segovia ended up being one of my favorite places I visited in Spain.

As we approached Segovia I could see in the distance that the old city seemed to be perched up on a rocky mount. The old city was surrounded by an old wall sitting high above the surrounding plain, and in the front, sticking out from the rocky mount, was an amazing castle with pointy towers and lookouts. It was something you would expect to see in a fairytale storybook. A couple of narrow openings in the city walls allow visitors to drive into the incredibly narrow streets of the old city. Some streets were so narrow that I had to open the car windows and fold in my side mirrors in order to get through! In the center of the city was an amazing old cathedral, and on the edge of town was an ancient aqueduct bridge that brought water to the city. It was from the Roman times and was believed to be around two thousand years old! During my entire time there it seemed as though I was pleasantly surprised every time I turned the corner! I was really impressed by the city walls that were built to defend in case of war, which is kind of sad if you think about it. We live in a sinful world, but our verse today shows us how, ideally, we should live at peace with everyone.

When in Greece

I am not saying this because I am in need, for I have learned to be content whatever the circumstances. I know what it is to be in need, and I know what it is to have plenty. I have learned the secret of being content in any and every situation, whether well fed or hungry, whether living in plenty or in want.
PHILIPPIANS 4:11,12, NIV

While visiting Athens we rode a bus from the airport to the city center that day. The buses were these neat double-decker buses, and, of course, we opted to sit on the top deck as far forward as possible. The city was in the midst of preparations for a festival as we arrived. All of a sudden we looked straight ahead of us and noticed there was a banner hanging from one side of the street to the other. The problem is that it was hanging too low, and we were heading straight for it! The bus never slowed down, and it ripped right through the banner, tearing it in half!

Later, as we walked to our cheap hotel, we saw what this unusual festival was about. People were armed with foam bats and cans of silly string, and they were walking around whacking each other with the harmless foam bats and spraying each other with silly string. We finally arrived at our hotel and discovered that major parts of the hotel were under construction. As usual, bathrooms were down the hall, but during the process of construction at this hotel, we had to climb out of our hotel window onto a scaffolding three stories up, walk down a little way on the scaffolding, and then climb back in through another window into the hall, where we could reach the bathroom! There's a first time for everything.

While some people might have gotten stressed out or bent out of shape by such an odd way to get to the bathroom, we simply chose to be flexible and adopt the attitude of, "When in Rome, do as the Romans do." Many of us are used to wanting things our way all the time, but sometimes we need to be flexible. The word the Bible uses is "content." Learn to be content with what God has given you; it's the secret to happiness!

Feeling Home Away From Home

Love one another with brotherly affection.
Outdo one another in showing honor.
ROMANS 12:10, ESV

Leaving home to attend school can be hard at first. I went away to academy my sophomore year in high school. I was excited about the idea of trying something new, and I was happy I could continue attending an Adventist school, but it was still hard. I remember the six-hour drive from my house to the academy, where, after getting me registered and checked in, my parents had to quickly turn around so they could get back home that same day. After they left, I remember going to my room and sitting on the edge of the bed and saying to myself, "What do I do now?" I didn't know a single person there.

Later, when I went to Europe to study for a year, it was also hard leaving home knowing I wouldn't see my family for a long time. Something interesting happened early on at the school in France. On Friday afternoons the tradition on campus was that anyone interested could go down to the athletic field to play soccer—probably the most popular sport in France. Some weeks we'd switch up and play rugby. I had never played rugby before and had to learn; it was a pretty rough sport, but we enjoyed playing. After about two months, something interesting happened—the European students on the field agreed to play American football with the American students. For the most part Europeans don't know anything about football, but they were willing to try and learn. It was a lot of fun. I know this sounds kind of silly, but those few hours playing football that day made us feel a lot less homesick. We really appreciated the Europeans recognizing that it was hard to be thousands of miles from home for so long, and even though we enjoyed playing soccer and rugby every week, that week they went out of their way to help the North American students feel less homesick. We could all learn a lot from our verse today. It says we are to "outdo one another" in showing honor.

I Have to Pay for That?

This is how one should regard us, as servants of Christ and stewards of the mysteries of God. Moreover, it is required of stewards that they be found faithful.
1 Corinthians 4:1, 2, ESV

Traveling comes with adventure and uncertainty. The "unknown" was part of the mystery and adventure that came with traveling to different parts of the world. One time, while studying in France, I travelled through Spain. I didn't have much money, so I stayed in places that were affordable. There was one factor about traveling through Spain that I remember being particularly difficult—the showers. I'm the kind of person who really appreciates a hot shower every day. I've never gotten used to taking the occasional cold shower. I find them very painful. During my visit to Spain as a student, practically every place I stayed at only came with cold showers, which were always housed in a central room down the hall from our room. There was an option though; if you wanted to pay a little extra, you could enjoy a hot shower. You could put a coin in, and for fifteen minutes there would be hot water. During the hours we stayed in the cheap hotel, I paid close attention to when other people in rooms down the hall took a shower. Most people showered for only five to eight minutes, so if I timed it perfectly, I could get in the shower after they had left and enjoy a quick five-minute *hot* shower! It worked several times, but a few times I had no choice but to take a cold shower because I refused to pay the extra money.

Some people might think, "Boy, he's cheap!" But I saw it differently. I believe God placed me as a steward of the little money I had. I made sure to be very responsible with what I was given to manage. That's stewardship. We each have things we are responsible to manage in life, such as our time, health, the environment, family, and our talents, and God wants us to be faithful in how we manage the resources He places in our care. Some would say I was a little extreme in Spain, but it did leave me more money to travel!

Sounds From a Cathedral

Oh come, let us sing to the LORD;
let us make a joyful noise to the rock of our salvation!
PSALM 95:1, ESV

While studying in France I became fascinated with a musical instrument I never would have expected—the pipe organ. I never learned how to play it; I simply became very appreciative of the music that can come out of a well-played organ. In North America many churches have organs, but to me they just don't sound the same. Maybe it's the quality of the organ or maybe it's the way the buildings are built. I don't know, but when I heard the organ playing in huge, lofty cathedrals in Europe, I was thrilled.

One of my friends studying in France with me was a great organ player. He would play for church, and on a couple of occasions we traveled together to cities to listen to organ concerts in some incredible buildings and locations. For a while, one of our traditions was that on Saturday night we'd travel to the nearby city of Geneva to the cathedral of St. Pierre where each week they would offer free organ concerts. As you might know, organs are played using both hands and feet, and while the organist is playing certain pieces, sometimes their entire body is consumed by the music as they quickly move their feet along foot pedals, tapping switches with their feet. There are another couple of pedals at their feet that are used to control the volume. Their hands are busy playing the keys on not just one keyboard but sometimes three and four keyboards that are stacked in front of the organist. On the sides of the keyboards some organs have dozens of hand stops and buttons that are pushed and pulled to create different sounds. Between the different stacks of keyboards there were even more little buttons they could quickly push to change the sound. Watching them play was incredible; it was like a one-person orchestra with many wonderful sounds being created!

Our verse today reminds us of God's love of music. There are many verses in the Bible that talk about the many ways to praise God, and there are so many instruments you can use to praise Him.

Round-Trip Love

Those who are kind benefit themselves,
but the cruel bring ruin on themselves.
PROVERBS 11:17, NIV

When in college I talked to my parents about taking a year to study French in France. They were open to the idea, so we talked about all the things that would be involved. Of course, we had to study the costs to make sure it could be done. We talked about how I would not see my family during the entire time because it would be too expensive to return to North America during any break. We also discussed how expensive it was to call between Europe and the United States. Remember, when I was there, there was no e-mail, no texting, no cell phones, no Skype or FaceTime or Facebook. The only options for communicating that year would be to either call using a pay phone or write a letter and mail it. Yes, I'm talking about paper, envelopes, and stamps. Since we were on a very tight budget, we calculated that I would be able to call home once a month for about ten minutes. That seemed very sad to consider, so I made sure the other cheaper option of mailing letters was used often.

During my year in France I sent dozens of letters home to my parents and siblings. Every time I traveled anywhere during my year there, I made sure to always send home a postcard from that place. Of course, every month I very much looked forward to my call home. About fifteen years later I was visiting my parents, and they pulled out a photo album I had never seen before. When I opened it I was surprised to find all the postcards I had sent them from Europe that year! Over the next few hours I thoroughly enjoyed going through the album and carefully looking at and reading every postcard I sent them. It was a wonderful trip down memory lane for us. Initially I sent all those postcards often to help my parents not miss me so much, but years later it was I who benefited from my own acts of kindness. Be thoughtful and kind to someone around you today. They will benefit from your kindness now, and you may also benefit later!

The Choir

Praise the LORD.
How good it is to sing praises to our God,
how pleasant and fitting to praise him!
PSALM 147:1, NIV

While traveling through Europe with some friends, I found myself in Vienna, the capital of Austria. We visited a magnificent cathedral in the city center and saw many fascinating street performers showcasing their talents all along the city sidewalks. We also visited the embassies of Hungary and Czechoslovakia because we needed to get visas to enter the country from their embassies. One of the other things we wanted to see while we were there was the world famous Vienna Boys' Choir. We didn't speak German, but we did our best to ask around where we could see or hear the choir. We got some information from a person and followed their directions to a chapel, where there was a worship going on. I have to admit the choir sang beautifully. The complete choir has about one hundred boys between the ages of ten and fourteen. The group is usually divided into four touring choirs that travel all over the world, performing about three hundred concerts to a total of about half a million people each year! We were excited that we got to hear them in their home church and in their home country.

If you are reading this book you may also be between the ages of ten and fourteen. Even if you're younger or older, the point is that any person of any age can use their talents to glorify God. He has given you special talents and abilities that you can use to bring honor to the God who made you. In one of Jesus' most famous parables, He reminded us that if we don't use our talents they may be taken away. I encourage you work to identify all your talents and to use them. You may not be 100 percent sure at the beginning, but there's nothing wrong with trying new things in order to discover where you have a natural gift. The cool part is that if you use them, He will give you more!

It's a Miracle!

For we walk by faith, not by sight.
2 Corinthians 5:7, ESV

I was driving back from Spain to France because the break was ending and school would be restarting soon. But I had heard about a little town in the southwest corner of France called Lourdes, and I wanted to visit it. Besides being a beautiful town with a castle up on the hill, this is one of the top sites of "religious tourism" in the world. I soon discovered that it is believed by many that Lourdes is a place where miracles happen. Because of that, millions of people each year make a pilgrimage to Lourdes. As a matter of fact, after Paris, Lourdes is the second most visited place in France. When we arrived, there were many people there on a pilgrimage—travelling to a place of religious significance. On that day there were hundreds of sick people from local hospitals gathered in a huge plaza. The majority of them were either lying in beds or sitting in wheelchairs.

I don't know that any miracles happened there that day, but I want to tell you that miracles do happen. A miracle is something that happens which can't be explained by nature or science. In 1980 I personally witnessed a miracle while in Dallas for the General Conference session meetings with my parents. On Sabbath afternoon in the main auditorium there was a skit about the Second Coming. In the skit, actors pretending to be sick and in wheelchairs were healed before going to heaven. All of a sudden a woman in the front who was really in a wheelchair watching was suddenly healed and stood up and walked to the platform! The program was stopped, and she told her story. It was incredible. I know this was a miracle because my parents had known that woman for years. Experiencing this miracle increased my faith. Faith is a big deal to God. Showing faith is our way of showing trust in what we can't see. Just as our verse says today, go out and walk by faith, not by sight.

My First Job

The rich rule over the poor,
and the borrower is slave to the lender.
PROVERBS 22:7, NIV

When I was about ten years old, I began to wonder when I would get my first job. One day at school we heard that a local farmer was looking to hire some kids to go with him after school to his apple orchard. I talked to my parents about it, and we agreed I would go. It was my first job!

The first day arrived, and the farmer came in a pickup truck to get us after school. Apple-picking season had already passed, but our job was to pick up the apples that had ripened and fallen off the tree. We would need to pick them up and toss them into a big wooden box. I figured this was easy enough, except I was a little disgusted when I found out most of the apples were rotten—even more so when I found out they used these kinds of apples to make apple sauce. Friday finally came: payday! I eagerly stood in line and got my very own crisp twenty-dollar bill! I know that doesn't sound like much to you today, but I figured I had just made about two dollars per hour working that week! I was rich!

Believe it or not, the Bible has a lot of advice for us regarding money. The one I want to point out today has to do with debt. They didn't have banks or credit cards back then, but the idea of borrowing money has been around for a long time. In North America many people have gotten in trouble because they borrow money they can't repay. Billions of dollars are borrowed each year because people don't want to save up and wait to buy things they want, so they get in debt hoping they can repay it in the future. As you can see in our verse today, when you borrow from someone, they control you, and you end up like a slave to them till you pay it off. This is not a position God wants you to be in. As you get older, do what you can to avoid getting in debt.

Ever Heard of Andorra?

For the entire law is fulfilled in keeping this one
command: "Love your neighbor as yourself."
GALATIANS 5:14, NIV

Have you ever heard of a country called Andorra? Most people I've run into have never heard of this country. For the few who have heard of it, many of them have no idea where it is. Could you tell me where it is without looking? Andorra is a small country sandwiched between Spain and France. That border is home to a mountain range called the Pyrenees. Once, while driving through Spain with friends, we decided to make the effort to visit this small, isolated country in the mountains. The country is only about twelve miles wide by about sixteen miles long, but I found it to be an amazing little country in a beautiful setting.

However, getting there was not easy, because there are no highways to take you up there, and you have to follow a winding road all the way up. When we got there, we explored for a little while and then decided to continue our trip. As we were driving away I thought to myself, "Well, that's another new country I've visited!" But then I suddenly felt unhappy with myself, because it occurred to me that I didn't know a single person in that little country and yet each person in that country was special to God.

In my family we try to visit a nursing home once a month to spend some time with some elderly folks who may feel lonely or isolated. We sing and tell stories and try to bring joy to them. Do we know all those people there? No, but we knew that, like the people in Andorra, they are special to God too. God has put people in your life, so make a point of always bringing joy to the people around you. Of course, be wise and safe and make sure a parent or leader is always involved when you encounter people you do not know. If you're still not sure just how much you should love the people around you, read today's verse.

Five Rationed Guys

For, as I have often told you before and now tell you again even with tears, many live as enemies of the cross of Christ. Their destiny is destruction, their god is their stomach, and their glory is in their shame. Their mind is set on earthly things.
PHILIPPIANS 3:18, 19, NIV

While living in France I was forced to be extremely careful with the few dollars that I was able to save from working the previous summer. When our first break came along in October, I, along with four other guys, planned a trip to Eastern Europe to see as much as we could while spending the least amount of money possible. We had already discovered that food and restaurants in Europe were extremely expensive, so one of the areas we decided to make a major effort to cut costs on was food. Obviously we had to eat every day, but we came up with a plan to reduce our food expense to a bare minimum.

We rented a tiny Fiat Uno and squished five guys in there for our two-week trip. In the days leading up to the break, we each took back to our rooms extra slices of bread from the cafeteria and a few other things such as jelly and cheese. Soon we were off on our trip. We tried to plan three meals a day, but most days it was two. The ration plan was that for each meal we'd each get one sandwich with bread and cheese. Someone had given us onion salt too, so if we wanted to add some flavor to our sandwich, that was an option. We also got hold of this big tin can with several compartments of pretzels, crackers, Chex snack mix, and popcorn. For each meal, we got to grab a big handful. Lastly, we somehow got a large industrial-size jar of fruit cocktail. Somehow we lived on this for almost two weeks, but I'm pretty sure we all lost weight. Now, I like food just as much as the next guy, and once in a while we're probably all guilty of "pigging out." Just be careful that it's not your stomach controlling your life, because our verse today reminds us to be careful of overeating.

Thirst of Life

"But whoever drinks the water I give them will never thirst. Indeed, the water I give them will become in them a spring of water welling up to eternal life."
JOHN 4:14, NIV

During our trek over the Iberian Peninsula we crossed the border from Spain into Portugal. Our first stop was to visit the town of Évora. The countryside in this part of Portugal is beautiful, and soon in the distance we could see Évora and its whitewashed buildings on the gentle slope of a hill. We chose to come to this city because of its amazing historical value. We drove through the well-preserved medieval outer city walls and into the old city center that looked like a page out of history. The town dated back about two thousand years, so there were buildings and monuments from many different historical periods. After parking, we started to walk around to visit the various monuments, the city wall, the cathedral, and the plaza.

One thing that really impressed me was the ancient Roman aqueduct. An aqueduct is a bridge designed to carry water from one place to another. In this case the aqueduct in Évora, which was built from stones and huge arches, brought water to Évora from six miles away. Building a six-mile bridge hundreds of years ago was no easy task! But it clearly reminds me of just how precious and important water is. Life on earth cannot survive without water.

Do you remember a time in the past that you experienced a kind of thirst unlike anything you've ever felt before? Remember feeling desperate to get water? It felt so good to gulp the water when you finally got hold of some. Can you imagine drinking a special kind of water that would remove your thirst forever? People on this planet are thirsting now, but not for water; they are thirsting for truth, and our verse today tells us that the truth and love that Jesus is offering the world will satisfy them for their entire life. Will you take a drink of that water today and also share it with others?

One Big Rock

"There is no one holy like the LORD;
there is no one besides you;
there is no Rock like our God."
1 SAMUEL 2:2, NIV

Driving though the south of Spain, we passed many wonderful towns with Moorish and medieval influence, but soon we arrived at the Strait of Gibraltar—a narrow body of water that connects the Atlantic Ocean and the Mediterranean Sea. The eight-mile-wide strait is all that separates Europe from Africa. From Algeciras we looked out across the strait and could clearly see the country of Morocco in northern Africa.

Just east of Algeciras was another destination we did not want to miss—the Rock of Gibraltar—a major landmark for the entire region. Gibraltar is actually a British Overseas Territory barely touching that southernmost point of Spain. We drove to Gibraltar and entered this tiny territory that is only 2.6 square miles in size. In the center of Gibraltar was the famous Rock of Gibraltar, which is a fourteen-hundred-foot-tall limestone mountain that seems to abruptly jut out of the water. The mountain was truly impressive because everything around it was pretty low, but then all of a sudden here was this giant rock coming up out of the water. I was very excited to see that there was a road that we could take and drive all the way to the top of the rock. Along the way we were surprised to learn that the rock had a huge population of wild monkeys—the only primates on the European continent. Most impressive was the view from the top of the rock. Now we had a really good view of Africa.

Growing up, I heard an expression that was used often when we wanted to say something was safe or firm: we said it was "solid as a rock." God is the rock we can stand on. He will never let us down. He will never leave us, and He will never crumble or erode. I'm so glad I can depend on God for anything and know that nothing in the universe is stronger!

Slow and Steady

Wealth from get-rich-quick schemes quickly disappears;
wealth from hard work grows over time.
PROVERBS 13:11, NLT

A few years back our family decided to take a trip to visit Las Vegas, Nevada. At first that did not bring a very positive idea in my mind, but we were told that Las Vegas had changed a lot and that it had become very family friendly, and we decided to give it a try. We found dates that worked for everyone and looked for the best ticket price we could find as well a place to stay. Soon the day came, and we headed to Las Vegas. Vegas is famous for many negative things. Gambling is one of the most obvious things you've probably heard of. People from all over the world come and spend millions of dollars at the casinos with the hopes that they'll get lucky and win money. In the meantime, casinos profit from people who spend millions hoping they will get lucky. Sadly, the money is often from people who can't afford to be losing money.

One thing I noticed about Las Vegas as we walked around were all the copies of famous places. There was a small replica of the Eiffel Tower in France, the canals of Venice, and even a mini New York City. Of course, the copy is never quite the same as the real thing, but some hotels in the area had amazing copies of the real thing. There are two distinct things I learned from my visit to Las Vegas. First of all, I appreciated how much effort these hotels made to copy the original. As Christians, we are to copy Jesus—that's what the word *Christian* means. We are followers of Christ and seek to copy the way He lived. Second, there were a lot of people trying to get rich fast. Did you know that the Bible actually warns about trying to get rich fast? Our Bible verse today can't say it any simpler—money that comes fast tends to go fast too. When we gather it little by little, we are more careful with it, and it will be easier to save up and increase it.

Liquid Poison

*What sorrow for those who are heroes at drinking wine
and boast about all the alcohol they can hold.*
Isaiah 5:22, NLT

I visited Great Britain while I was a student in Europe, but once I was married I decided to return so that my wife could visit the many wonderful things there are to see in this amazing and diverse country. For many people, when they think of Europe, they think of castles. We decided we wanted to see an authentic royal castle, so we decided to visit the outskirts of London to see Windsor Castle, the largest inhabited royal residence in the world. The original castle was built in the eleventh century, making it one of the oldest places in England. When we arrived, we were very impressed with the size! We were also amazed to think that all this was the home of a single family. In actuality, about 150 people live and work there. During World War II, they were worried the castle would be bombed, so they darkened the windows and moved many of the most valuable works of art away. During the war, the general public was led to believe that the royal family was sleeping at Buckingham Palace in the city, but the truth was that they were staying at Windsor Castle for safety.

The castle is always well stocked and ready for anything, but one thing that concerned me about the castle is that the wine cellar at the castle held more than eighteen hundred bottles of wine. Is that really necessary? When I was younger, I had a friend who was killed by a drunk driver, so I hope this helps you understand why the thought of anyone drinking alcohol upsets me. The Bible clearly forbids drunkenness. Every day we need to keep our minds and bodies clean and pure. Every day we make choices about what we put into our bodies. Make choices today that glorify God.

Eighth-Grade Class Trip

"It is easier for a camel to go through the eye of a needle than for someone who is rich to enter the kingdom of God."
MARK 10:25, NIV

When I was in eighth grade I lived in Massachusetts. It was quite exciting when I heard the news that our eighth-grade class would be going to Washington DC for our class trip. It was the first time I took a trip without my family, so I was nervous and excited all at the same time. The school provided us with a list of things to bring for the one-week trip. We would be camping out in the basement of some church offices, so we needed to bring sleeping bags and pillows. The day came, and we piled onto the bus for the eight-hour bus ride to the nation's capital.

One day we visited the Capitol Building with its huge dome. We sure felt small in there! Another day we visited the Washington monument—a giant obelisk in the middle of the mall area. We also visited the Lincoln and Jefferson memorials and a couple of the Smithsonian museums. We even got to visit Ford's Theatre, where President Lincoln was shot while sitting in the balcony enjoying a play. Although all those places were amazing, there is no doubt in my mind what impressed me the most—the Bureau of Engraving and Printing, where they print money! As a kid, I was fascinated when they took us on the tour to show us how the government made money, including showing us from behind a super-thick glass window a huge pile of money, more money than I had ever seen in my entire life.

Why do we spend time daydreaming about being rich? Maybe you've asked a friend before, "What would you buy first if you had a million dollars?" Today I need to warn you about something. One of the most dangerous threats to a Christian is the love of money. Just look at our verse today for proof. It says it would be easier to stuff a camel through a tiny hole than for a wealthy person to go to heaven. That's pretty scary. That's how evil the "love of money" is. It's true that we need money to live; just don't let it run your life.

Consequences of Sin

For the wages of sin is death, but the gift of
God is eternal life in Christ Jesus our Lord.
ROMANS 6:23, NIV

If you pull out a map and look at the middle of Utah you'd probably say there's not much there. Wrong. Near the center of the state there is a town called Delta. One time we drove west from Delta for about thirty miles. On the left was a huge, white salt flat. On the right, a mountain range rose from the desert floor. We got off the paved road and onto a gravel road and headed toward the mountain twenty miles ahead of us. The gravel road was in decent shape, but it was obvious that only a few cars used this road. Soon we started to gently climb the mountain slopes.

We arrived at a place in the desert where there is a special layer of shale rock exposed by erosion caused by water and wind. Embedded in this layer of rock you can dig for trilobite fossils. Trilobites are marine creatures that appear to have become extinct during the Flood because they are found rapidly buried and preserved in this rock layer. We paid a small fee and received a little bucket with tools to split the pieces of shale in the quarry. We'd pick up a rock, split it with the tool, and see if there was a trilobite hidden there. It was like searching for hidden treasure! My family and I spent about two hours there, and collectively we found about one hundred trilobite fossils of various sizes. I think the biggest one we found was almost two inches wide! I know this sounds creepy, but we were surprised how much fun we had digging for dead creatures.

Even though death is a horrible thing, humans on this planet seem to have gotten used to it. You've probably heard someone say, "Death is part of life." Actually, it's not. Death is a terrible consequence of sin. When God made life, death was not part of the plan. That's why forgiveness from sin is so important. That's also why I can't wait to get to heaven, where there will be no sin or death.

Don't Judge the Desert

"Do not judge, or you too will be judged. For in the same way you judge others, you will be judged, and with the measure you use, it will be measured to you."
MATTHEW 7:1, 2, NIV

Driving through a desert would seem like a boring thing to do, but one day we drove through southeast Utah and were amazed at some of the landscapes in this part of the world. We headed south from a town called Moab into an amazing desert filled with canyons and cliff walls. All of a sudden ahead of us was a massive snowcapped mountain range that seemed to pop up out of nowhere. Nearing the Arizona border, we then arrived at an unforgettable place called Goosenecks State Park, where the San Juan River meanders in huge S-curves along the bottom of a one-thousand-foot, shockingly deep canyon. I remember walking up to the edge of that canyon. I had to catch my breath at the sight. Soon we passed a town with a memorable name—Mexican Hat.

Continuing on Highway 163, we next drove through an incredible piece of the southwest desert called Monument Valley. It's a region of the expansive Colorado Plateau, where a cluster of huge sandstone buttes rises dramatically off the valley floor, the largest shooting up one thousand feet in the air. If you've never been to the old west, this is probably what you would imagine the American West looking like. All of these places I mentioned seem to be in the middle of nowhere, but it's thrilling to see stunning landscapes like these in some of the remotest places in the world. This is why I love road trips. You never quite fully know what you're going to see till you are standing there in front of it. Some people assume there's nothing in the desert, but they have judged prematurely. In the same way, sometimes people judge each other based on something someone said or on the outward appearance. This almost always backfires and ends up causing bigger problems. Our verse today says it pretty simply: Don't judge other people. Instead, look for the positive in people!

Twenty-Five Years

Do not be anxious about anything, but in every situation, by prayer and petition, with thanksgiving, present your requests to God.
PHILIPPIANS 4:6, NIV

The first time I visited Prague was in 1989, when it was part of Czechoslovakia and a stronghold of Eastern European communism. The second time I went to Prague, in 2014, it was free from communism and belonged to a country called the Czech Republic. I was shocked when I visited the city the second time after more than twenty-five years. Although pretty much all of the buildings were still there and they still looked the same, I was surprised to see how commercialism made a huge impact and changed the city.

In 1989 the six-hundred-year-old Charles Bridge between one side of the city and the other was a quiet misty walk over the Vltava River. Now it was crowded with street performers and vendors doing everything possible to squeeze a Euro or two out of tourists. The last time I stood in the main plaza in 1989, there was not a single store or kiosk or cart in sight. There was nothing to buy, and the only thing to see were the magnificent old baroque buildings surrounding the plaza. In 1989 as we stood in the plaza we were not able to identify one other tourist. Today, the plaza is a busy, bustling center of commerce and shops with hundreds and even thousands of tourists walking around taking pictures, buying souvenirs, drinking something at a café, or munching on a snack. The change I witnessed in twenty-five years was unfathomable.

Change is an inevitable part of life. Maybe you've moved, maybe your family dynamic has changed, maybe you're at a new school, or maybe you're anxious about something that might happen. God says we should trust Him and come to Him in prayer with thanksgiving and requests. Stressing and worrying does nothing to help. That's why our verse today reminds us to not worry and just humbly present our requests to God.

Hot Stick

Can a man walk on hot coals
without his feet being scorched?
PROVERBS 6:28, NIV

Our flight landed in Kona on the big island of Hawaii, and my number-one destination was Volcanoes National Park. After entering the park, we first visited a huge crater that was on the side of the volcano called Kilauea and had sulfur clouds rising from the crater floor. Next we took the Chain of Craters Road that would lead us down the mountainside toward the ocean. An older flow had covered up the road we were driving on, so we parked and continued over the hardened lava field on foot.

Before entering the lava field, I found a wooden stick to carry with me in case I encountered flowing lava and I could poke it. About two hours into the hike, the temperature suddenly jumped by fifteen to twenty degrees—I knew lava was close by! I looked around and, sure enough, about twenty feet away I spotted a slow-moving stream of lava. I carefully walked toward the lava and pulled out the wooden stick I had with me. The heat was intense, and I could only stay within a couple of feet for a moment. I poked the lava, and the stick immediately caught fire!

Have you ever heard the expression, "If you play with fire, you're going to get burned"? Well, I'm glad I didn't get burned that day, but later I concluded that I had put myself a little too close to danger. There are many things around us that can hurt us, such as drugs, alcohol, smoking, bad food, violent video games, inappropriate books and movies, and destructive music. Some people think it's smart to see how close you can get to those things without getting "burned," but if you ask me, that's foolish. A wise person would stay far away from those harmful things. Ask God today to help you have the courage to stay away from things that will hurt you and separate you from Him.

The Right Idol

"You shall have no other gods before me."
EXODUS *20:3, NIV*

Several years ago I was in central California visiting my parents with my family. We rented a car at the airport in San Francisco and decided that part of our trip would include a visit to Southern California. We drove down and spent a couple of days visiting some of the main sights in that area. During one of our days in Southern California we drove to Hollywood and Beverly Hills to look around. In Hollywood we drove as close as we could to the big Hollywood sign and also looked at all the big studios that filled up several entire city blocks. These are the places where actors and actresses come to make movies, TV shows, and other productions.

One of the last stops we made was to Mann's Chinese Theater—where actors and actresses come and put their hands and feet in fresh cement on the sidewalk. Along the sidewalk in front of the theater there were stars embedded into the sidewalk with the names of Hollywood people who made a contribution to the industry. That's when I started thinking to myself, "What are these people really contributing to the world? Entertainment. Is that it?" I realized that some of these people were making millions and millions of dollars working in film or TV while many people practically worship the ground they walk on, following everything they do in the news, on Twitter, or Instagram. People line up on the street by the thousands to just get a quick peek at their idol, sometimes screaming and waving uncontrollably. Is it right to give glory to other people like that? It made me think about the first commandment. It simply states that we should have no other gods before God. Nevertheless, our sneaky enemy has convinced people to treat other people like gods while treating God as though He doesn't exist. In all you do, remember every day to keep God number one in your life. Worship the true God of the universe!

The Oracle

It is better to take refuge in the LORD
than to trust in humans.
PSALM 118:8, NIV

As my wife and I spent time exploring Greece, my love for ancient architecture and famous landmarks led us to make plans to travel to a city called Delphi, which is several hours from Athens by bus. The ancient Greeks were famous for building temples, and the ruins of many temples could be seen throughout the countryside. Traveling in Greece during this trip was difficult due to the language barrier, but we managed to buy tickets to Delphi.

After arriving, we walked around and explored the ancient ruins dating to a time several hundred years before Jesus walked on earth. The centerpiece of the ruins was the Temple of Apollo, dedicated to a mythical god they believed in. If you wanted to ask the god for something, you spoke to the oracle— a priestess who claimed to talk to the gods and claimed to predict the future. In life I've noticed that sometimes people are so desperate to know the future, they will believe anyone who claims to have the ability to tell the future. But only God can tell the future.

The Bible is filled with hundreds of prophecies of things that would happen in the future. I love the fact that many biblical prophecies have already come true. The oracle at Delphi tried to tell about the future, but the answers were usually vague. If someone asked, "Will the frost be gone tomorrow so I can plant my crops?" She would answer something vague like, "The frost will be gone if the gods will it." It was an answer that didn't say much. The true power of prophecy found in the Bible is another wonderful clue to show us that the Bible is God's Holy Word. Prophecy tells us that the Bible is God's Word and that it can be trusted.

God Knows Best

He will cover you with his feathers,
and under his wings you will find refuge;
his faithfulness will be your shield and rampart.
PSALM 91:4, NIV

My wife and I drove through the southern part of Africa in early 2000. Naturally we had a basic idea of the places we wanted to visit during our time there. As our time in Africa started to wind down we found ourselves driving south through Zimbabwe into South Africa, where we'd eventually turn east and drive toward the city of Maputo in Mozambique. Unfortunately, in the weeks leading up to our trip to Africa we had heard about Mozambique in the news. Several months earlier, five straight weeks of heavy rainfall pounded parts of the country and caused a lot of destruction. The flooding caused many of the main rivers in the country to flood. We checked the news to see if the situation had improved in time for us to visit. A couple of weeks before our trip, the flooding began to recede, and now as we drove toward Mozambique the situation took a terrible turn for the worse. Cyclone Eline made landfall in Mozambique, bringing so much destruction that it is still considered the country's worst natural disaster in a century.

We never made it to Mozambique. The border closed a couple of days before we arrived, which was a blessing in disguise. If we had gone in just a few days earlier we might have gotten trapped in the country during the terrible storm. Instead we veered south and visited Swaziland, missing the effects of the storm. Nevertheless, our hearts and prayers were with those people in Mozambique just a few hundred miles away as they dealt with the fury of the storm. As you grow, you will encounter storms in your life. There's no way to avoid them, it's part of living in this sinful world. The best thing you can do is to be prepared for when the storms arrive by putting your faith in God and taking shelter under His wings.

A Visit to Arches

Commit to the LORD whatever you do,
and he will establish your plans.
PROVERBS 16:3, NIV

Our destination that day was Arches National Park—a desert known for containing more than two thousand natural sandstone arches. Just outside the town of Moab we arrived at the entrance of the park, but to reach the higher plains where the arches were located we had to drive up a huge cliff wall on a trail with several switchbacks. Our first stop was at the Park Avenue trailhead—a wonderful trail down the middle of a dry streambed with towering red cliff walls on either side. Driving in farther, we encountered many trails where we could hike and explore many different natural arches formed by erosion.

One interesting feature of the park is the petroglyphs. Petroglyphs are images created by removing part of a rock surface by carving or picking. The petroglyphs showed horses with riders surrounded by bighorn sheep. Historians believe that they were made hundreds of years ago. It made me wonder about those people back then. Did a native just decide to draw himself up on a horse surrounded by sheep one day? Or was it drawn by a young native dreaming about being a brave member of his tribe someday?

When you were little, did you ever draw pictures of how you thought you might be when you grew up? God has a plan for each one of us. He has a plan for you. The question is, will you trust Him to let His plan come through in your life? He's not trying to run your life for you; He just wants you to commit whatever you do to Him, and He has promised to help guide you on your path. Remember, when you trust your life to the Creator of the universe, your life is in good hands.

City Center Surprise

Obey your leaders and submit to them, for they are keeping watch over your souls, as those who will have to give an account. Let them do this with joy and not with groaning, for that would be of no advantage to you.
HEBREWS 13:17, ESV

A few years back I traveled to El Salvador for some speaking events. When I travel to unique places, I usually try to make time to go to a few locations and film. This time I wrote a script to use while filming at three locations in El Salvador. By the last day of my trip, I had only shot at two of the three locations—this meant trouble because unless I shot that last part, I did not have enough footage for a complete episode.

On that last day I was responsible for two final presentations in the convention center in downtown San Salvador. It would be dark after my final presentation, and my flight the next morning was very early. It seemed hopeless. But when I talked to the leader of the event, we saw that there was a two-hour break between my two presentations. She knew I was trying to shoot this video, so when I asked her what she thought about me going out to film between programs, she told me to go for it. When we got to the site of the volcano, we worked quickly through our scenes and finished the recording. Then I made it back just in time for my second presentation.

I was very grateful that the organizers decided I had time to shoot the video, but if they had said there wasn't time, what would have happened? Would I have gone anyway? No. Would I have been grumpy or in a bad mood? No. I accepted that the people who invited me had authority over what I would be able to do. Whether we like it or not, there will be people in our lives that God has placed there to have authority over us, such as parents, teachers, mayors, coaches, or bosses. They may not always be perfect, but they have been given that authority, and it is our job to be obedient.

Ten Days, Ten Cities

This is the confidence we have in approaching God:
that if we ask anything according to his will, he hears us.
1 JOHN 5:14, NIV

I landed in Munich, Germany and headed through customs and immigration. Two leaders from the local church picked me up, and we immediately drove to the first place on the tour of Austria to present the "Austria Creation Tour" in ten cities. It was very well organized and promoted, and all that was left was to start the tour.

Arriving in Dornbirn, the first town, we quickly set up a huge screen and projector, a large exhibit area with a couple dozen banners and exhibits, and even an area for kids to play and learn. After the event, we tore down everything and headed to a nearby church, where we were given an area to lay out our sleeping bags. In the morning, the local church members came and provided us with a delicious breakfast, and then we headed out to the next city in order to start setting up for the evening program. We did this for ten days straight.

The tour took us to many wonderful towns, including the capital, Vienna, but I will never forget when we arrived in the city of Graz. In this city, the event would occur in a place called Dom im Berg, a cave cut out of the side of a mountain created so the local people could hide from air raids during World War II. Now this huge cave had been converted into a hall for events, banquets, concerts, and other functions. The arched ceiling and walls had been cut out of rock, and all the necessary wiring and lighting and seating had been installed to make this the most unusual place I had ever spoken at. Even though I was deep under a mountain, I prayed to God to bless that event. Do you think He heard my prayer? Yes. There is nowhere you can go on this planet where God won't hear your prayers! Not even in a deep underground cave.

First Taste of Freedom

*It is for freedom that Christ has set us free. Stand firm, then, and
do not let yourselves be burdened again by a yoke of slavery.*
GALATIANS 5:1, NIV

The year 1989 was a pivotal year for the country of Hungary. It was one of the first communist countries in Eastern Europe to visibly start to distance itself from the Soviet Union and embrace the fall of communism. During this time, I visited Hungary with a few friends. Prior to our visit, Hungary began taking down its barbed-wire fence along the Austrian border, representing the first tear in the "Iron Curtain" that had divided Europe since the end of World War II. A few weeks before we arrived in Budapest, the first McDonald's restaurant in the country had opened! Little by little, many small changes were happening. The people in Hungary were eager for change and freedom, but for some it did not come quick enough. Some people were still very poor and dependent on the government.

While in Hungary, my friends and I were hungry and asked where we could find a restaurant (there were only a few places that had opened). We had already reluctantly eaten at McDonald's once and didn't want to go back, so we were happy to hear about a pizzeria that had just opened. When we arrived we wondered if this was the only pizzeria in the city—it looked like it had opened *that day!* The people in Hungary hadn't had that kind of freedom in almost fifty years. We were shocked when we noticed that a personal "plate-size" pizza was only $1.50. We noticed a couple sharing one of those plate-size pizzas, and it made us think how this was probably the first time these people had ever eaten out in their life. Possibly, it was their first taste of freedom. In North America we are blessed with freedom, but unfortunately we are still slaves to sin. Today, ask God to free you from the bondage of sin so you can live every day in God's freedom.

The Snowstorm Trap

A perverse person stirs up conflict,
and a gossip separates close friends.
PROVERBS 16:28, NIV

I love experiencing the four seasons each year in Michigan. During the spring everything comes back to life in full color. The summer days are warm and pleasant. Fall is my favorite season as the temperatures start to cool and the tree leaves turn into magnificent colors and then fall to the ground. When winter arrives there is usually no shortage of snow and cold.

A few years ago during a particularly intense winter storm, the forecast called for the triple whammy of (1) heavy amounts of snowfall, (2) strong winds, and (3) very cold temperatures. One morning during this storm, my wife had to leave for work at 6:00 A.M. I plowed the drive so she could get out, and we prayed she would make it to work safely. Less than a minute later I got a call from her. Just up the street, a massive eight-foot-deep snowdrift had covered the street, and because of the whiteout conditions she had plowed into the drift and gotten stuck. I drove my Jeep up the street to get her. We then drove down the street in the opposite direction to see if we could get out a different way, but we discovered that the winds had knocked over a huge tree and it blocked the entire street. We were trapped!

This reminded me that Satan is constantly trying to trap us with bad habits. One of the most destructive habits people get trapped in seems harmless, but it's not—gossip. There are two major problems with gossip. First, the one who gossips often does it to make themselves look good while making others look bad. Second, the gossip often involves lies or embarrassing details that shouldn't be shared. Gossip is very un-Christlike, and it's a sure way to destroy a relationship. Don't be a gossip, and if you hear someone else gossiping, make a statement by leaving.

Surprise Castle

*For just as the body is one and has many members, and all the members
of the body, though many, are one body, so it is with Christ. For in one
Spirit we were all baptized into one body—Jews or Greeks, slaves or
free—and all were made to drink of one Spirit.*
1 CORINTHIANS 12:12, 13, ESV

A couple of years ago I was invited to be part of a ten-day "Creation Tour" through Austria, where we presented outreach events in ten different Austrian cities. I was excited to have my family join me after the tour to spend a little time exploring Europe. It was the first time our boys had visited Europe, so as we planned our tour, I asked the boys one question: Do you prefer to spend time soaking in a few neat locations, or would you rather quickly move through a lot of locations in order to see as much as possible? Of course, they wanted to see as much as possible.

We picked up our rental car from Vienna, Austria and headed out. We had laid out a plan that would take us to the maximum number of locations and countries we could squeeze into the time we had. As we left Prague in the Czech Republic, we all knew our next stop would be Berlin, Germany. A few hours later, we stopped and parked. I told the boys we were going to make a little stop to visit a neat old castle. Just before we walked through the outer walls of the castle, I stopped the boys and told them I had a surprise for them. They looked at me with curiosity as I simply looked at them and said, "We're in Poland." You can imagine their surprise when they found out they were standing in a country they had never expected to visit!

There are about two hundred countries in the world and many different cultures. Because Satan is out to destroy God's creations, he works to create hate wherever he can. He has convinced people all over that they must hate people because they're different. Do not fall for his tricks! God created everyone, and I think it's cool that there is so much variety! Celebrate variety; it's a beautiful thing.

Big Talk

Let no corrupting talk come out of your mouths, but only such as is good for building up, as fits the occasion, that it may give grace to those who hear.
EPHESIANS 4:29, ESV

For many years I've lived in and around the small town of Berrien Springs, Michigan—the home of Andrews University. Students from all over the world come to Andrews to study for a few years. Berrien Springs has one of the oldest courthouses in the United States. For many years this little town was also the home to one of the most famous people in the world. I'll tell you who it was in a moment. Now, each year Berrien Springs hosts the county youth fair, where thousands of people come during a fun week in August. There are rides, food, exhibits, animals, and many other fun things to see and do.

One year, as my wife and I were leaving the fair, I was surprised to see a famous person approaching. I immediately knew who he was because I had heard he lived in Berrien Springs. I even knew where his house was, but I had never run into him before. Walking toward us was Muhammad Ali, considered by many to be the greatest heavyweight boxer in the history of the sport and probably one of the most recognizable sports figures of all time. I stopped and greeted him and shook his hand.

Ali was a great boxer, but he was also famous because of his "trash talking." Before and even during his fights, he would insult and bait his opponents with words, trying to get them to lose their focus and composure. In addition to that, he loved to tell the press that he was "the greatest." The words we use every day should be chosen very carefully. Bragging to build one up and bullying to tear others down are not the kind of words that bring God honor. Some people don't think before they talk. But if you really want to honor God, think before you speak, and use words that build other people up!

Your Daily Bread

Very early in the morning, while it was still dark, Jesus got up, left the house and went off to a solitary place, where he prayed.
MARK 1:35, NIV

From Santiago, the capital of Chile, my wife and I boarded a bus that would take us north to the city of La Serena—a coastal town and Chile's second-oldest city. It was about a seven-hour drive, but we were happy to spend a few days with some of my relatives there. My uncle picked us up at the bus station when we finally arrived. Because it's closer to the equator, La Serena is one of the most popular summer beach destinations in Chile. The warm weather and miles of beautiful beaches bring thousands each year from all over the continent.

During our days there, my uncle took us around to visit the area. One day he decided to drive us inland toward the Andes mountain range, which is in the background of practically every city in Chile. As we drove higher I made a fascinating realization; we were entering a very hot and arid desert region of Chile that has become an important agricultural area. Because of the warm weather and annual melting snow coming down off the Andes, it has become an ideal place to grow food. The only problem is that the waters were plentiful mostly during the spring. My uncle took me higher into the mountains till we reached a huge reservoir created by a massive dam that had been built recently. The dam was built to collect water and let it through to the farms little by little so that water was available all year long.

In order to grow healthy crops, plants need a little water on a regular basis. You can't water a plant once and expect it to grow from that one watering. God has asked us to do the same with our devotional time. We need to spend time with God on a regular basis, not just once a month or a few times a year. Our relationship with God will grow as we spend time with Him every day, all year long. Spend some quiet time alone with God today!

Egyptian Train Trek

*"The stranger who dwells among you shall be to you as one
born among you, and you shall love him as yourself; for you
were strangers in the land of Egypt: I am the LORD your God."*
LEVITICUS 19:34, NKJV

During our trip to Egypt, my friends and I decided to see if we could visit Luxor, a city in the southern part of Egypt. Luxor was home to two of the most famous Egyptian temples: the Temple of Luxor and the Temple of Karnak. We soon found out that the best way to get there was by train. We proceeded to the train station and asked about tickets and prices. As it turns out, we couldn't afford first-class or second-class tickets, but fortunately third-class tickets were within our budget. It was an overnight twelve-hour train ride, and by 7:00 P.M. we were on our way.

Riding third class was quite an interesting experience. Besides the car having animals in it and hay on the floor, the people were incredibly friendly. One man in particular set out to make friends with us. Along with about eight or ten other Egyptians, they surrounded our seats, and over the next two or three hours proceeded to teach us Arabic words. They would say the words, we would repeat, and they would laugh. I'm sure we had a funny accent, but we had a great time. After a few hours of sleep, we were awakened by the intense sunlight beaming through the windows. A couple of hours before arriving in Luxor, the train slowed down while passing through a village. Someone must have bought a huge bunch of sugarcane stalks, because they were tossed onto our car, and everyone was handed a huge seven-foot-tall stalk to eat. None of us had ever tried eating sugarcane before, but they showed us how to use our teeth to peel the stalk and enjoy sucking on the sweet cane juice over the next hour or two. During that ride, my friends and I were very impressed at how friendly and hospitable the Egyptian people were to us. I believe their attitude toward my friends and me is the same way Jesus treated every stranger that He met. By the way, look at today's verse and you will see why it especially means a lot to me.

My Trial at the Nile

My brethren, count it all joy when you fall into various trials,
knowing that the testing of your faith produces patience.
JAMES 1:2, 3, NKJV

My friends and I arrived in a city called Luxor, Egypt after a twelve-hour train ride. Our plan was to visit the Valley of the Kings, where many pharaohs were buried. From the train station, a horse-and-cart taxi took us to a small hotel. We were hungry, so we found a little stand on wheels with a man selling fresh bread. It looked and smelled so good that we offered to buy every piece of bread in his cart, but he only sold us two each because many other people were expecting to get bread too.

Our first obstacle was that the Valley of the Kings was on the other side of the Nile River. After walking a little we found a place that rented bicycles. They looked about fifty years old, but we didn't see any better options. We rode straight toward the River Nile and found another obstacle—no bridge! The only way across was by boat or ferry. An Egyptian man saw our dilemma, so he approached us with his broken English and offered to help us find a way across. He took us downriver a little way to an elderly man who had a tiny sailboat. He insisted there was room for all four of us and our bikes on the boat. About halfway across we hit another obstacle; the wind completely died, and we were now stuck in the middle of the Nile. Fortunately the river was not deep, and the man had a long pole on the boat, so he started to push us across the Nile with the pole. It took almost an hour, but we finally made it across!

Trials and obstacles are a guaranteed part of life; isn't that great? I'm serious; the Bible encourages us to take a different approach to how we look at trials. Our verse today says we should be joyful when trials come our way, because the testing of our faith will produce patience. We can all use more patience!

Valley of the Kings and Queens

For the living know that they will die;
But the dead know nothing,
And they have no more reward,
For the memory of them is forgotten.
ECCLESIASTES 9:5, NKJV

We finally managed to get across the Nile River in Luxor, Egypt with our rented bikes. We didn't have a very good map, but we had an idea of where we were going, so we rode off on our bikes. Every time we rode through a village, the kids who lived there would run out to the street and run alongside our bikes, laughing and screaming out the two or three words they knew how to say in English. Some would say, "Hello!" while others would say, "Good morning, America," even though it was the middle of the afternoon. Sometimes we would stop to say hello and try to talk with them for a few minutes.

As we rode deeper and deeper into the desert, we passed huge Egyptian temples and monuments that were thousands of years old. There were so many temples that we ended up selecting random temples to stop and explore. Part way through our excursion, three of our four bikes started breaking. On one, the chain kept falling off; on another, the breaks were malfunctioning; and on the third, one of the tires was mostly flat. We pressed on, knowing this was a once-in-a-lifetime opportunity, and we weren't about to let anything stop us from visiting some of the most incredible ruins in the world. Toward the end of the day we made it to the burial temple of Queen Hatshepsut, which was built into the side of an escarpment. The temple had a huge set of steps that extended from the temple, giving it a very majestic feel.

Standing in front of these impressive temples made me wonder why people would build such enormous temples for the dead. The dead people can't see or enjoy the buildings, because the Bible teaches us that the dead don't know anything.

Odyssey to the Red Sea

So God led the people around by way of the wilderness of the Red Sea.
And the children of Israel went up in orderly ranks out of the land of Egypt.
Exodus 13:18, NKJV

We left Luxor, Egypt and headed east toward the Red Sea. We all remembered the exciting stories of the children of Israel as they left Egypt and as God parted the waters of the Red Sea. When we got off the bus in Hurghada we were met with several surprises. First of all, there were about thirty hotel representatives trying to get us to stay at their hotel. Since we were the only four tourists that got off the bus, all thirty men surrounded us and started shouting over each other, trying to get us to come stay at their hotel. Over the next few minutes it escalated even further as the men pushed and fought to get close to us. It was insane. My friends and I didn't know what to do, so I finally took action and shouted at the top of my voice, "We're only passing through. We're not staying here tonight!" We really didn't know where we would sleep that night, but that seemed to work as they all slowly left.

As we walked toward the Red Sea, a second surprise unfolded. We quickly noticed that at every intersection of the city there were several well-armed Egyptian army soldiers. We soon found out why. About an hour later, Egyptian president Hosni Mubarak passed through in his motorcade. With him was Libyan president Muammar Gaddafi. They were touring Egyptian military bases nearby. I never dreamed I would see those two presidents that day in Egypt. But we did finally make it to the Red Sea.

As I travel, I particularly enjoy visiting places that are mentioned in the Bible, such as the Red Sea, because they make the Bible even more real to me. Some people believe the Bible isn't true, but history and archeology have confirmed many examples of places, events, and people from the Bible as being real. We can use these discoveries to build our faith in the Bible.

The Horrible Bus Ride

For you were bought at a price;
therefore glorify God in your body
and in your spirit, which are God's.
1 CORINTHIANS 6:20, NKJV

We left Hurghada, Egypt and headed north to the city of Suez, along the Suez Canal. This bus ride would prove to be one of the hardest moments of our trip. When we boarded the bus, it was packed with people, so we had to sit separately. The next challenge we faced on this trip was that the only seats available for us to sit in were toward the back of the bus. The reason that was a problem was that at the very front of the bus there was a small television mounted to the ceiling showing old Egyptian movies, but the only speakers on the bus that were working were in the back. In order for every person on the bus to hear the movie, including the people at the front of the bus, the driver had the volume on max. For ten hours I had deafening audio from Arabic movies blasting my ears.

Believe it or not, there was one more devastating part of this bus ride. About 75 percent of the people on the bus were constantly smoking, and because the Egyptians considered this time of year to be winter, all the windows of the bus were closed. If I ever contract lung cancer, I'll know where it came from! Thankfully, I got a window seat, and thankfully, I was able to have my window inconspicuously cracked about two inches. My neighbors complained once in a while, but I always managed to keep it a little open. I spent the entire ten-hour ride straining to press my nose against the two-inch-window crack, gasping for fresh air. When we finally arrived in Suez, my neck was incredibly sore, and I wasn't able to move it for twenty-four hours after that.

Smoking is incredibly destructive to our bodies. The Bible says we were purchased by Jesus' blood; therefore, we should glorify God with our body. Pay attention to what you do with your body, not just what you put in it but how you use it. Honor God with your body.

Shaky Ground

He will wipe every tear from their eyes. There will be no more death or
mourning or crying or pain, for the old order of things has passed away.
REVELATION 21:4, NIV

Just outside La Serena, Chile, a dam was built to collect water. The interesting thing about the area is that it's a desert, but because of the dam, the Elqui Valley below it has become a lush agricultural zone. There's another unusual aspect about this area I want to tell you about; there are a lot of earthquakes. In an earthquake, the surface of the earth shakes because of the sudden release of energy from the earth's crust. I was shocked to find out that in the area surrounding La Serena there is an average of one earthquake per day!

Chile has suffered many terrible earthquakes in its past. In 1960, the most powerful earthquake in Chile was recorded near Valdivia; but twenty-one years before that, in 1939, the deadliest earthquake ever to hit Chile struck the city of Chillán, where my father was living. He was sixteen years old at the time. The violent earthquake struck the city around 11:30 P.M. and immediately destroyed about half of the city. Aftershocks followed, leaving the city completely destroyed. The death toll from that event was around fifty thousand people, and another sixty thousand were injured. In the city of Chillán, one-fourth of the people died. My father and his family were spared that day; he survived to tell others about his experience. Occasionally, he told me about that day and the neighbors, teachers, and friends he lost.

When God created us there was no death—everything was perfect—but because of Satan's lies, humanity fell to sin. Have you had someone close to you die? It's a horrible thing, and we have no choice but to continue on. I can't wait till Jesus returns, because the dead in Christ will rise again. Our verse today reminds us that there will be no death in heaven. No crying, no pain, no mourning. We are blessed to live with that hope!

A Secret Place

"Do not store up for yourselves treasures on earth, where moths and vermin destroy, and where thieves break in and steal. But store up for yourselves treasures in heaven, where moths and vermin do not destroy, and where thieves do not break in and steal. For where your treasure is, there your heart will be also."
MATTHEW 6:19–21, NIV

As a pastor's kid, I moved around a lot, but I'm happy that during my elementary years we lived in one place for about six years. We lived in a country town in Massachusetts with a population of about five hundred. We had very few neighbors, but it was a fun way to grow up, and I enjoyed having plenty of countryside to play in.

One day, one of my friends told me that he had heard about a place nearby called Forty Caves. It was not an official park or destination, and it was a hard place to find unless someone told you how to get there. It all sounded very exciting and mysterious. The place was only a mile or two from my home, so one day my friend and I jumped on our bikes and we followed the directions given to us. First, we had to ride on a small country road for about a mile till we reached a railroad crossing. Next, we carefully left the road and carefully followed the railroad tracks, being sure there were no trains coming. After a while, we came to a certain tree on the left that supposedly had a small dirt trailhead forming there. After a few minutes of searching we found the trail into the dense woods. We walked in, and with almost no warning we suddenly arrived in a deep rocky ravine where huge boulders had created a maze of little caves between the rocks. Arriving at this place was like finding a treasure! We never knew such an exciting place to explore had been there all along!

No treasure compares to the treasure that awaits us in heaven. Earthly treasures are temporary and will one day be gone. Don't live your life for short-term treasures; make sure your heart longs for the real treasure. The treasure that God is offering us will last for all eternity!

ABC in 1-2-3

"Therefore go and make disciples of all nations, baptizing them in the name of the Father and of the Son and of the Holy Spirit."
MATTHEW 28:19, NIV

Have you ever heard of the ABC islands? They're not actually called the ABC islands, but that is a nickname they were given because they are a set of three islands in the Caribbean Sea, off the coast of Venezuela. The islands are called Aruba, Bonaire, and Curaçao, and they are part of the Kingdom of the Netherlands. Recently my family and I were invited to come down to do a series of meetings on the three islands in three days. We gladly accepted and were blessed during our time there. Our tour finished on Aruba, and we gave ourselves an extra day to stay and explore the island. We decided to rent a four-person ATV to explore Arikok National Park. One thing about the ABC islands that intrigued me was that they had their own language called *Papiamento*—the only place in the world where it's spoken.

According to some calculations, it's estimated that there are almost seven thousand languages in the world! I read recently that the Bible has been translated into almost three thousand of those languages. The next most translated book only has about six hundred translations. Even though three thousand is a lot, it's a reminder that there are still about four thousand languages that do not yet have a Bible translation. Many people haven't been able to read the Bible.

Today, let's remember the Great Commission given to us by Jesus as He ascended into heaven, telling us to go and make disciples of all the nations. In order to reach all those people, we're going to have to be smart and work together. That is the beautiful thing about the church; it's our team of believers that are working together to spread the word. Even if you're young, you are part of God's team and can help get the work done right where you are!

The Laws of Life

But whoever looks intently into the perfect law that gives freedom, and continues in it—not forgetting what they have heard, but doing it—they will be blessed in what they do.
JAMES 1:25, NIV

It seems like at least once a year my family drives from Michigan to Florida. Sometimes it's for work and meetings, sometimes it's to visit family, and other times it's to simply rest or take a break from the winter weather. Just recently we were coming back from a trip to Florida, and we decided to pick a place to stop and do something fun. Previously, I had found a place in the little town of Horse Cave, Kentucky. Right in the center of the little downtown we found Hidden River Cave. I thought it was unusual to find a cave right in the middle of a town, but there it was, a huge hole in the ground about the size of a city block. After getting our tickets, we were led down some steps to the entrance to the cave and were given a tour. After the cave tour, we decided to try two other activities they offered there at the cave.

First of all, we were each fitted with a harness and taken to the top ledge of the cave, where we would get to zip-line over and above the giant hole in the ground that led down to the cave opening. After we each zip-lined across the hole, we were taken to another part of that huge hole where we were tied into another rope that was dangling down a seventy-five-foot-tall rock face to the bottom of the hole. One by one we each backed out over the edge of the rock cliff and rappelled down the face of the rock to the bottom. When you rappel, you are tied into a rope and you let yourself down the rock face a little at a time, or you can let the rope out faster and descend quite quickly. The natural laws of gravity made that whole experience possible. People have also made laws made to govern people. Those are important to obey too. The most important laws are the ones given by God. Keep them in your heart and you will be blessed!

Got a Brother or Sister?

"But I say to you that everyone who is angry with his brother shall be guilty before the court; and whoever says to his brother, 'You good-for-nothing,' shall be guilty before the supreme court; and whoever says, 'You fool,' shall be guilty enough to go into the fiery hell."
MATTHEW 5:22, NASB

When my boys were little, I had the privilege of staying home with them at least three days each week while my wife worked part time. During those three days we had a routine of going to three or four places they loved to visit. We had a wonderful, historical train station in our town where they loved to watch the trains come and go. During rainy and cold days we'd head to the public library to read a bunch of books. Another day of the week we went to the nearby zoo. The boys knew their way around the zoo, and they anticipated each animal that was coming up—and even named some of them. There was an area where they could feed ducks. There was also a pair of emus there that must have loved the boys because my boys would collect dandelions all over the zoo so that when they arrived at the emu corral they would hand-feed them. The emus loved it and would run to them when they saw the boys approaching.

On the campus of Andrews University near our home there was a dairy farm. Every week we went to see the cows eating and being milked. My sons' favorite part was visiting the barn with the baby calves. My boys had a wonderful time in these places even though once in a while they didn't always get along perfectly. Siblings can be like that sometimes.

The Bible talks about brothers—even though most of the time I think it's referring to Christians as brothers in Christ—but if you have a sibling you don't always get along with, our verse today applies to you. It's a strong reminder that God expects us to be kind to our brothers and sisters in Christ, as well as our real brothers and sisters. Siblings are meant to be a blessing. Don't let Satan divide you and trick you into fighting. Be a blessing to each other!

What Are You Reflecting?

"In the same way, let your light shine before others, that they may see your good deeds and glorify your Father in heaven."
MATTHEW 5:16, NIV

I love to visit national parks. A few years back I took a summer road trip with my family, driving north from California toward Oregon. Before leaving home, I studied the map and identified all the national parks within range of our route. I was excited to discover that we would be passing near a national park I had never been to before—Crater Lake National Park in Oregon.

Crater Lake is exactly what the name says; it's a volcanic crater that was filled with water and is now a big lake. The water is super clear and very deep. It's actually the deepest lake in the United States, measuring almost two thousand feet deep! The National Park Service built a road all around the rim of the volcano, so no matter where we went there was an amazing view. What was even more amazing was the deep blue color of the water. As kids we usually draw the water blue when we color, but when we look at a bottle of water, it's transparent. So what color is water? There is a very slight tint of blue in water, but you only start to notice it if you are looking through a large volume of water. That's what we saw at Crater Lake. As I stood there gazing over this huge crater, it was easy to appreciate another reason why the water looks blue. The sky above the lake was a very deep blue, so the water acted as a mirror reflecting the color of the sky.

In life we sometimes like to get credit for doing something good or winning something, but the best position to take is one where you can reflect God and give Him the glory and honor for what you've accomplished. Don't be tempted to take the glory for yourself. Be a reflector and let others see God in you!

The Big Surprise

Honor your father and your mother, so that you may
live long in the land the LORD your God is giving you.
EXODUS 20:12, NIV

A few years back my brother, sister, and I decided to throw a surprise eightieth birthday party for my father. At that time, my parents lived in central California. My sister lived nearby, and my brother lived about four hours away in northern California. I was the farthest away in Michigan. We made a plan where my brother and I would secretly travel to my sister's house and hide out in her house while my sister invited my parents to come over to her house to eat. We also gave the party a theme by having everyone dress up in traditional Chilean garb, since my father is from Chile. The day arrived, and we flew to the Bay Area in California, and along with my brother and his family, we drove to my sister's house and hid in the bedrooms. When my parents arrived, my dad was surprised to see my sister dressed in Chilean garb as she exclaimed, "Happy birthday!" A few moments later, my brother and his family came out of the bedroom and also yelled out, "Happy birthday," surprising them even more! After a quick hug, it was my family's turn to jump out of a bedroom and yell, "Happy birthday!" Of course, they were extra surprised to see us since we had to come all the way from Michigan in order to surprise them. Over the next couple of hours we celebrated together by honoring my dad with stories and video clips of ways he had impacted and molded our lives. As a special gift, my siblings and I got them tickets to visit the Canary Islands, a set of islands off the coast of Africa that belong to Spain. They had always wanted to go since my mother's parents had emigrated from there many years ago.

There's no such thing as a perfect parent; it's a hard job being a mom or a dad. Still, even when they make mistakes, God says we are to honor them. You can honor your parents today by thanking them for their sacrifices and for all the things they lovingly do for you every day.

Thirty Hungry Hours

Whoever is kind to the poor lends to the Lord,
and he will reward them for what they have done.
PROVERBS 19:17, NIV

For almost twenty-five years I've enjoyed serving at church as a Sabbath School teacher for Juniors, Earliteens, and teens. For several years we hosted an annual event with the teens at church called "The 30-Hour Famine." The idea was that the kids would experience hunger in order to help hungry kids. The kids would get sponsors for the thirty hours they would go without food one weekend. Skipping several meals in a row was especially hard for the typical teenager. During the thirty hours we would basically lock the group in a location from Friday afternoon till Saturday night. The kids brought their sleeping bags and clothes and a good attitude. During our time together we would do games, activities, and worships that would focus on the seventeen thousand kids who die every day, many from preventable causes. We were reminded of how blessed we are, and together we experienced the pains of hunger in order to raise money to feed hungry children. At the end of the thirty hours we'd bring them all together and give them a little something to eat.

One year at the end of the thirty hours, we decided to try something different. We sat them around a table and brought out three trash cans—each with a clean liner—but we took a bunch of mashed sandwiches and crackers and fruit and tossed them all together in a nasty-looking mix, and we put the three trashcans on the table in front of them to see what would happen. We explained that for some homeless people, this is what some meals were like. They were so hungry after thirty hours, they did not hesitate to dig through the "trash" to eat anything they could get hold of.

God wants us to have compassion for the poor. Maybe if you skip a meal or two it might help you understand how much it hurts to be hungry. Be kind to the poor and feed the hungry. God will reward you for your compassion.

Hang On, Cowboy

For he will command his angels concerning you
to guard you in all your ways.
PSALM 91:11, NIV

One of my favorite national parks in the United States is Yellowstone National Park—the first national park in the U.S. park system. During one visit to Yellowstone, my family decided to stay outside the park boundaries in a town called Cody, Wyoming, which is just east of the park's eastern entrance. Cody is famous for several things. First of all, it's named after William Cody, better known as Buffalo Bill. Buffalo Bill was one of the most famous characters of the American Old West. He founded his "Buffalo Bill's Wild West" traveling rodeo show in 1883 and toured all over the United States with his large cast and crew.

During our stay in Cody, we had heard that there was a year-round rodeo that was held each night in an arena. I had been to a rodeo one other time in my life and remembered enjoying it, so we decided to go as a family. We got our tickets, found our seats, and soon the show started as horses and riders came out and did a variety of fascinating stunts on horseback. During another part of the rodeo, a small calf was released into the arena and a cowboy on horseback rode out and tried to lasso the calf as quickly as possible. The most impressive part of the show was the bull riding. A cowboy sat on a bull that was anxious to remove the rider from its back. The bull kicks and bucks wildly while the rider tries to stay on the bull for at least eight seconds. Eventually the rider flies off. During this part of the show we noticed several colorful rodeo clowns were in the arena to help the rider in case he got into trouble, or to distract the bull long enough for the rider to get to safety after falling off. I know this may sound kind of silly, but those clowns are kind of like our guardian angels. God has sent them to be with us at all times and to guard us in everything we do, especially when there is danger nearby. Thank You, God!

Old Wood

"But ask the animals, and they will teach you,
or the birds in the sky, and they will tell you;
or speak to the earth, and it will teach you,
or let the fish in the sea inform you.
Which of all these does not know
that the hand of the LORD has done this?
In his hand is the life of every creature
and the breath of all mankind."
JOB 12:7–10, NIV

My parents live in Merced, California, and I love visiting them every chance I get. In case you didn't know, Merced is also known as the "gateway to Yosemite Park," one of the most amazing national parks in the United States. One of my favorite places to visit in the park was a place called Mariposa Grove. This is a part of the park where a grove of giant sequoia trees grows. Sequoia trees are well known as being the largest living trees in the world. The Coastal Redwoods grow taller, but there is no other tree that is as massive as these giant sequoias. As a kid I clearly remember seeing these huge trees reaching high into the sky. One tree in particular stuck in my mind, because many decades ago a huge hole was cut into the trunk— big enough for a car to drive through! I also remember enjoying a bus ride though the park on a huge double-decker bus that didn't have a roof on top. We always sat on top so that we could look up in awe at these magnificent trees God created.

It's neat visiting the park now as an adult, because the guides tell the visitors that some of these trees are more than three thousand five hundred years old, and they are some of the oldest trees in the world. The other thing they say is that scientists think they can grow for many thousands more. I think that's great because, according to Bible calculations, the Flood happened about four thousand five hundred years ago, so the oldest trees we find are from *after* the Flood. Evidence of biblical truths can be found in all the nature around us! It's another way of telling us that the Bible is a book we can trust!

Talking Heads

I sought the LORD, and he answered me;
he delivered me from all my fears.
PSALM 34:4, NIV

When my younger son was born, my older son was about two and a half years old. My wife was able to take a three-month maternity leave from work, so we decided to take a family road trip to South Dakota before she had to return to work. Our first destination was a visit to the Badlands National Park. Our second stop was to visit Mount Rushmore— a huge stone sculpture carved into the side of a mountain. The sculpture features the heads of four U.S. presidents, George Washington, Thomas Jefferson, Theodore Roosevelt, and Abraham Lincoln. Each head is about sixty feet tall! We got there a few hours before sunset because I had read they did something special after dark. That gave us time to take some pictures and walk the Presidential Trail that takes tourists right under the faces for a very up-close look at the sculptures. As evening neared, we headed toward the outdoor auditorium area for the evening program. Finally, a park ranger came out and spoke for a few minutes then we watched a video about the United States. At the end, powerful lights lit up the four heads and someone played the U.S. national anthem, "The Star-Spangled Banner." At this point, my older son started to cry in fear. Since he was barely two years old, his communication skills were still limited, but he was able to give us a couple of words to help us figure out why he was scared. He basically said, "Those giant heads are singing!" My wife and I smiled at each other, and of course we immediately tried to comfort his fear and tell him that it was not the giant heads that were singing and that it was just a recording.

Fears are scary, and we each go through life with certain things that we fear. Fortunately we don't have to face them alone, because if you seek out God, He will deliver you from all your fears. Trust Him today!

The Real Deal

But God demonstrates his own love for us in this:
While we were still sinners, Christ died for us.
ROMANS 5:8, NIV

Each year a large production of the Passion Play is presented at Andrews University. For many years the event spanned two days as the scenes of the story took place in different parts around campus. Every half hour, a new tour would depart from the first station. Over the next ninety minutes or so, each group of about one hundred people would walk around campus to watch actors present the story of Jesus, including His death and resurrection. This was a major production. Some years there were up to six hundred volunteers working to make this event possible. Over the course of the two days, thousands of people would come through to see the story of Jesus. A huge marketplace set was built, complete with shops and blacksmiths, animals, and basket weavers. There were dozens of Romans soldiers—even some riding around on horseback. The scene where Jesus was brought before Pilate was one of the most intense scenes of the journey. By far the most emotional scene was when Jesus would be laid to rest in the tomb followed by His resurrection on the third day. There were even angels flying around!

For several years I was cast to play the part of Pontius Pilate. Each time a new group would come around I would argue with the priests about what they wanted to do with Jesus until I eventually washed my hands and condemned him to be crucified. Of course, I was simply acting and playing a role in the cast, but once in a while it would hit me that a real man named Pontius Pilate ultimately gave the go-ahead to crucify Jesus. In reality, each of us is responsible, because the reason Jesus died was to take the punishment we deserved so that we could be saved. Each year at Easter we remember and celebrate this wonderful sacrifice. Let's thank Jesus today for suffering and taking our punishment so we could be saved!

Traditions of Life

Dear friends, let us love one another, for love comes from God.
Everyone who loves has been born of God and knows God.
Whoever does not love does not know God, because God is love.
1 JOHN 4:7, 8, NIV

There's something fun about traditions. When I was a kid, our family had several traditions, and when I grew up and had my own family, we started our own traditions. For example, every summer we'd get a big group together from church and go to a water park. It was an automatic annual tradition. I've been married for more than twenty years now, and every year we've hosted a party called the Super-Duper Bowl Party, which of course is a gathering to watch the Super Bowl every February. Every year we went to our local county fair in August to see the farm animals, tour the new RVs they were selling, ride a bunch of rides, and eat elephant ears. Each winter when the first sticky snow fell, we went out to the yard and made a snowman named "Mr. Snowy." Each Christmas we'd go caroling. Every Fourth of July we'd organize a big celebration. Some traditions went on for years, while others faded after a few years. But there's one thing all of the traditions I mentioned have in common—they require more than one person. God created us as social beings, so it's His plan that we make connections with other people. Our culture is changing though. Social networking is supposed to bring us closer to each other, but many people complain that it's actually alienating us.

I want to encourage you today, so make a point of actually connecting with the people around you. Build friendships and bonds by actually spending time with people. More than anything, seek out those who are lonely or don't have many friends. God may have put them in your life because they have no one else to connect with. Social networking is cool, but don't let it take the place of really connecting with people. Remember, God is love, and He wants us to love one another.

The Taxi Ride

There is neither Jew nor Gentile, neither slave nor free, nor is there male and female, for you are all one in Christ Jesus.
GALATIANS 3:28, NIV

In order to visit my wife's family in Cuba, I had to get permission from the U.S. State Department. Once we arrived in Havana, we connected with our family and made plans to visit a little of the city center. The plan was to go by taxi, but in order to do that, my wife and I would need to try to pass off as current Cuban residents. Sadly, at the time in Cuba, there were two different versions of many things; there was the beach that Cubans could visit, and there was the beach only for tourists. There was an entire monetary currency that the Cubans were supposed to use, and there was a separate currency for tourists. Yes, two currencies in one country! It was confusing. Taking a taxi to the center turned out to be an adventure. Like everything else, there were taxis for tourists and taxis for residents, but in our case, since they were taking us sightseeing, we wanted to all go together. Which taxi do we take? Since they were only familiar with their taxis, we decided to take theirs. But they were worried that they would get in trouble if they took us "tourists" with them in their taxi, so they told us to stay quiet during our taxi ride, because the driver would immediately know we were tourists if we said anything. I sure didn't want to deceive anyone, but I also didn't want to get in trouble, so we just went along with their suggestion and silently rode the taxi to our destination.

Segregation occurs when people are divided from each other for one reason or another. Sometimes it's because of race, sometimes because of nationality, and sometimes because of money. Abraham Lincoln put it nicely when he stated, "All men are created equal." Cultural diversity is something Satan uses against us. He's fooling many people into hating people because they're different. In God's eyes we are all His children, so be sure to love and treat everyone equally.

The Easy Ride Up

He tends his flock like a shepherd:
He gathers the lambs in his arms
and carries them close to his heart;
he gently leads those that have young.
Isaiah 40:11, NIV

When my boys were about four and two, we took a family vacation to Hawaii. While there, we decided to hike up to Diamond Head State Monument. This monument is a volcanic cone whose top forms the shape of a crater. The rim sits overlooking the city of Honolulu and Waikiki. A tunnel took us to the center of the crater, where we parked our car. From there we began our hike up the inside of the crater toward the rim. We had heard the view from the top was amazing, and we were determined to experience it for ourselves.

The hike started off easy and flat, but after a few minutes it started to get steeper and steeper as we went up a series of switchbacks. We could see our destination up above us—an old bunker built in the early 1900s that served as a lookout, now a popular destination for hikers. About halfway up, my youngest son ran out of gas—after all, he wasn't even two years old yet, and I was amazed he'd made it that far. At this point we had a choice: turn back or carry him the rest of the way up. We chose to carry him up, so I lifted him up onto my shoulders. I was tired by the time I made it up there, but I was reminded about how our Father in heaven is ready to carry us when we face challenges. No matter what you may go through today, remember that God is with you every step of the way, and during the hard times, He will help carry you through.

The Quiet Pain

*Do not lie to each other, since you have taken off your old
self with its practices and have put on the new self, which
is being renewed in knowledge in the image of its Creator.*
COLOSSIANS 3:9,10, NIV

I was six years old when we moved from Miami, Florida to Boston, Massachusetts. In Miami we lived in a house with a flat roof and palm trees in the yard. When we arrived in Massachusetts there were no palm trees and all the houses had steep roofs. The weather was different too. We went from wearing shorts and t-shirts all the time to having four clearly pronounced seasons to dress for. Of course, when the first winter came, my brother and sister and I were thrilled when the snow started falling.

When we first arrived, we stayed on campus at Atlantic Union College until our house was ready to move into. Every day we would eat in the campus cafeteria. One day when it was cold and wintery we ate at the cafeteria, and as we exited the building, my brother—who is eight years older than I—ran to the bottom of the steps outside, and then I ran off the top step, jumped, and landed on his back. Immediately he started running while I climbed up to sit on his shoulders. On this one particular day, my brother slipped on the ice as he was running, and I landed hard on the concrete sidewalk on my shoulder. My brother didn't want to get in trouble, so when we got in the car he tried to convince me not tell my parents. I lasted about five minutes, but the pain was too much, and I finally spilled the beans. At the hospital we discovered that I had broken my collarbone.

Sometimes we all try to hide the truth, maybe because we made a mistake. Usually that means we end up lying too. Sometimes we have to lie again to cover up the first lie. What a mess. We all make mistakes. Don't make it worse by lying to cover it up. Take responsibility and own your mistake instead of trying to hide from it. It's the proper way to deal with mistakes. Ask God to give you the courage to own your mistakes.

Things of Great Value

"Again, the kingdom of heaven is like a merchant in search of fine pearls, who, on finding one pearl of great value, went and sold all that he had and bought it."
Matthew 13:45, 46, ESV

When I was a little boy, I was rambunctious. I always wanted to be outside even if it was raining or snowing. I was always up in a tree or exploring the woods or riding my bicycle. Once, I saw a toy I liked in the store but I had no money, so I started trying to think of ways I could get some money. While playing in my yard I found a neat-looking rock, so I decided I would try to sell it. I also looked around for other valuable-looking things I could sell. I found a few flowers, an old bottle, and what I thought was a really cool-looking tree branch. I put a "for sale" sign on a little table and sat by the road for at least half an hour selling my things. Not a single person stopped. I was determined to sell something, so I cleared off the table and thought for a moment. "There's got to be something valuable I could sell." That's when I came up with a brilliant idea. I decided I would try to sell our house. I went back inside and got a new piece of paper and made a new sign. Along with some tape, I went back outside to my table and put my new sign up. It said, "House for Sale, $10." I was sure I would get some buyers now. After all I was now selling a valuable house for only ten dollars. I sat there another half hour, and again, not a single person stopped to try to buy my house. I was disappointed, but only for about five seconds. I eventually put the table away and went off to play something else.

Sometimes we think certain things are incredibly valuable, but to others they're not. I'm sure my house had value, but in my case, I didn't even properly understand the value since I was trying to sell it for ten dollars. Sometimes we don't realize how valuable things are so we don't appreciate them. The most valuable thing we could ever have is our relationship with God. Treasure the time you spend with God every day!

Who's in Charge Here?

For it is by grace you have been saved, through faith—
and this is not from yourselves, it is the gift of God.
EPHESIANS 2:8, NIV

While in Buenos Aires, Argentina we decided to take our rental car and drive to the northern part of the country. When we looked at the map, we discovered that we could actually take a shortcut by cutting through the country of Uruguay. The first step of the journey would be by ferry from Buenos Aires to Colonia del Sacramento in Uruguay. We drove down to the dock and bought our tickets and drove onto the ferry. We left our car parked and went to the upper deck as we rode across the Rio de la Plata. Since we had now entered a new country, we had to go through customs and immigration to make our entry into Uruguay official. We were surprised to discover that Colonia was a small town of great historical significance and one of the oldest towns in Uruguay, dating back to the 1600s. As we explored the town we found a wonderful historic quarter with city walls, a wooden drawbridge, an old lighthouse, and more. One of the interesting things I learned was that the town of Colonia was originally founded by Portugal in 1680. The following year it was conquered by Spain, but the following year Portugal took it back. A few years later, Spain took over again, and soon after, Portugal took it back again.

From 1680 till today, Colonia has changed hands from crown to crown eleven times! This made me think of how life is sometimes. We ask God to enter into our lives, but then we fail. We ask God for forgiveness and ask Him to rule our lives, but Satan works hard to tempt us and make us fall away again. The wonderful news is that it doesn't matter how many times we fail, God forgives us and welcomes us back. That's what grace is. We've sinned and we don't deserve forgiveness, but God forgives us anyway because He loves us so much. Tell God today that you are sorry for your mistakes and ask Him to forgive you. His forgiveness is the best gift!

Andes Hot Springs

The law of the LORD is perfect,
reviving the soul.
PSALM 19:7, ESV

There's a wonderful area in Patagonia called the Lake District. Patagonia is the southern part of the South American continent shared by Argentina and Chile. My family flew down and landed in a beautiful little town called Bariloche, located in the foothills of the Andes Mountains and on the shores of a huge lake. The area is known as the Lake District because of the countless lakes found nestled in the Andes mountain range. Over the next few days, our trek led us west through the Lake District in Argentina to the Lake District in Chile. Once in Chile, we entered Puyehue National Park, the most visited national park in Chile, where visitors can enjoy abundant thermal hot springs, waterfalls, ancient forests, pristine lakes, and amazing mountain views. I had read about a beautiful hotel called the Grand Hotel Puyehue in the park that allowed guests who were not staying in the hotel to come and enjoy the hot springs as a day guest. We went into a huge building with an enormous hot spring pool area where they had pools of varying degrees in temperature. Visitors started in the less hot pools and worked their way to the hotter ones. In order to enjoy the pools, each guest received a blue cap similar to the ones competitive swimmers wear. The journey driving through the mountains had been tiring, so I was looking forward to relaxing in the pools with my family, but my younger son, who was less than two years old at the time, didn't like the idea of wearing the cap—he didn't understand the rules.

Rules are placed in our lives sometimes, and it's important to keep them. Oftentimes we resist the rules because we don't understand them, but rules are made to keep us safe and happy. Imagine how many accidents there would be in the world if there were no stop-sign rules. Let's follow the rules God has given us to live by.

Creepy Catacombs

"Blessed are you when people insult you, persecute you and falsely say all kinds of evil against you because of me. Rejoice and be glad, because great is your reward in heaven, for in the same way they persecuted the prophets who were before you."
MATTHEW 5:11, 12, NIV

My friends and I were only going to have a couple of days to visit Rome, so it was necessary to plan ahead. Of course, the main landmarks were on everyone's list: the Coliseum, the Roman Forum, the Spanish Steps, and St. Peters. Everyone also had a place or two that was a little more unusual that they wanted to visit. I was happy that one of my suggestions interested the whole group—probably because it was a creepy idea. We hopped on a bus and went just outside the city walls on the historic Appian Way. We got off, and there in front of us was the Catacombs of St. Sebastian—a cemetery. This is no ordinary cemetery, though, because the tombs were all housed in an elaborate underground tunnel system. Almost two thousand years ago the area was used as a mine, but shortly after, it was abandoned and used by Christians as a cemetery.

Our guide led us through hundreds of feet of passages in the dimly lit tunnel system. Carved into the sides of the dirt walls were shelves where the Christians were laid to rest. These catacombs got their name from Sebastian, a Christian who was persecuted and killed in the year A.D. 288 for being a follower of Jesus. He was one of the early martyrs who was willing to give his life for his belief in Jesus. He was laid to rest here at this underground cemetery.

Giving up your life for something you believe in is no small matter. Even today, there are still parts of the world where Christians are being persecuted and killed for following Jesus. Our verse today is from the Beatitudes, where Jesus says He will bless you when you are insulted and persecuted in His name. It also says that the kingdom of heaven will be yours and that we are to rejoice and be glad for the reward God has in store for us in heaven!

The Deserted Desert Drive

He heals the brokenhearted
and binds up their wounds.
PSALM 147:3, NIV

There are some parts of the United States that are incredibly desolate. You can drive for miles and miles without seeing anyone else. A couple of years ago my family and I were driving from Michigan to California to visit family. I love experimenting with different routes, so on this particular trip I drove to Denver and through the Rocky Mountains and into Utah, where the I-70 highway ends and you either have to go north to Salt Lake City or south toward Las Vegas. I decided to do neither, so we got off the highway and continued heading west into Nevada on smaller roads.

The drive through those couple of hundred miles in the middle of Nevada is something I won't forget anytime soon. We drove through incredible mountain formations, through rocky canyons, and amazing salt flats. I've been to many national parks, and I was surprised that some of these areas we were driving through were not a national park. It wasn't even a state park or even a protected area! It was nothing, just miles and miles of amazing desert. There were hundreds of miles, and in one hour we might see a car here and there but no towns.

Sometimes in life we feel lonely and isolated. This is the not the way God created us to be. We were designed as social beings who need interaction with others. Do you ever feel lonely? Tell God how you feel and ask Him to heal your broken heart. Are there any kids in your class or neighborhood who look like they're all alone in the middle of a desert? Make a point today to connect with them. It may feel awkward, and that person may even treat you badly in return, but remember that they may be like that because they're hurting inside. Those are exactly the kind of people God needs us to help heal.

Roughing the Eastern Block

And do not forget to do good and to share with others,
for with such sacrifices God is pleased.
HEBREWS 13:16, NIV

During my travels there's no way to avoid the fact that some trips are going to be rough while other trips will be more comfortable. It all depends on where I go, who I go with, and my budget. I'm going to tell you about a trip I once took with some friends that was done on a shoestring budget. That means we didn't have a lot of money for the trip but we still wanted to see the most we could. I was studying in France at the time, and during the October break, myself and four other guys decided to rent a tiny Fiat Uno and travel around Eastern Europe as much as we could for the least amount of money possible. It was very crowded in the car to the point that we had to unroll our sleeping bags and lay them across the back seat over everyone's laps.

During our two-week trip we camped every single night on the side of a quiet road. Two people would sleep in the front seats of the car while the other three slept in a two-man pup tent. Since we didn't have the luxury of having a hotel every night, that also means we didn't have the luxury of getting a shower every day. As a matter of fact, we only got one bath during the two weeks. While in Budapest, Hungary we discovered the Gellert public bathhouse, featuring water from a thermal hot spring where we could get cleaned up for about a dollar. That bath refreshed us so that we could go another week without a shower. We saw a lot during those two weeks, but our trip was rough. Luxuries like brushing your teeth or changing clothes or eating food didn't happen regularly, but it was the sacrifice we decided to make in order to see as much as we could.

God asks us to make sacrifices, but not for our own benefit. In our verse today we see that God is pleased when we make personal sacrifices in order to do good and share our faith with others.

Button Pushers

For this very reason, make every effort to add to your faith goodness;
and to goodness, knowledge; and to knowledge, self-control; and
to self-control, perseverance; and to perseverance, godliness.
2 Peter 1:5,6, NIV

Howdy cowboys and cowgirls! In the United States cowboys are famous because of their rich history from the Old West and also because of movies and TV shows. Of course, there are plenty of real-world cowboys in the rural parts of the country who truly live as cowboys and cowgirls today. Naturally, cowboys are found in many other countries too, and they're all a little different. I remember being in awe of my father's Chilean cowboy outfit: the hat, the poncho, the shirt, and many other small details that were part of his national costume. He would tell me that this is what the Chilean cowboys traditionally wore. When I was a little older and I traveled to Chile, I was able to see a Chilean rodeo, and I got to see their cowboys in action. Their rodeos are quite different from the rodeos in the United States. For example, only Chilean horses can be used, and riders must wear the traditional *huaso* cowboy costume I just mentioned.

During the rodeo, two riders on horseback ride laps around an arena and try to stop a calf by pinning it against large cushions. They earn points when they properly drive the calf around the arena and pin it correctly. There are also deductions for faults. The crowd cheers wildly when they get a perfect pin. The horseback riding has to be extremely accurate, and the rider must have total control of their horse in order to earn points. The rider must be very disciplined in order to control the powerful creature they're riding.

Self-control is important, but it is often not an easy thing to do. Sometimes in life, people will push your buttons, and we can lose control of our words and actions. Ask God to give you self-control over everything you do and say today so that your words and actions may be godly.

Impossible to Describe

And I saw the holy city, new Jerusalem, coming down out of heaven from God, prepared as a bride adorned for her husband. And I heard a loud voice from the throne saying, Behold, the dwelling place of God is with man. He will dwell with them, and they will be his people, and God himself will be with them as their God.
Revelation 21:2, 3, ESV

A couple of summers ago I went to the state of Hawaii with a camera crew to shoot a couple of videos. I had been there a few years before with my family, so I was familiar with the area and I knew about some of the things available to do on the island. One of the things I had done previously was to swim with green sea turtles. When I returned the second time I asked the locals to tell me where the best spot to find sea turtles was. I love talking to the locals because they really know all the secrets and back roads of where they live. After talking to several locals, we made the decision and drove to that spot. It was a wonderful spot because, as I expected, there was no one there. The beautiful spot we found was a quiet, isolated beach with a rocky reef system that provided the perfect backdrop to look for marine life in the water. I got my gear on and slipped into the water. Within a minute or two, I had spotted a sea turtle swimming. Soon after, I spotted another and then another! The water was crystal clear, and the turtles didn't seem to mind one bit that we were swimming around their environment. I was careful not to get too close; I wanted to simply enjoy watching them naturally interact with their habitats from a distance, even though some of them were curious and came to check me out.

We have gotten used to the idea that earth is our natural habitat. It's true that there are many wonderful places that God has created on earth, but the Bible tells us that our real home is in heaven. If we think it's amazing here, can you imagine how awesome heaven is going to be? There are several passages in the Bible that try to describe what heaven will be like, but I get the idea there simply aren't words to describe it! I can't wait to get to our real home; how about you?

Attacking Good Things

*If anyone does not know how to manage his own
family, how can he take care of God's church?*
1 TIMOTHY 3:5, NIV

Several years ago, our extended family decided to save up and go together
on a trip during the winter. It was cold in Michigan, so our list only
included places that were warm. The decision was finally made—we would
go to Cancun, Mexico. We had never attempted an international trip with all
the families, so this was new and exciting even though we were only going
for a long weekend. We landed in Cancun and took a bus to our hotel.

My niece was only a couple of years old and had never experienced a
tropical beach before. It was cute to see her at the beach. She rolled around
in the sand and splashed in the water. The next day someone found a glass-
bottom boat that looked like a submarine, and we took that out to observe
the marine creatures in the waters there. For those of us who were a little
more adventurous, that afternoon we took a bus down to a place where one
could snorkel in the ocean right off the beach. On our last night there, we
went to the city center to walk around and eat ice cream.

The reason I'm sharing this with you is that it's important for families to
spend time together in order to build bonds. There used to be a man in an
office I worked in who once told me that he lived about a mile from his
brother, but he hadn't seen him in several years. This broke my heart, and it
really made me think of how God wants families to be strong. Sadly, Satan
has made a major effort to attack and destroy families. Remember, Satan will
attack every good thing that God has created. Some day you may have your
own family. Make up your mind that you will do everything necessary to
manage and defend your family against Satan's efforts. Do that by keeping
God in the center of everything you do, starting today!

Trekking the Black Hills

The prudent see danger and take refuge,
but the simple keep going and pay the penalty.
PROVERBS 22:3, NIV

You would think that the *national* parks system has all the best parks in the United States, but I'd like to tell you that there are some incredible *state* parks too. Just recently I visited one of the most amazing state parks in the country, called Custer State Park, in the Black Hills of South Dakota—a small isolated mountain range that rises from the Great Plains.

The first thing we did was drive on the Wildlife Loop, where you are certain to run into quite a bit of wildlife, including a famous herd of about fifteen hundred free-roaming bison that will pass a couple of feet from your car. You can pull over to watch them as they move around looking for new grasses to graze. There were also several prairie dog towns to visit as well as lots of elk, bighorn sheep, and mountain goats. Some of the most famous residents are called the "begging burros"—a band of wild donkeys that spend a lot of time on the side of the road approaching cars that have stopped so they can stick their heads into cars in an effort to find food.

Another part of the park contains the scenic Needles Highway. The engineers did an amazing job building a road through this section of the park because this area is filled with tall, pointy granite rock formations that shoot up into the sky. These granite spires are referred to as "needles." In order to for people to visit them, these engineers designed and built fourteen miles of incredibly curvy switchbacks and sharp turns through the Black Hills. This route is closed in the winter because it's dangerous. Satan is constantly trying to get us to pick paths in life that are harmful and dangerous. That's why it's important to recognize danger and run away from it. Don't let him tempt you into hanging around to wait and see what the consequences of sin are. Ask God to deliver you from temptations every day!

The Strangest City

But in your hearts revere Christ as Lord. Always be prepared to give an answer to everyone who asks you to give the reason for the hope that you have. But do this with gentleness and respect.
1 PETER 3:15, NIV

My family and I entered a shop on the island of Grand Cayman where we planned to sign up for a unique tour. We boarded a small bus with a few other people, and the driver took us to a boat. There we sailed out about four miles while putting on masks and snorkels. Soon in the distance we could see a spot where another eight or ten boats had congregated. We were miles from the shore, but in this spot there was a shallow sandbar that was only about waist deep. When the boat anchored, we all jumped into Sting Ray City. Every day, dozens of stingrays come because the tourists feed them. It's a little concerning at first, because these creatures have a barb on their serrated tail that is covered with venomous mucous, but it's only used for self-defense.

Fortunately, many of the rays here have become tame. The boat drivers recognize some of them as individuals, and they even have names for them! Our boat driver called us over to where he was interacting with one of the tame rays that was about three feet wide. He told me to extend my arms so he could position the ray in a way that I could cradle it in my arms for a picture. I did as he told me to, and the stingray was gently put in my arms. Its skin was soft and smooth, and of course we avoided putting our hands anywhere near its barb. I found them to be quite gentle creatures. But because they have a prominent defense mechanism, it is often assumed they are aggressive. The defense mechanism is only used when it feels threatened.

The Bible says that if someone challenges our faith, we are also to defend what we believe. People will see us being very different, so our verse today reminds us that we should be prepared to respond to people and do it in a very gentle and respectful way.

The Stormy Boat Ride

The disciples went and woke him, saying, "Lord, save us! We're going to drown!"
He replied, "You of little faith, why are you so afraid?" Then he got up and
rebuked the winds and the waves, and it was completely calm.
MATTHEW 8:25, 26, NIV

Chile is a long, skinny country in South America that runs more than twenty-six hundred miles from north to south, but it is only about two hundred miles wide at its widest location. The southern part of the country is not connected by road to the rest of the country. During a recent trip there, we were to Puerto Montt in the south-central part of the country, where the highway through Chile ends and the landscape is taken over by volcanoes, islands, fjords, mountains, and glaciers. Just south of this spot was a place my father had told me about for years—an island called Chiloé.

We drove as far south as we could before taking a ferry to Chiloé. Once there, we had to take a second ferry just to get from one side of the island to the other. I read that there was a tiny village there with people who would take tourists out on a small boat. Eventually the road to the village ended, and we had to drive the car right on the beach in order to get to this village, which was accessible only during low tide. We were given huge heavy raincoats and boots to wear, and the four of us trudged out to the edge of the ocean, where a little boat was waiting on the sandy beach. The waves were heavy that day, but we stayed along the rocky coast, where we were able to view amazing rock formations as well as sea otters, penguins, and sea lions.

The heavy waves that day almost made us sick, but it reminded me of the boat Jesus and His disciples were on, where the disciples didn't think they were going to make it. The disciples woke Jesus in a panic, and, as you know, Jesus spoke to the waves and told them to be calm. Since Jesus created nature, He also has control over it. Jesus also created us, so every day we should entrust our lives to Him and live according to His will.

A Little Too Real?

For the word of God is alive and active. Sharper than any double-edged sword, it penetrates even to dividing soul and spirit, joints and marrow; it judges the thoughts and attitudes of the heart.
HEBREWS 4:12, NIV

Every five years, the Seventh-day Adventist church leaders gather for an important event commonly known as the General Conference session. During the events, you will learn about other ministries, see people dressed in amazing cultural outfits from their countries, and meet up with friends you haven't seen in a while. The 2015 General Conference Session was held in San Antonio, Texas, and I was asked to lead out in the Primary Sabbath School class.

The lesson that week was teaching about the children of Israel and the crossing of the Red Sea. I wanted to make this a memorable class that kids would never forget, so we first built a huge thirty-five-foot backdrop from foam that looked like a desert on the horizon. We built palm trees for the desert and created a Red Sea crossing effect using blue fabrics that kids would have to escape through. Using music and lights and sound effects, the story unfolded as several large Egyptian soldiers chased the kids across the room toward the Red Sea. As the actor playing Moses raised his arms, an eight-foot-tall wall of blue fabric was lifted to create a narrow passage of escape. The kids were squirted with water as they ran through the Red Sea, and one kid got so consumed in the story that he not only sprinted through our fabric sea, he continued running till he crashed into the desert foam backdrop, knocking it over! I was excited that we were able to make the Bible story come to life for that young boy.

God gave us the stories of the Bible to remind us that He is alive and active in our lives. We can each gain strength and understanding from others, who have trusted God in the past. So, go out today and be one of God's stories!

Lights, Camera, Action

I will set nothing wicked before my eyes;
I hate the work of those who fall away;
It shall not cling to me.
PSALM 101:3, NKJV

While visiting the island of Oahu, we enjoyed many unique sights, sounds, and tastes. We even stopped at a huge pineapple plantation and got to eat fresh pineapple! But before coming to Hawaii, my brother had told me to be sure to also stop at a very specific place and try something called "shave ice." It was like a snow cone, but the ice was shaved into a fine granulated snow that just melted in your mouth.

One of our last stops was to visit a beautiful and popular beach on the North Shore. When we got there, we noticed immediately that something was happening. There were lots of huge trucks parked around the beach parking lot as well as lots of roped-off areas and signs. We parked our car and proceeded toward the beach. The signs said that a movie was being filmed that day on the beach! They also said that by being on the beach that day, we were giving them permission to let us appear in the background of the movie they were filming. We found a spot about one hundred fifty feet away from where the actors and cameras were filming. All we had to do was pretend like we were visiting the beach, which turned out to be pretty easy because that's exactly what we came to do. The movie being filmed was a Disney movie called *The Shaggy Dog*.

Movies are fun, and they're a big part of our culture. I'm not here to tell you what to watch or not watch, but I am here to say you should be very protective of what you allow your eyes to see. Next time you are deciding what to watch, ask yourself, would Jesus watch this with me? A lot of the movies made today are worthless. Honor God with what you watch.

The Unlikely Victors

*For it is God who works in you to will and to act
in order to fulfill his good purpose.*
PHILIPPIANS 2:13, NIV

Dominoes is a very popular game in many parts of the world. The game is played using small domino tiles with different numbers of dots on them. You can either play as an individual or as a team, and your goal is to get rid of all your tiles while blocking and preventing others from being able to place theirs. Some people love the game so much that they play every day. In some countries the competition is fierce, and people get very worked up during the game. In my family, dominoes was often played at gatherings and family functions. I learned how to play by watching others play, but I never played enough to fully understand the various rules and strategies that can be used to help your team win. I just knew that if there was a six on the table, my goal was to match the six so I could get rid of another tile. For the extreme fans of dominoes, there was a much more involved technique and strategy to be used.

One Fourth of July party, my brother-in-law and I were invited to play dominoes against two other players, who were arguably the best players in the whole town. Since my brother-in-law and I barely knew how to play, our style of innocent play confused the other team so much that their complex strategy didn't work. They would say we "should have" played this domino, but instead we played another that made no sense to them. They were so completely confused by our random, reckless approach that we ended up beating them!

The Bible contains many stories in which the small, inexperienced underdog beats an army or a giant that should have easily won. I'm quickly reminded of the story of David defeating Goliath or of Gideon's army of three hundred. When you are on God's team, you always win, but you must first give yourself completely to God so that He can work through you to do amazing things.

Weigh Me, Not the Basket

But the fruit of the Spirit is love, joy, peace, forbearance, kindness, goodness, faithfulness, gentleness and self-control. Against such things there is no law.
GALATIANS 5:22, 23, NIV

Where I live in Michigan, we are blessed with abundant fresh produce to enjoy. Early in the season we see asparagus, and soon after, strawberries. Corn and soybeans are never far away, and our county is big on apples, grapes, and peaches. In the late summer we see huge trucks hauling thousands of watermelons to the market, and in the fall I drive by the farms where you can see pumpkins of all sizes. There are also tomatoes and wheat and all the veggies you can imagine.

The wonderful thing about being surrounded by so many farms is that you are never too far from a "u-pick" farm that allows customers to come onto the farm and pick their own goodies. Without a doubt, our favorite fruit to pick over the years has been blueberries. When you arrive, the farmer gives you a basket-type thing that you can tie around your waist. Next you head into the long aisles of blueberry bushes and start to pick. Here's where it gets interesting: you are encouraged to enjoy eating the blueberries while you are picking. When you are done picking, they weigh the blueberries you have in your basket and you pay for those. I've always found it interesting that you can eat all you want while you are on the farm! I would have thought that maybe they should be weighing our kids on the way out too, but they let them eat to their hearts' content. At home, the fun continues as we eat some of them, and others we freeze to eat later in a smoothie recipe with other yummy fruits.

In the Bible, God refers to fruit when talking about the qualities of a Christian. He calls them "fruit of the Spirit." The idea is that as a Christian, you are like a tree that bears fruit, and good trees bear good fruit. Look at today's verse and make this list your goal of fruits to bear today as you come in contact with people wherever you go.

Rockies on Horseback

A man who is right with God cares for his animal,
but the sinful man is hard and has no pity.
PROVERBS 12:10, NLV

A few years ago our family drove from Michigan to California to visit my parents. It's quite a long drive, and we took our time driving across the country, stopping to see as much as we could along the way. You'd be surprised at the kinds of fun things you find when you drive across the country. At one stop we found an original Pony Express cabin-turned-museum in Iowa. A few hours later, in North Platte, Nebraska we discovered the largest train yard in the world! In this one place, the train yard splits into two hundred different tracks about two miles wide!

Soon we made it to the Rocky Mountains and decided to stop at a ranch to go horseback riding. No one in my family rides horses often, so it was pretty exciting for us to climb up on a horse and ride off into the mountains—with a guide, of course. The horse ranch was tucked right in the middle of the mountains. During our tour we climbed to a point where we got an amazing view of the continental divide and snowcapped mountains. It was amazingly peaceful and quiet up there during the hour or two we rode through the pine forests and mountain paths to places cars could not reach. At all times, our horses behaved wonderfully; they never complained, nor did we feel threatened.

If you think about it, none of us would like to have to carry someone around all day long, but when God created the animals of the world, He said in Genesis that we were to rule over the animals and fish and birds. Of course, ruling over the animals also means that we are to be kind to them. God has made us stewards, or caretakers, of this world and all that's in it. Make sure you treat everything God created with respect. Naturally that means we must treat each other with respect as well.

The Big Ocean Adventure

He replied, "Blessed rather are those who hear the word of God and obey it."
LUKE 11:28, NIV

So far, I have had the privilege of going on three different whale-watching tours. The first time was from Monterrey Bay in California, the second time was from Oahu in Hawaii, and the third time was in the Puget Sound in Washington. However, going on a whale-watching trip doesn't guarantee you will see whales. Since they are wild and unpredictable creatures, they do not appear at a certain time, nor do they stay in one place for very long. The ocean is definitely not an aquarium! You have to be lucky you are in the right place at the right time in order to get a good look at them in their natural environment.

Although during our whale-watching trip in Washington I was excited to see a lot of orcas, our trip in Monterrey was definitely the most successful whale-watching trip I've taken.

Right away as we headed out into the ocean on a small boat, there were dolphins swimming a few feet from our boat. Once we were out far enough, we spotted a pod of humpback whales as well. In several instances the whales came to the surface about ten to fifteen feet away from our boat! Then, toward the end of our tour, our captain spotted a giant blue whale swimming almost right under us! All the way back to port the captain kept saying over and over that in ten years of giving tours he had never seen as much as he did on this one trip.

I am reminded of the story of Jonah and how he spent three days in the belly of a big fish. In the story, God calls but Jonah runs. We can each be stubborn at times, insisting that we get our way, but God's way is better. Sometimes we may not understand God's plan, but we must trust and obey Him. Jonah finally figured that out. Hopefully we can figure it out too, before going through what he went through!

The Monkey Whisperer

You alone are the LORD. You made the heavens, even the highest heavens, and all their starry host, the earth and all that is on it, the seas and all that is in them. You give life to everything, and the multitudes of heaven worship you.
NEHEMIAH 9:6, NIV

My wife and I decided to take our eighteen-month-old son on his first trip to the beautiful Central American country of Costa Rica. At that time, zip lines were unheard of in North America, and we decided to give it a try. We had to wear harnesses and follow the safety measures, but once we were ready, we started the tour, zipping along on twelve different cable runs high in the trees. Even though our son was only eighteen months old, he got to go too, except his harness was attached to the cable as well as to the guide who went with him. Since the zip-line tour would take us from treetop platform to treetop platform, there was a lot to see up in the canopy of the forest. We saw birds, monkeys, insects, reptiles, and all sorts of plant life. When we finished the tour, there was a little outdoor cafeteria that allowed guests to rest or get something to eat or drink after their adventure. While we were standing around reflecting on the adventure we had just experienced, a little monkey came out of nowhere and started to play with our son Leo. He danced around and tugged on his arms and squealed. Our son wasn't sure what to make of this little creature, but we enjoyed watching them interact.

As you know, there are many people in the world who believe humans evolved from ape-like creatures over millions of years. It's a trick Satan is using to separate people from God by saying He didn't create anything—that incredibly complex living machines simply created themselves and that the universe exploded itself into existence. Scientifically, it's impossible for something to create itself. And as for evolution, the actual process of one creature slowly turning into another has never been scientifically observed. Don't fall for Satan's tricks.

A Little Too Close

*Then the fire of the L*ORD *fell and burned up the sacrifice, the wood, the stones and the soil, and also licked up the water in the trench. When all the people saw this, they fell prostrate and cried, "The L*ORD*—he is God! The L*ORD*—he is God!"*
1 KINGS 18:38, 39, NIV

After graduating from Andrews University with a degree in architecture, I worked in various areas of architecture for the next seventeen years. One day I had a meeting with a client in their home. When I arrived, we sat down at a table near a large picture window overlooking their yard. The meeting started and we discussed the plans for their new home. It was a stormy day, and as we met, rain fell, and every once in a while we'd hear a distant crack of thunder. Suddenly I heard *BOOM* unlike any boom I had ever heard in my life. It felt as though a crash of thunder exploded ten feet from where I was sitting. We were in a daze after it happened, because I had never heard such a loud noise before. Suddenly, we looked out the window and realized that a lightning bolt had struck the ground ten feet away from us! It created a hole in the ground, and the hole was filling with water, but there was a flame of fire on the water! The puddle of water was on fire! We quickly realized that a natural gas line ran through that part of the yard, so we called 9-1-1. Shortly after, the fire and police departments arrived as well as the gas company to shut off the gas valve to the house.

This experience reminded me of the story of Elijah on Mount Carmel, when he prayed to God, and God answered with fire from heaven. Prayer is a powerful thing, and God is always listening. Call on Him today for all your worries and concerns. As happened to Elijah on Mount Carmel, you can ask Him to use you today so that people will know, *"The Lord—He is God!"*

Giving God the Glory

We have different gifts, according to the grace given to each of us.
If your gift is prophesying, then prophesy in accordance with your faith.
ROMANS 12:6, NIV

The large city of Chicago is about ninety minutes from my house. It's a wonderfully diverse city with lots of neat things to do and a bunch of ethnic neighborhoods to visit. When my kids were smaller, they loved visiting the many great museums in the city. Another favorite was a visit to Lincoln Park Zoo on the north side of the city. We even have our favorite pizzeria we always visit in Chicago that makes an amazingly delicious pizza. Every time we came into the city we marveled at all the tall buildings. The most famous building in the city was arguably the Chicago Sears Tower, which was renamed a few years ago as the Willis Tower.

For twenty-five years, the Willis Tower held the title of being the tallest building in the world. One day we decided to go up to the observation tower, which was 1,353 feet above the street level. We were sure glad we wouldn't have to climb the stairs! We got our tickets and waited in line for our turn to ride the elevator. Once in the elevator, the door closed, and it almost felt like a space launch. It took the elevator sixty seconds to get to the top, and we could feel the pressure changing as we went up, going an average of twenty-two feet per second! As you can imagine, the view at the top was spectacular. In 1999 a French daredevil went to Chicago and began climbing this building from the outside. He used only his hands and feet, climbing the entire building in about an hour! That's quite a talent, although a bit risky if you ask me.

Each of us has been given talents, but I want to ask you today—how are you using them? Are you using them to make you look good, or are you using them to bring glory to God? God has been generous in giving us gifts; go and use them today to give God honor and glory!

A Weird Duck

You shall not make any cuts on your body for the dead or tattoo yourselves: I am the LORD.
LEVITICUS 19:28, ESV

One weekend my wife and I decided to take a long trip to the Wisconsin Dells, which is about six hours from our home. As usual, I immediately set out to find something fun and unique to do that involves nature. That's when I discovered the duck tours. No, I'm not talking about the bird; I'm talking about a very unusual vehicle. We arrived at the location of the tour and bought our tickets to ride a unique vehicle called a "duck."

The duck is an amphibious vehicle built during World War II. We boarded the duck, and a driver came out to greet us and start us on the tour. As we cruised down the street, the driver told us about different aspects of the vehicle and its history. That's when we arrived at the edge of the river and we suddenly found ourselves speeding down the pathway toward the water's edge. When we reached the water, the duck entered the water with a huge splash. Moments later, we were afloat, cruising down the river! This amphibious duck was a six-wheel vehicle made to operate on land and water, originally named the DUKW. During the war, troops sometimes needed to land on a beach or to transport supplies between land and sea, and this vehicle was made to be able to change back and forth between truck and boat.

In our culture we see a lot of people who do extreme things to change how they look. People in North America spend billions of dollars in surgeries and procedures to change the way they look. Others try to change the way they look by piercing holes in their body or getting tattoos by injecting ink into their skin. God clearly says in the Bible that we shouldn't deface our own bodies with cuts or tattoos. Our bodies are to be used to glorify God. Do things with your body that will honor Him today.

Growing From the Bad Times

Not only that, but we rejoice in our sufferings,
knowing that suffering produces endurance.
ROMANS 5:3, ESV

As a kid in school, I longed for field trips. Living in Massachusetts, I once got to go on a school field trip to Plymouth, Massachusetts. We arrived at school and piled onto the bus with our sack lunches. Plymouth is the site where the pilgrims arrived on the *Mayflower* in 1620. During our field trip we got to visit Plymouth Rock, where, it's believed, the pilgrims landed. We were also taken to a re-created colonial village, where people dressed up as colonists from that time period do various reenactments.

My favorite part of the trip was when we were taken to a replica of the *Mayflower*. As we explored the ship, I was surprised at just how small it was. I was amazed to think that for two months about 130 people lived in this vessel as it slowly came across the ocean. Many of those people were fleeing religious persecution back home. The pilgrims arrived in Plymouth in November, just in time for winter. Even though they had arrived in the New World, everyone continued living on board until March because the weather was so rough. Historical records show that about half the people who made that difficult voyage across the Atlantic Ocean got sick and died during the first winter. These people really had it rough that first year.

The Bible says that in the end, God's people will flee from persecution again. It's no fun going through hard times. We have hard times now, and we are guaranteed to have hard times ahead. Our verse today reminds us that we are challenged to do something very difficult; it says we are to rejoice in our sufferings. That doesn't seem like a very easy thing to do, but when we go through difficult times, we grow and we learn and our faith increases. Ask God today to turn your challenges into opportunities to grow as a Christian.

They're Not Dogs

*So then, as we have opportunity, let us do good to everyone,
and especially to those who are of the household of faith.*
GALATIANS 6:10, ESV

Driving across the middle of South Dakota is a great way to appreciate the endless prairies in the middle of the United States. There are hundreds of miles of grassy prairies and rolling hills to cross, and one of my favorite features of the prairies is the prairie dogs. There is a zoo near my house in Michigan that we used to visit a lot when our boys were little, and one of their favorite exhibits was the prairie dogs who dart around their little community of tunnels. In the wild, we noticed, there were hundreds if not thousands of prairie dogs living in one area. Prairie dogs are famous for standing up on their hind legs in order to gain those extra few inches of height, allowing them to get a better view of their surroundings. They're like little lookouts working to keep their community safe.

Have you ever wondered why the word *dog* is part of their name? They are not dogs, but they make this cute barking sound that I never heard from the ones living at the zoo. Out in their natural habitat, they all worked together observing their environment for any danger. If any one of them saw something potentially suspicious or dangerous they would start barking. The babies would immediately dart back to the safety of their holes, while the adults would partially retreat but also keep looking for where danger might still be threatening their community.

As Christians we are to do the same. Have you ever noticed that it's easy to help and protect the people we know at church? Our verse today is a reminder that God not only expects us to help our Christian brothers and sisters but we are also responsible to do good to everyone in our community. Look around in your community today and look for an opportunity to be good to someone around you. It's a wonderful way to be a witness for God.

The Launch

"Therefore you also must be ready, for the Son of Man is coming at an hour you do not expect."
MATTHEW 24:44, ESV

Adults often ask kids, "What do you want to be when you grow up?" Most kids don't know all the endless career choices available today, but they often respond with things like a firefighter, a doctor, a teacher, or a police officer. When I was in the third and fourth grade, my standard reply was that I wanted to be an astronaut. The final NASA trip to the moon had occurred a few years earlier, and there was still a lot of excitement about the idea of traveling to the moon. Soon after, NASA started its space shuttle missions.

In 2010 I found myself in Florida with my family for a few days. I found out that on the second day we were there, one of the space shuttles was scheduled to launch. I had always wanted to see a shuttle launch, so we made plans to drive to Cape Canaveral to see it. Just as we were about to head out, we heard the news that the launch had been "scrubbed," or postponed. I was sad at first but then hopeful, because it had been rescheduled for the next day. The day came, and again we made our plans to go see the launch, but once again the launch was postponed. We only had one more day left in Florida, and the news finally reported that they would try again that evening! A few hours before the launch we checked again; the countdown was still on. We drove out to Titusville and found the spot where all the people positioned themselves to view. Would the launch take place, or would they postpone again? The minutes counted down to zero, and it launched! We stared in amazement as it blasted its way toward the heavens.

No one knows when Jesus will return. There's no point trying to count down because the Bible says not even the angels know when that day is. Our job is to simply be ready every day and live every day for Jesus.

A God-Fearing Museum

For I am not ashamed of the gospel, because it is the power of God that brings salvation to everyone who believes: first to the Jew, then to the Gentile.
ROMANS 1:16, NIV

When I was in grade school, I loved field trips. It could be a trip to the nearby aquarium, farm, or museum. No matter where we were going, it was fun and exciting to go somewhere different with my friends and learn by seeing and experiencing something new. When I was younger, public museums never had any religious or spiritual displays or comments. As a matter of fact, it was totally the opposite. They usually taught that there was no God or creator. They taught that life appeared by itself and evolved over millions of years into amazingly complex creatures by chance. As an adult, when I took my own children to those museums, I was always ready to remind them that many of these explanations were contrary to the Bible because they relied on faulty human ideas.

A few years ago I heard about a new museum. I was very excited that someone was building a state-of-the-art museum that gave God the credit for what He had done. It was built in Kentucky, just outside of Cincinnati, Ohio, and it was simply called The Creation Museum. Shortly after it opened, I planned a trip with my family to visit the museum. I was amazed. I had previously visited all the Smithsonian museums in Washington, DC and several prominent university museums in the United States, but the new Creation Museum had interactive displays, lots of TV screens with short video clips explaining things, amazing robotic creatures, and exhibits that talked or made sounds. There were painstakingly recreated historical scenes and even a planetarium and 4-D theater! The best part was that the entire museum credited God and gave Him the glory for being the Creator. Sometimes we find ourselves trying to blend into this world, but God has called us to go out and boldly proclaim the truth!

The Power of Community

Carry each other's burdens, and in this way you will fulfill the law of Christ.
GALATIANS 6:2, NIV

A few years ago, my brother-in-law decided to open an office for his business. He found a building and rented it. The next step was for him to buy the necessary furniture and equipment so that it could function as a business. Before we could move any furniture in, there was some work that needed to be done such as removing wallpaper, repairing drywall, and doing lots of painting and cleaning. He decided to get a group together to work on the office, and I was happy to go help. As you can imagine, the work was quickly finished.

Not too far from where I live, there are a lot of Amish communities. The Amish are Christian believers who live a simple life and usually live out on a country farm far from any city. Within their culture there is something fascinating called a "barn raising." Each Amish family usually has a big barn for their hay or animals. If a fire destroys someone's barn, the members of the community bring materials and supplies to build this family a new barn. Sometimes hundreds of men will all come together at once and quickly build this family a new barn. I think this is a wonderful Christian attitude, because it turns tragedy into hope. Because we live in a sinful world, life comes with many hardships and burdens. But wouldn't life be so much simpler if we worked together to help each other get through the difficult times?

We should always be aware of the people around us and take action to help them when they're struggling with a hardship. There are many ways to help people every single day in our own communities. God tells us in our verse today that it's important for us to work together to help each other. The more we work together, the lighter the load will be for everyone!

Short Temper, Big Boom

*A quick-tempered person does foolish things,
and the one who devises evil schemes is hated.*
PROVERBS 14:17, NIV

I've been blessed with the opportunity of visiting Mount St. Helens several times in recent years. Every time I go, I explore a new part of this mountain. Mount St. Helens is a volcano in the state of Washington. On May 18, 1980, it erupted violently. An earthquake triggered a landslide, and then the mountaintop exploded, releasing tons of energy. Because of this huge event, the area around Mount St. Helens has been turned into a national monument, preserving the history of what happened there and providing a great place to learn about volcanoes.

The first time, we visited Johnson Ridge, an overlook right in front of the mile-wide crater. The second time, we drove to the back side of the mountain and hiked to the rim. On the third trip there, we decided to get a close-up look at the middle of the crater, so we found a company nearby that offered helicopter tours to the crater. After buying our tickets, we arrived at the designated time, the pilot gave us a brief safety talk, and then we took off. Helicopters are usually not very roomy inside, but the doors and even part of the floors on this one were transparent, allowing us to see below and all around us. The helicopter lifted off and sped toward the volcano, flying over the South Fork Toutle River and up the side of the mountain to the crater. In the center of the crater there's a lava dome where new lava continues to come out.

People with short tempers are explosive, like volcanoes. You never know when they're going to blow up, and there's usually some damage to deal with afterward. God says people with short tempers end up doing foolish things because they do not have self-control. Oftentimes people get hurt because we say something we don't mean. Be wise; ask God to help you think before you speak.

Late-Night Antics

But each person is tempted when they are dragged away
by their own evil desire and enticed.
JAMES 1:14, NIV

During my years studying in architecture school, there were a few challenges I had to deal with. First of all, every semester we were required to take a studio class, which meant we had to spend a lot of time at our drafting tables drawing buildings. Drafting tables are huge desks where you can change the angle of the surface by tilting it upward. We would then take a giant sheet of paper and tape it to the desk and start drawing. The architecture building had several studios—a large room with a bunch of these drafting tables, one for each student. Every once in a while we'd get a large project to do. While most university students simply go to the library or study in their dorm room, we architecture students had to do our projects at the studio because we couldn't have a drafting table in our dorm room. Because of that, the university allowed us to stay in the building into the wee hours of the morning working on our projects.

Once in a while at 1:00 A.M. we would get so tired we'd take a break and do something unusual to help wake us up. One time we played indoor "archi-baseball," using cardboard tubes and wads of paper rolled up into a ball. Another time we moved drafting tables into a giant circle and rode our bikes around the top of them as if it were a track. Although nothing was damaged, I didn't figure out till later that it wasn't a very good idea to do that, since something may have broken or someone may have gotten hurt.

In life we often make poor decisions. Sometimes we don't even realize it till years later. Our feelings and desires cause us to make bad decisions, and when that happens the consequences can be hurtful. When we are close to God, His desires become our desires. Ask God to help you with each decision you make today!

The Beautiful Game

There is neither Jew nor Gentile, neither slave nor free, nor is there male and female, for you are all one in Christ Jesus.
GALATIANS 3:28, NIV

As a fan of soccer, I was excited to learn that the 1999 Women's World Cup would be played in the United States. I was even more excited when I found out that some of the matches would be played in Chicago, only two hours away from my home. We got a group of friends together and made plans to go, counting down the days till the game. We packed a lunch and did our best to find red, white, and blue clothing to wear. We drove in two cars to Chicago; we parked, and made it to our seats. We were ready! We were excited!

Two great things were about to happen before our eyes. First of all, not only were we going to be able to experience a match, we were going to experience two matches! It turned out that on this particular day in Chicago there would be a double header! Second, we were thrilled to find out that the first game would be between Brazil and Italy and the second game would be between the United States and Nigeria! It took several hours to make it through both games, but we had a wonderful time being there with a group of friends and cheering on the U.S. women's soccer team that represented our country. We also thoroughly enjoyed watching Brazil play soccer because it is obvious that they believe soccer is, as it is called around the world, "The Beautiful Game." Their footwork was amazing, and their passing was sharp. These women were good!

There are many cultures in the world where women are not allowed to do certain things or where they're mistreated. If you are a girl, I'm here to tell you that God can use you to do amazing things. If you are a boy, I'm here to tell you that girls can be incredibly talented and that you need to always treat girls with respect. Remember, we are all children of God.

Fire in Your Mouth

Our tongues are small too, and yet they brag about big things.
It takes only a spark to start a forest fire!
JAMES 3:5, CEV

One evening as we returned home, about half a mile from our house we saw that there were a bunch of fire trucks in the middle of the road. My heart always sinks when I see fire trucks or ambulances or police cars going somewhere with their lights on because I worry that someone is hurt. As we approached the fire trucks we could clearly see a house fully engulfed in flames. One of the neighbors told us that fortunately there was no one in the house. I was relieved to hear that but sad because, the following morning when I drove by, the house was pretty much totally gone.

Then a couple of years later while driving home from a road trip to Florida, we came around a corner and there was a car stopped in the middle of the road. I thought that was odd, but suddenly I noticed why. There was a house right in front of us that was on fire! Immediately I called 9-1-1 and told them what I could see and where I was. About five minutes later, the flames were spilling out the windows and catching the roof on fire. That's when the fire trucks arrived. They pulled in and quickly set up, but it was too late; the fire was out of control. Fortunately no one was in the house, but we were surprised to see yet another home destroyed by fire in our community.

Fires start small, but they can grow and cause a lot of destruction. Your tongue is also small, and just the same, it can also cause a lot of destruction if you are not careful of the things you say. Of course, the opposite is true; you can use your tongue to do great things as well. Use your words to do good things today!

The Sign I Ignored

For it is by grace you have been saved, through faith—and this is not from yourselves, it is the gift of God—not by works, so that no one can boast.
EPHESIANS 2:8, 9, NIV

Once in Oahu, Hawaii, we decided to rent a car so that we could get around and visit different parts of the island. Our boys were still little at this time, so we were always looking for things that they would also enjoy. Our plan on this particular day was to drive clockwise around the perimeter of the island along a highway that hugs the coast for long sections. That means the first major thing we needed to do was cross over a heavily wooded mountain range between Oahu and Kaneohe.

As we drove over the pass, we noticed that there was a pull-off overlook area. Since we weren't in a hurry, we pulled off and decided to check it out. There was a parking lot and a path that went a few hundred feet to a lookout platform that looked over the Kaneohe and the beach beyond. As we started walking toward the platform, we noticed a warning sign posted next to the sidewalk. It was warning about bees in the area. I had never seen a warning sign about bees before, so we weren't really sure what to make of it. We made it to the lookout and enjoyed the view and took some pictures. At that point, as you can probably imagine, a bee came along and stung my oldest son on the hand. Bee stings are painful, and he cried in pain.

As his parents, we felt horrible that this had happened. We felt even worse since we were given fair warning that this could happen. I remember wishing I could take his place and bear the pain on his behalf. Why would I want to do that? You know the answer. It's because of my deep love for him. It's exactly what Jesus did for us. Because of His deep love for us, He took our punishment on the cross so that we could be saved. The price of salvation has been paid. The question we must answer now is whether we will live today accepting that wonderful gift.

The Disappearing City

*But the Lord is faithful, and he will strengthen you and
protect you from the evil one.*
2 THESSALONIANS 3:3, NIV

A few years ago, my parents flew from California to Michigan to visit my family and me—an event that didn't happen very often. Usually we traveled to California to visit them. On this occasion, though, I was blessed with two wonderful weeks with my parents at my home. We did lots of things together. One of their favorite activities was to watch my boys play soccer with their soccer little league. Each evening from Monday through Thursday, one of my boys had a game. We'd pack our camping chairs and head to the field to cheer and support the kids.

One of the days we decided to take a day trip to a nearby town called Saugatuck, Michigan that is located along Lake Michigan. We were going to an attraction that puts you in a convertible truck and drives you up and down the towering sand dunes, providing wonderful views of the lake. It was a lot of fun! One of the stops on the tour featured a ghost town called Singapore. In 1871, three huge fires consumed three nearby cities. In order to rebuild those cities, thousands of trees surrounding the town of Singapore were cut down to make lumber. Because the protective tree cover was now gone, the winds and sands off Lake Michigan came toward the town and brought it to ruin. Within only four years, the entire town of Singapore disappeared. It was completely buried by sand!

Satan wants to bury you with temptation and sin, but fortunately God offers us safety and protection from the evil one. Sometimes in life we feel as though we want to do our thing and go our own way. Just like when the trees around Singapore were cut down, it's hard for God to protect us when we intentionally put ourselves in a dangerous situation. Part of asking for God's protection is to decide to stay away from Satan's temptations.

Didn't You Wear That Yesterday?

Your beauty should not come from outward adornment, such as
elaborate hairstyles and the wearing of gold jewelry or fine clothes.
Rather, it should be that of your inner self, the unfading beauty of a
gentle and quiet spirit, which is of great worth in God's sight.

1 PETER 3:3, 4, NIV

For a long time, American citizens were not allowed to travel to Cuba. Eventually an arrangement was made so that people could travel there to visit immediate family or go on a mission trip. Occasionally I work with *Your Story Hour* and their Spanish division, *Tu Historia Preferida*, which oversees the production and distribution to Spanish-speaking countries. A few years back, a handful of us got permission to go to Cuba to connect with the kids and leaders, but getting there was still complicated. At the time there were no direct flights from the United States to Cuba, even though the bottom tip of Florida is only ninety miles from Cuba.

First, we drove from Michigan to Chicago, where we took a flight to Miami. Once in Miami, we were to fly to Nassau, Bahamas, change planes and take a flight to Cuba. At the airport there were complications, and our flight was canceled. They worked to figure out how to get us there, and the only solution was to put us on a flight to Cancun, Mexico, and then on to Cuba. However, when we got to Cancun, we were stuck. The flight from Mexico to Cuba wouldn't leave till the next day; even worse, half of our luggage didn't arrive in Cancun. The following day we flew to Cuba hoping the rest of our luggage would catch up—but it never arrived. Those of us who had extra clothes were happy to share with those who didn't, because there were no stores in Cuba to buy clothes!

Clothing can be a big deal for people in North America. Malls and stores sell billions of dollars of clothing each year. What should Christians wear? The Bible only provides a few simple principles for us to follow. Our verse today clearly says what is most important to God.

Black Gold

"For where your treasure is, there your heart will be also."
LUKE 12:34, NIV

A few years ago I filmed a video in Bakersfield, California, at the Kern River Oil Field. Oil is also known as "crude oil" or "petroleum," and it's made from algae and tiny marine creatures called zooplankton buried in layers under the surface. Evolution-believing scientists think these living things were buried there millions of year ago, but since I believe the Bible is God's word, I'm aware that when we see living things that were buried underground in layers, it's probably related to the Flood described in Genesis, which uprooted and buried all kinds of living things all over the world. The layers of the earth were deposited by water, so a huge flood covering even the highest hills fits perfectly with what we see in nature today.

In Bakersfield, there is a neat overlook at the field that allowed me to see the entire oil field. It's the fifth largest oilfield in the United States with more than nine thousand wells!

After finishing there, we went to the California coast at Huntington Beach to film. We went because about a mile into the ocean, several giant oil platforms are visible; they are drilling for oil under the bottom of the sea floor. Oil has become an incredibly important resource in the world. Ninety percent of the vehicles in the world run on some sort of oil product, and many homes are heated by oil.

Since oil is buried in the ground, it's really like a buried treasure! Treasure sounds great, but it can be very dangerous for our spiritual life. Our verse today reminds us that our heart is always with the things we treasure, but you have to ask yourself where that is. It's OK to like certain things, but don't let them consume your heart and all your attention. Make sure God has the spot in the center of your heart.

The Miracle Buggy

*And we know that in all things God works for the good of those
who love him, who have been called according to his purpose.*
ROMANS 8:28, NIV

A few years ago I was in the Pacific Northwest for a five-day filming shoot. We were on a very tight schedule and did not have much room for problems that could arise. On the last day of the shoot, before we were to fly home, the schedule called for us to drive to Tillamook, Oregon, right on the Pacific Ocean in the northern part of the state. That day we needed to shoot at a sand dune riding around in a dune buggy. As I prepared for the filming trip, I called a dune buggy rental place, and I asked about renting one for a couple of hours. They said there would be no problem at all, and because I was coming on a weekday during the low season, we wouldn't even need a reservation. We arrived, and the lady in the office was shocked and embarrassed to tell me that out of nowhere a huge group arrived unannounced about an hour before me and rented every single vehicle they had—for the entire day. She said in the past ten years, nothing like that had ever happened. I prayed with my crew, and I told them that we'd drive to the dunes anyway. A few minutes after we got there, a man drove up to the parking lot in a dune buggy. Something inside me told me to go over to him and tell him about our filming situation. Right on the spot he offered to allow us to film our scenes with his buggy!

Unexpected things happen in life all the time. We try to make plans, but they don't always work. Don't be stressed out; instead, ask God to let His purpose be fulfilled in your life. In Tillamook, we were able to save time and money, plus we were able to witness to this man when we told him about our filming project. God's plan is always better than ours. Remember to always listen for the Holy Spirit's leading!

Turn Your Light On

*"You are the light of the world. A town built on a hill cannot be hidden.
Neither do people light a lamp and put it under a bowl. Instead they
put it on its stand, and it gives light to everyone in the house."*
MATTHEW 5:14, 15, NIV

If you've ever used electricity to turn on a light, you are probably utilizing the power of coal. Coal is a fossil fuel made from dead plant matter, and it's actually the single largest source of energy for the generation of electricity in the whole world. There are two types of coal mines—surface mines and underground mines. Underground mines are exactly what the name says, mines that are located deep underground, where tunnel systems are created and coal is removed. In a surface mine, the coal is located closer to the surface, so machines on the surface dig down into the ground till they reach coal and then the coal is removed. Then, the hole is usually filled back in with dirt, and a few years later you would never know it had once been a coal mine.

A couple of years ago I visited a coal mine in the state of Wyoming. First, from a platform we looked into the pit where gigantic machines were scooping the coal out and shoveling it into huge dump trucks. During my visit I walked around one of those huge trucks; the tires were twice as tall as me! Once the coal was on the truck, it was brought to another part of the mine, where it was crushed and loaded onto train cars that were lined up. Once the train was full, the coal was taken to its final destination, usually an electric power plant that runs on coal.

It's amazing to think that the energy we use to turn on light comes from a hidden source underground; but unless the coal is uncovered, it can't be used to make electricity. Our verse today is very similar. God has given us a light to shine in the world, but you have to ask yourself, am I shining it for everyone to see, or is it covered up and hidden away? There is too much darkness in the world; choose today to bring God's light out for everyone to see!

The Dinosaur Dilemma

All Scripture is God-breathed and is useful for teaching,
rebuking, correcting and training in righteousness.
2 TIMOTHY 3:16, NIV

Everyone is fascinated by dinosaurs. When I was a kid, I was intrigued by dinosaurs and knew the names of several of them. In church and in school I was often told that dinosaurs never existed and that they were mythical. Sometimes we were told that they were real animals but that they lived long ago and were now extinct. On TV and in museums, people taught that dinosaurs lived millions of years ago. The more I learned about them, the more confused I got.

As an adult I visited the Natural History Museum in Washington, DC, and marveled at the amazing dinosaur displays, and I was convinced that there were too many different explanations about dinosaurs. And I knew they couldn't all be true. It came to a point that I had to decide where I would get my truths from—God or people. For example, the Bible teaches that God first created life on earth six thousand years ago, while some people think dinosaurs lived millions of years ago. First, I discovered that there is a lot of physical evidence showing that these animals lived, so I knew that these were indeed real creatures. Next, from reading the Bible I knew that only God has the power to create a living thing. That means that in the beginning, the original dinosaur ancestors must have been created by God before sin came along, and they became aggressive and violent after sin entered the world. Finally, I started discovering scientific evidence clearly pointing to the idea that these creatures lived thousands of years ago, not millions of years ago, which fits with what the Bible says.

I'm still very fascinated by dinosaurs, and I still love to visit museums, but I rely on God's word to understand the truth about the world we live in. People's knowledge is limited, but God's word never changes.

Making an Oregon Trail

You will go out in joy
and be led forth in peace;
the mountains and hills
will burst into song before you,
and all the trees of the field
will clap their hands.
ISAIAH 55:12, NIV

A few years ago I stopped to visit some friends in Oregon—a beautiful state with a variety of environments to appreciate. My friends lived in an area of tall rolling hills, dense forests, quick moving rivers, and away from highways and heavy traffic. On the day that I spent with them, they told me about their surroundings and how there were paths and wonderful wooded areas to explore along the river. All this sounded very nice, especially since I had driven for many hours before arriving. I mentioned how nice it would be to explore all this land, but I made the observation that there was not enough time to explore it all. They admitted that it would take a while to explore all their land, since they had about fifty acres. But then they offered me an alternative. They took me out to the barn and showed me their four-wheel ATV. They said, "Why don't you go and take it out! You'll get to explore a lot more ground if you're riding one of these!" That made a lot of sense, but I had never driven one before. They gave me a quick lesson on how to turn it on, how the throttle and brakes worked, and so on. After a few minutes, I felt prepared and ventured out into the wild. For the next hour or so, I drove around grassy plains, pine forests, and alongside a rocky mountain river.

There is a lot of nature in the world for us to explore—it's like God's personal artwork! Nature is a great place to retreat to when you want to spend some quiet time with God. Make time once in a while to find a quiet spot in nature and spend time talking to God. I've discovered that by being surrounded by nature you will feel very close to Him.

The Real Sugar Juice

Create in me a pure heart, O God,
and renew a steadfast spirit within me.
PSALM 51:10, NIV

Trinidad is a colonial city in Cuba and one of the UNESCO World Heritage sites. Walking through the streets made me feel as though I had time-traveled hundreds of years into the past. That's when we came across a vendor selling *guarapo*—a popular drink in Cuba. I told the vendor that we wanted to buy four cups of guarapo for our family. The man reached around the corner and grabbed four stalks of sugar cane that were each almost eight feet long. Next, he went over to this large metal machine and pushed a button, and wheels started turning and a loud noise followed. He took one of the stalks of sugar cane and put it into the back part of the machine and fed it into the machine, which proceeded to smash it. As it went through the machine, the liquid sugar cane juice came out and filled a pitcher near the front of the machine. After the sugar cane went through once, he put it through the machine again, and again. He did this to all four of the stalks, and all the while we curiously watched. In Cuba it is common to order something to drink and have them make it right there in front of you. When he was done, the floor in his shop was littered with the stalks, which had been smashed so hard they had become like dry, flakey hay all over the floor. Next, he filled up four cups of the guarapo and gave it to us. It was delicious, and I was amazed that he had transformed those long stalks into this yummy, sweet drink.

God has a special transformation in store for you too. When we accept Christ into our life we are transformed and born again. Have you been baptized? Baptism is how you publicly accept Jesus as your Savior. If you want God to forever be the center of your life, look into being baptized and let God create in you a pure heart.

The Big Ocean Surprise

The LORD himself goes before you and will be with you; he will never leave you nor forsake you. Do not be afraid; do not be discouraged.
DEUTERONOMY 31:8, NIV

Before my first son was born, my wife and I spent a week on the island of Cozumel in the Caribbean Sea, just off the coast of Mexico. Our hotel was right on the beach, and every day we'd sit by the water and talk, read, or listen to music. Every day I'd spend an hour or two in the water snorkeling on the nearby reef. At night we'd get on a moped and go into town to find a restaurant to eat at. Later we'd hang out for a while in the park where children and families came to be together each night.

One day we decided to venture to the southern tip of the island, where, I was told, the snorkeling was supposed to be better. I wasn't sure what to expect but when I got there; as a matter of fact, there was no one else there. I had been told that the reef was a couple hundred feet out, so I got in and started swimming out. I was a little nervous going all the way out there alone, but the reef turned out to be amazing, and I spent a good half hour exploring the reef before I started heading back. That's when I saw something ahead of me that startled me. It was a huge manta ray with a wing span of at least fourteen or fifteen feet. My heart pounded, and once the ray disappeared I remember suddenly feeling very alone.

Loneliness is something a lot of people struggle with. If you are a person who sometimes feels lonely, know that God Himself is with you always. If you know someone who seems lonely, consider that maybe God has placed you within reach of that person to help bring them out of loneliness and despair. May God be with you today!

My Fortress of Mesh

The Lord will rescue me from every evil attack and will bring me safely to his heavenly kingdom. To him be glory for ever and ever. Amen.
2 TIMOTHY 4:18, NIV

Several years ago my wife and I decided to take a trip to Africa. But traveling to Africa is not something you take lightly, and we decided to consult our doctor to see how we needed to prepare. One month before traveling, we ended up returning to his office to get a few vaccinations we needed. For the next month we also had to take a pill every day, as well as each day during our time there, and also for one month after returning. All this was part of an effort to reduce the risk of getting malaria and other infections from a mosquito bite or contaminated water. When it came to our health, we didn't want to take any chances, so we faithfully took all our pills in preparation for the trip. But that's not all we did.

Before leaving the United States, I bought a mosquito net that was meant to cover our entire bed. I had never used one before, so I wasn't sure how to put it up. That first night I pulled out the mosquito net and started to try to figure out how I was going to set it up in our hotel room. There was no obvious way to hang it, but I had come prepared with a ziplock bag full of cord and pushpins. Over the next forty-five minutes I managed to somehow hang the mosquito net with an amazing system of string all over the room in order to hold the netting in place. It was a lot of work to put up, but let me tell you, I slept a lot better each night knowing the net was there.

There are many dangers in the world that can hurt our body, but there are also many dangers out there that will hurt our spiritual life. Remember, your body is temporary, but God wants to recreate you to have eternal life! That is why it is more important to protect your spiritual life. Every day, ask God to protect your spiritual life.

Leaving the Past in the Past

"Forget the former things;
do not dwell on the past.
See I am doing a new thing!
Now it springs up; do you not perceive it?
I am making a way in the wilderness
and streams in the wasteland."
Isaiah 43:18, 19, NIV

In 1952 my father decided to leave Chile to come to the United States to pursue a college education. He traveled by boat up the Pacific coast of South America, making stops in Lima and Panama City. He crossed the Panama Canal and steamed on toward Cuba, the last stop before arriving in Miami, his final destination. His stop in Cuba turned out to last longer than he thought—by several years. He ended up attending the Adventist college in Cuba, Antillean College, which later moved to Puerto Rico because of the Cuban Revolution. There he met my mother and eventually got married and found a job.

During the mid 1950s my parents were working in Cuba while a rebel army fought to bring down the Cuban government. In 1958, the rebels marched into Havana, and the war was over. Unfortunately, three years later, the revolution made changes that caused the college to be shut down. The buildings were locked up, and the college campus remained abandoned for decades. In 1999, almost forty years later, I visited the campus for the first time. All my life I had heard stories about this place where my parents had met and studied, but the place was now a ghost town. The buildings were overgrown with bushes and trees, windows were broken, the walls were black with dirt, and some buildings were falling down. My heart was broken seeing it like that.

Bad things happen, but humans were not created to dwell on the past and continually suffer for bad things that happened. God says in our verse today that He has wonderful plans for your future, not your past. You won't heal until you are able to forget the past and live in the present and look to the future—keeping God close at all times.

JUNE 3

A Stinging Surprise

*The L*ORD* tests the righteous,*
but his soul hates the wicked and the one who loves violence.
PSALM 11:5, ESV

A few years ago I bought an old farmhouse in Michigan on five acres that was previously abandoned for ten years. The inside was trashed, and the whole place was a terrible mess, but it was in a wonderful location. I challenged myself to restore the farmhouse to its full glory. I asked my workers to remove all the plaster from the walls and ceilings. As we removed materials from the farmhouse, we made several fascinating discoveries—nothing of major value, but we found interesting things such as newspapers dating back one hundred years stuffed into the walls to serve as insulation. We also found a few glass jars and a very old Coke bottle.

As my workers removed the plaster from the ceiling of a one-story area of the old farmhouse, they made an alarming discovery—there was an enormous wasp's nest in the attic space. The guys called me, and I came. It was about eight feet wide and about twelve feet long and between one and three feet thick. I had never seen anything like it before. The thing that saved us was that we were working in the cold month of January. Although we encountered tens of thousands of wasps in the nest as we removed it, we were safe because they were all in a drowsy, inactive state because they are dormant during the cold winter months.

Sometimes we walk around in life not knowing that danger is lurking just a few feet away. Satan wants to surround us with danger to make us fall and get hurt. One of his most powerful tools is violence. Have you noticed violence is everywhere around us? It's found in movies, TV, music, video games, and books. Satan wants us to see violence as "normal," and because of that, young people sometimes copy the violence and act it out in real life. Exposing yourself to violent images or content is like asking Satan to expose you to danger. Ask God today to help you make good decisions that keep you far from violent media.

Do as I Say, Not as I Do

For at one time you were in darkness, but now you are light in the Lord. Walk as children of light.
Ephesians 5:8, ESV

Recently we decided to visit the Florida Everglades National Park—a huge area of wetlands where a shallow sixty-mile-wide river flows southward for about one hundred miles. As part of our day trip to the everglades, we decided to drive to Everglades City in the southwest corner of Florida. Our plan was to take an airboat ride. Airboats have a giant fan mounted on the back of the boat that pushes the boat forward through the shallow water. When we got to the Everglades, we found a company that offered airboat tours and purchased tickets. At the dock, we boarded the airboat, and we were each given noise-blocking headsets.

Soon we were navigating down a narrow river and entered an area dense with mangroves. Moments later, the driver hit the throttle and started speeding along the surface. We were surrounded on both sides by the mangrove forest. After a while, we pulled over because our driver/guide had spotted a family of raccoons in the mangroves. He proceeded to tell us about them and reminded us we should never feed them. Deciding to illustrate his point of how attracted they are to "human things," he pulled out a bottle of soda and poured a little on the branch. Right away, a large raccoon scurried over and started licking the branch. Then the raccoon grabbed the bottle of soda out of the driver's hand and took off into the mangrove! Our guide was embarrassed because he was accidentally breaking the law right in front of us.

Did you know that every day God has asked you to be a good example to the people around you? There are many ways to witness to people, but I would say the easiest way to let your light shine is by letting people see the way you live, by doing good works, and by always being kind to others.

Never Give Up

Do everything without grumbling or arguing, so that you may become blameless and pure, "children of God without fault in a warped and crooked generation." Then you will shine among them like stars in the sky.
PHILIPPIANS 2:14, 15, NIV

D uring the 1990s, Cuba went through a very difficult period, and the people struggled due to shortages. While visiting there, I decided to spend a few days in the capital, Havana, and then drive east to a town called Camajuaní, where another group of my relatives lived. Because of the shortages, even getting around the island was difficult. It was finally decided that a cousin from Camajuaní would drive to Havana to pick us up. The distance from Havana to Camajuaní is about 170 miles, so under normal circumstances, it should've taken us about three hours to get there. We got on the national highway and left Havana behind, but I soon discovered that the shortages in Cuba had also affected the highway system—it was full of enormous potholes! We were driving in a small Russian car called a Lada from the 1960s, and as we left the city, we had to slow down to about twenty-five to thirty miles per hour in order to dodge the hundreds of potholes. But it was impossible to miss every single one. After an hour, one of our tires went flat—but people there didn't replace tires, they repaired them, and so we did just that. A couple of hours later, we got another flat. Again, we repaired it. A couple of hours later, the car broke down. We pulled over, and our cousin pulled out a bunch of tools from the trunk, and he fixed the car. I was so impressed by our cousin's never-quit attitude! It took us almost ten hours to drive the 170 miles, but our cousin never gave up, and he never got upset.

Do you ever grumble and complain about things when they don't go your way? Make a choice today to always have a good attitude. Don't be a complainer. Let your words be positive. Ask God to help your attitude shine like a star in the sky!

Shoestring Budget

For the love of money is a root of all kinds of evil. Some people, eager for money, have wandered from the faith and pierced themselves with many griefs.
1 TIMOTHY 6:10, NIV

People often ask me if I'm wealthy when they learn how much traveling I do. I can tell you with all assurance that I am not wealthy. In college I learned that there were secrets to traveling on a shoestring budget. I decided early on that I would be willing to travel under very non-luxurious conditions in order to travel and see as much of the world as I could. Shortly after getting married, my wife and I decided to travel to the Yucatán Peninsula in Mexico. By going in the off-season, we were able to find extremely cheap airline tickets to the city of Cancun. At the airport, we took the bus to the city center and found a cheap hotel that most of you would probably never dream of staying in. It was a bit rough by our standards since there was no air conditioning and the bathroom was down the hall.

The first day there, we paid less than a dollar to take the bus to a beautiful nearby beach. Another day we went down to the local bus station to see how far the local bus would go. It turns out that one of them went several hours west near the ruins of Chichén Itzá. It was only a few dollars, so we went for it. Traveling with the locals was fun, and we met interesting people along the way. We made it to the Mayan ruins and spent the day exploring pyramids and ancient buildings. The ruins were expansive, and we spent hours upon hours walking around, climbing things, and entering structures that were almost one thousand five hundred years old. We had a wonderful adventure together, even though we spent very little money taking this trip.

As you grow, be careful that you aren't driven to love money. It's true that we need money to live, but don't let it be the center of your life. Instead, let your life with God be the ultimate adventure, because it will bring you true happiness and joy that money simply cannot buy.

The Joy of Contentment

Keep your life free from love of money, and be content with what you have, for he has said, "I will never leave you nor forsake you."
HEBREWS 13:5, ESV

In yesterday's devotional, I shared with you about our low-budget trip to Mexico awhile back. After visiting Chichén Itzá that day, we went back to the entrance of the ruins to catch our bus back to Cancun. Soon we found out that we had missed the last bus going back. Since we spoke Spanish, I was able to find out that there were more buses that went to Cancun, but they left from a city called Valladolid, about forty-five minutes away. You're probably thinking, *Now what?* We walked out to the street, and I stuck my thumb out. Although hitchhiking is not very popular in North America, it's quite a common form of getting around in many other countries, especially if you're traveling on a tight budget! After a few minutes, my wife and I were picked up by a man in a pickup truck. He said he was heading to Valladolid, but he only had room for us to ride in the bed of the pickup truck. We were not in any kind of position to be picky, so we jumped in. It was only a forty-five-minute ride; what could go wrong? Ten minutes into our ride it started raining.

My wife thought I was crazy, but eventually we made it to the bus station in Valladolid, and from there we were able to take a bus back to Cancun that evening. In the end, since we had hitchhiked part of the way back, the return trip cost even less than the cost to get there! I know what you're thinking: *Boy, he's cheap!* I've learned that in order to travel a lot, you have to be willing to adapt to situations and be content.

Learning to be content will build your character and help you deal with challenges in life. It will also bring you joy and peace from constantly wanting things you don't have. Be joyful, simply knowing that God is with you and He will never leave you!

Your Story Hour in Cuba

In everything I did, I showed you that by this kind of hard work we must help the weak, remembering the words the Lord Jesus himself said: "It is more blessed to give than to receive."
ACTS 20:35, NIV

A few years ago I traveled to Cuba on a mission trip with *Your Story Hour.* The dramatized stories teach about developing good values and often feature Bible stories. Many people don't know that they also produce stories in Spanish and Russian; in Spanish, they're known as *Tu Historia Preferida.* During this particular trip we traveled to Cuba with the hosts of the Spanish stories, Tio Daniel and Tia Elena. Our goal was to travel across the entire island nation to bring nightly special events to churches jammed with hundreds of kids. At the time of our trip, Cuba was going through a rough period. There was a lot of poverty, and people had very few possessions.

Every time we arrived at a new city we were welcomed with open arms by the local leaders, who used the stories to minister to the kids of that city. Because of the political situation there, the stories were not allowed to be broadcast by radio, so the only way to reach the kids was by having local leaders and teachers bring kids into their homes to listen to the stories on a CD player. Many of these incredibly poor leaders would work hard to also provide a small snack and even a coloring sheet for the kids as they came. I got to meet several of these leaders during the couple of weeks we were there, and I was impressed because it seemed that the poorer the people were, the more generous they were. One woman had saved up all her money to transform her home into a gathering space for kids, leaving only a tiny corner of the house for bedrooms.

In North America, our society teaches us to want things. It teaches that we deserve things and that receiving is better than giving. We are reminded today that you will be blessed more when you are generous and give to the weak and needy.

The Worst Game Ever

*Be alert and of sober mind. Your enemy the devil prowls
around like a roaring lion looking for someone to devour.*
1 PETER 5:8, NIV

The first time I went to an NFL football game was an experience that left me telling myself I would never go to a game again. Let me explain. I had just graduated from college, and I was working at an office. One day, the owner of the company I worked for was given four tickets to a Chicago Bears home game in late November, and I was invited to use one of those tickets. I was excited since it would be my first time attending an NFL game. We drove to Chicago, but right away, there were two things working against us: first, it was very cold; and second, it was raining. This is a terrible combination, because Soldier Field is not an indoor stadium. Even though I had brought a rain poncho, being in the cold, wet rain for three hours was not going to be fun. The next thing I discovered was that all four of our seats were in different parts of the stadium, so we'd each have to sit alone. *Wonderful, now I'll be alone in the cold, wet rain for three hours!* Since I was the newest employee, I got the last pick of the seats—in the highest seats of the stadium. Last of all, the game was terrible. Because of the rain and cold, and because of the rivalry between the Bears and the Vikings, the final score was a whopping 0-3. The only exciting thing to happen the entire game was a Vikings field goal, which lost the game for the home team.

What was the lesson learned? Things do not always seem as they appear. A ticket to an NFL game sounded good, but it turned out to be terrible. Satan is trying to get the world to think that drugs and alcohol are good but things are not as they appear. These things are terrible and destructive, and they will destroy your body, your family, your friendships, your money, and your life. Don't even be curious; stay away from Satan's traps.

Zip-Line Surprise

*And we urge you, brothers, admonish the idle, encourage the
fainthearted, help the weak, be patient with them all.*
1 THESSALONIANS 5:14, ESV

My family spent two weeks on a mission project in Central America. As usual, the travel was exciting and tiring all at once, but it was a joy to work in three countries. During our days in Costa Rica, the church assigned us a driver to take us to the places we needed to visit. Our driver always had a wonderful attitude and was ready to help and do anything necessary to make our work there successful. When our work in Costa Rica was complete, we were given a free day to do something fun as a family. I asked the driver about a good place to zip-line. He told me about one that he drove by almost every week and was supposedly the best one in Costa Rica. This sounded great, so we decided on that one. When we got there, we found out that the tour was about two to three hours long, so our driver dropped us off and went to run some errands. When the tour was over, he was there to pick us up. That's when I asked him, "Have you ever gone on a zip line?" He told me that even though he'd been driving by this place for more than twenty years, he had never zip-lined before. I made him get out of the car right there, and I marched him over to the office. I bought him a ticket to ride on the final zip of the tour, which happened to be one of the longest zip cables in the country, going over one-third of a mile over a forested valley between two mountains. He was quite nervous, but I encouraged him and told him I believed he would love it, and he did!

Sometimes we get caught up just thinking about ourselves. That's our sinful nature. With God's help we can be the kind of person who thinks of others. Encouraging others is one of the easiest ways to help someone because all it takes is kind words. Look for someone who looks discouraged today and use kind words to encourage them!

The Gift of Sacrifice

"This is my commandment, that you love one another as I have loved you. Greater love has no one than this, that someone lay down his life for his friends. You are my friends if you do what I command you."
JOHN 15:12–14, ESV

Life is very fragile. When God originally created us, we were made perfect. But because of sin, death was introduced into the world and has been a part of humanity ever since the time of Adam and Eve. Death is something we eventually have to deal with.

A few years ago, our family traveled to Panama City, Florida for a little escape from the northern winter weather. We rented a condo with several bedrooms and drove down to spend a few days in the warm weather. For the first day or two, everyone had a great time relaxing and playing on the beach. The waves weren't too big, and the weather was nice. On the third day there was a red flag on the beach that day, which meant the currents were strong, and you swam at your own risk. Our children were ten and twelve, and they were not allowed to get in the water more than knee deep that day. A bit farther in, a teenager was playing in the water and he was suddenly trapped by the current. In a flash, his father rushed out to save his son who was struggling less than seventy-five feet away. The father reached his son and saved him, but in a horrible turn of events the father was caught by the current and drowned. As you can imagine, this affected the remainder of our time there, and it really made us think about how delicate life is. It also made me think of how the father never hesitated to sacrifice himself to save his son.

We are all sons and daughters of God, and Jesus also came and sacrificed His life so that we could be saved. Sin is a horrible thing, but salvation from sin is the best news we could ever get. Jesus' sacrifice will give us eternal salvation. In the meantime I suggest we treat every day of life as a precious gift!

Welcome Home, It's 2:00 A.M.

A joyful heart is good medicine,
but a crushed spirit dries up the bones.
PROVERBS 17:22, ESV

I grew up as a PK—"pastor's kid." Being a PK had its advantages and its disadvantages. While living in New England, my father was usually responsible for three or four churches at once. Of course, this also meant that every Sabbath of the month we'd attend a different church and I'd only get to see my church friends once a month. On the flip side, this also meant that I had a bunch of sets of friends all over the state. My dad pastored Spanish churches, and the great majority of the members in my father's churches in Massachusetts were from Puerto Rico. This meant that I learned to love to eat all the Puerto Rican dishes and appreciate their traditions.

One tradition was especially interesting. On an unannounced night between Christmas and New Year's, a large group of people went door to door, bringing all kinds of instruments and singing traditional Puerto Rican holiday music until the person opened the door. The songs were lively, catchy, and even humorous. The group would go around for hours, surprising their friends with music and joy. Since my dad was the pastor, our home was reserved as the last stop of the night—usually arriving around 2:00 A.M. They'd park in our driveway and sneak up to the front door and suddenly break into loud, joyful song. We didn't have any Puerto Rican neighbors where we lived, so every year my dad's goal was to hurry and get them into the house as quickly as possible so as to not disturb the neighborhood. I've always remembered our Puerto Rican friends as very joyful people. Even when faced with challenges, they were upbeat and smiling.

More and more it seems like we are surrounded by grumpy, long-faced people. Many people think joy is something you have to achieve, but it's not; joy is a choice. Will you choose to be joyful today? Want to know a secret? People love to be around happy people.

A Very Special Beach

"Honor your father and your mother, so that you may live long in the land the Lord your God is giving you."
Exodus 20:12, NIV

Since I've lived the majority of my life in cold climates, the cold has never bothered me much, and each year we embrace the changes that come with the season. Fortunately, every once in a while I get to travel to someplace warm during winter. A few years back I had the privilege of traveling to Cuba. Cuba is special for me for two simple reasons: my mother is Cuban, and my wife is Cuban. Because my wife is Cuban, she still had a lot of direct family members living there. Even though travel to Cuba was not allowed by the US government at that time, she was given special permission to travel to Cuba to visit her family. Since I was her husband, I was allowed to accompany her. During that trip, we spent more than a week visiting family. One day we were able to get away and went to the beach. There was one beach that I had always wanted to visit since I was a child—Varadero. This was an important beach to our family because I was often told that my parents spent their honeymoon on the beaches of Varadero. My parents would often comment on how beautiful the beaches were, and now I was anxious to finally discover this place for myself. From Havana we boarded a bus and headed toward Varadero. We spent the day there, and I was not disappointed. The beaches were beautiful, the water was great, and the weather was magnificent. Of course, I couldn't help but reflect that a few decades earlier, my parents were right there too.

Parents are special people who are given the tough job of raising kids. They make mistakes, and they may not always be right or perfect, but it's still our responsibility to love, honor, and be respectful of our parents. Go give them a big hug today.

Historic Encounter

But our citizenship is in heaven. And we eagerly
await a Savior from there, the Lord Jesus Christ.
PHILIPPIANS 3:20, NIV

After the Cuban Revolution in 1959, Fidel Castro became the new president of Cuba. One of his most famous partners in the revolution, Ernesto "Che" Guevara, became the president of the National Bank of Cuba. At this time, my father was an employee of the church in Cuba, and one of his responsibilities was to take a group of colporteurs from Cuba to the neighboring island of Puerto Rico for an event. To do so, my father needed to go to the National Bank of Cuba and ask for permission to take money for this trip. Arriving at the bank, my father was surprised to learn that he needed to make this request in person—to Che himself. As they chatted about the trip, their conversation included Che's appreciation of my father's work with the youth of Cuba. My father carried a journal with him that day, and at the end of the meeting he asked Che to sign his journal. Instead, Che took the journal and wrote several sentences of encouragement to the youth who were embarking on this trip. Che Guevara left Cuba shortly after, but a few years later he was killed in Bolivia. During my several trips to Cuba, I noticed that images of Che were seen all over the place. They were on t-shirts, mugs, paintings, and all sorts of souvenirs. The interesting thing is that he was not even from Cuba; he was from Argentina.

Did you know Satan works hard to divide people by color, by country, by beliefs, and any other thing he can use to make us feel threatened by each other? The Bible reminds us that we are all created by God and that our citizenship is in heaven. Don't let Satan deceive you into missing out what God has in store for you. It doesn't matter what country you are from; you are a child of God!

Lost in Athens

Do not get drunk on wine, which leads to
debauchery. Instead, be filled with the Spirit.
EPHESIANS 5:18, NIV

After traveling by train from France to Greece, we arrived in Athens with a plan to immediately find a travel agency because we wanted to find a flight to Cairo, Egypt. First, let me tell you that we were in the old sector of the city. That means the streets were laid out in a very random pattern. There was no grid or blocks. There was not a single street that was parallel to another; they just went in every direction. To make matters more difficult, the language in Greece uses different alphabet characters, so even reading the street-name signs was complicated and disorienting. We asked for directions and wiggled our way through the streets, closer and closer till we finally found the travel agency! We were so relieved!

Fortunately the travel agent spoke English, and we found out that we could catch a flight that same day—we just had to hurry and make our way straight to the airport. That's when we remembered that we had no idea where we were. Again, we started to ask directions from anyone who spoke English. We wandered the streets of Athens for a long time, frustrated that we were lost and worried that we were going to miss our flight. We finally found the bus and headed to the airport, but it was too late—we had missed our flight to Cairo.

We felt so disoriented during that time we were lost. Alcohol has a similar effect, and drunkenness will slowly destroy your family, your finances, your friendships, and your life. As you get older, Satan will tempt you by making alcohol appear fun and exciting. Don't fall for his tricks; he just wants to ruin your life. Don't even fall for the temptation of "just trying it once," because addiction is also part of his trap to snare you. Instead, I suggest you simply stay as far away as possible. Ask the Holy Spirit to guide your steps today and always!

Pushing the Bus Uphill

Sing to God, sing in praise of his name,
extol him who rides on the clouds;
rejoice before him—his name is the LORD.
PSALM 68:4, NIV

While studying in France, I joined the school choir. In April of that school year we took a ten-day choir tour of Italy. One of the places on our tour was the Adventist school in Florence. The Adventist school is located on a hill overlooking the city. The road up the hill was quite steep. Along with the choir, our bus carried all our luggage and sleeping bags for the trip, plus it towed a small trailer containing all the chairs, stands, and instruments used in our concerts.

As we slowly chugged up the hill the bus suddenly stopped—it simply did not have the strength to make it up the hill. The guys got out and tried to push the bus. I've pushed cars out of snow before, but this was the first time I tried pushing a bus—up a hill no less! Somehow, we made it up the hill, only sustaining one injury along the way. One of the guys pinched his hand near the hitch that towed the trailer. After we pushed the bus and trailer up the steep part of the road, the bus was able to make it up the last portion all by itself. Still, when we made it to the top, it turned out that my friend's hand had a big cut, so I volunteered to go with him to the hospital to get his cut checked out. The nurse patched him up and we made it back to the concert just in time.

Music is probably a big part of your life, and your musical choices can have a big influence on you. Usually they lead you toward God or away from God. What kind of music do you listen to? I encourage you to pick music that honors God.

The Accidental Approach

"Go in through the narrow gate. The gate to destruction is wide, and the road that leads there is easy to follow. A lot of people go through that gate."
MATTHEW 7:13, CEV

After a fifty-two-hour train ride from Switzerland to Greece, my three friends and I were happy to arrive in Athens, the capital of Greece. Since my friends and I had basically starved during our fifty-two-hour train ride, we decided to get food first. We found a restaurant just below the Acropolis where we could eat in the shadow of this amazing historical site. Seeing that it was the first time any of us had been to Greece, we concluded that we needed to eat food at a traditional Greek restaurant. While three of us ordered traditional Greek plates, one guy from our group decided to have pizza—we teased him about that!

Soon we were hiking our way up toward the entrance of the Acropolis—the most important historical monument in the city. We tried to take a short-cut from the restaurant since the normal tourist approach would have taken us way around a much longer route. This got us lost trying to get there, but in the process we were able to see authentic parts of the surrounding city that most tourists do not see. We found ourselves walking through people's yards, alleyways, and through marketplaces, meeting interesting people. We finally made the climb up the steps till we were standing face to face with one of the most famous Greek buildings—the Parthenon, which was built more than four hundred years before the time of Christ!

Even though our shortcut was hard, we enjoyed the journey to the Acropolis so much more than if we had taken the path chosen by most tourists. The Bible says the path to heaven is narrow. Like our path in Athens, it means the path to heaven is less traveled and more difficult, but in the end, it's rewarding. Many people choose the easy path, which leads to destruction. There are no other paths to pick from. Which path will you choose?

Everyone's Castle, Everyone's Fortress

So Christ was sacrificed once to take away the sins of many; and he will appear a second time, not to bear sin, but to bring salvation to those who are waiting for him.
HEBREWS 9:28, NIV

As I drove through Europe on a recent trip with my family, it was amazing how quickly everything would change: the style of buildings, the language, the climate, and the culture. One moment we'd be driving through the Alps, the next we'd be driving through rolling hills covered in vineyards.

Europe also contains a lot of history. Once, we arrived in a city called Granada in the south of Spain. Granada is home to a huge palace and fortress perched up on a hill overlooking the city below. As we explored this amazing complex, we learned that the first part of this fortress was built more than one thousand one hundred years ago by the Spaniards. A few hundred years later, the Moorish people came and rebuilt and expanded the palace dramatically. Then a few hundred years after that, the Christians took over again and more of the palace was added. Not long after, the palace was abandoned for a while, until finally in the 1800s it was rediscovered by historians and turned into a major tourist attraction. What a bizarre history! As we walked around the palace, it was clear which parts were from the different kingdoms that controlled it and added on to it.

Many parts of our world have been conquered by various kingdoms over the years. A new one rises, dominates for a while, and then it's replaced. The Bible prophecies found in Daniel and Revelation tell us about different kingdoms that will rise and fall leading up to the final judgment and the Second Coming. Many prophecies have already been fulfilled. The first time Jesus came, He died for our sins on the cross. We are now waiting for Jesus to return to take us to heaven. The good thing is that His kingdom will last for eternity. I definitely want to belong to that kingdom! Don't you?

The Dig

The soul of a lazy man desires, and has nothing;
But the soul of the diligent shall be made rich.
PROVERBS 13:4, NKJV

The summer I spent in Jordan was by far one of the most fascinating experiences of my life. During my time there, we had a very simple routine each day. We usually started the day at 5:00 A.M. with an early breakfast and worship. Before the sunrise, we boarded a bus and drove thirty minutes into the Jordanian desert to the location of our dig site, arriving as the sun rose. Since we were at the dig site by the time the sun was rising, we were able to dig before the hottest part of the day. Most of the time our digging in the desert was over by noon, at which time we would go back to camp and have lunch.

After lunch, we were given time to clean up and change out of our dusty clothes. Next, we would clean and sort out our discoveries we had dug up earlier, while one of the archeologists would help us understand each of the findings. Later we'd explore nearby ruins or the marketplace in town. Sometimes I'd just find a neat spot and sketch an interesting view in my journal. Our days were long and busy but very rewarding and memorable.

The Bible warns about lazy people who don't do anything with their life. Are you being lazy and wasting it? Do you spend too much time watching TV or playing video games? Life is a gift given to us by God. He wants you to fill your life with new experiences, friendships, and discoveries, but that's probably not going to happen if you're lazy. Go out today and every day and live life to the fullest!

The Tradition of the Sheik

Therefore, brethren, stand fast and hold the traditions which you were taught, whether by word or our epistle.
2 THESSALONIANS 2:15, NKJV

While in Jordan, we had breakfast early in the morning, but lunch wouldn't happen till we were back in camp around one o'clock. That's a lot of hours in between! Fortunately, each day around 9:30 A.M. we would stop working and take a break to have what we called "second breakfast," made up of delicious falafels. In Jordan, falafels are as common as hamburgers are in the United States or tacos in Mexico. They consist of pita bread that is stuffed with a chickpea patty, lettuce, tomatoes, cucumbers, and a yummy white sauce.

Our dig site was located on land that belonged to a local sheik, who gave us permission to dig there. Because the sheik allowed our team to dig on his land, we were considered to be his guests. The tradition is that guests are served tea at 11:00 A.M. while they are on your property. Every day, from a mile away, we saw an elderly Jordanian man with his servant walking toward our dig site. His servant carried a tray with a tea kettle and a bunch of tiny cups. When he arrived at the site, he was all smiles, and he would tell our interpreter that because we were his guests, we had to stop working and drink tea with him. He did this every single day for weeks!

Does your family have traditions? Does your church? In 2 Thessalonians we are reminded that traditions help us to be faithful about the things we've been taught. There is one very important tradition I would like to encourage you to add to your life: morning devotions. For morning devotions to really be of value, you have to spend time doing it every morning. The reason "morning" is important is that it sets the tone for the rest of your day. Don't you want to make sure you start each day right? Start each day by spending time with God. In no time you will notice the changes in your life!

The Long Job

I praise you because I am fearfully and wonderfully made;
your works are wonderful,
I know that full well.
PSALM 139:14, NIV

When I was attending architecture school at Andrews University, we took classes about the history of architecture. It's valuable to understand how things were done in the past in order to properly plan for the buildings of the future. As the class progressed, each student developed favorite architects and styles of architecture. My favorite architect was a Spaniard named Antonio Gaudi. When I had the opportunity to study in Europe for a year, I hopped on a train to Barcelona to see my favorite building that Gaudi designed—La Sagrada Familia, a church. Construction started in 1882, but when I finally went to see it, it was still not even half-built yet. I arrived in Barcelona and took the subway to the part of the city where this church was being built. I finally stood there in front of it, marveling at the building even though it was incomplete. Building this church was not as simple as you might think. They're not using truckloads of steel beams or concrete blocks. This building is being made one block of stone at a time. Practically every stone was carved and formed to a very exact and specific shape.

I went back to Barcelona about fifteen years later, but it still wasn't finished. They say it will be done in 2026. The Bible says that God is also building in heaven—He's building homes for us! And if I had to guess, I doubt He's using common beams and blocks. I would guess that every inch will be specifically designed for us by the ultimate Creator and Builder. Just as each person is a unique creation of God, it's exciting to know that He's planning a special home just for each one of us in heaven!

Fighting Giants

*Do not envy the violent
or choose any of their ways.*
PROVERBS 3:31, NIV

While my wife and I were traveling through the British Isles, we decided to visit Ireland and Northern Ireland. We took a train from London to Holyhead in Wales on the coast, where we would take a ferry over to Ireland. As we waited for the ferry, the wind picked up, and rain came down harder and harder with every passing hour; we could tell this was going to be a rough voyage. Once we departed we encountered the most intense waves I had ever experienced in my life. For several seconds the ferry would go up on a steep incline, and then the ferry would come down the other side of the wave in a steep drop. No one on the ferry got any rest that night as we wondered if we were ever going to make it to Ireland—but we did.

The following morning we spent the day exploring Dublin, and then we took a train north to Belfast in Northern Ireland. After exploring the city, we took one more bus to the very northern coast to a place called the Giant's Causeway, our final destination. A causeway is an elevated path built to cross a body of water. There was no actual causeway here, just a fascinating natural occurrence where about forty thousand interlocking basalt columns hardened into intriguing shapes due to a past volcanic eruption, extending out into the sea several hundred feet. Old legends say that a giant from Ireland and a giant from Scotland challenged each other to a fight, and so they built a causeway in order to cross the sea between their islands.

Satan works hard to convince people that the best way to solve a problem is by fighting. He's even figured out a way to make people admire and envy people who fight. Many movies and TV shows include as much fighting as possible. Satan is doing this to convince you that violence is the normal way to resolve problems. Don't fall for Satan's tricks.

Close-Up and Christian

But the fruit of the Spirit is love, joy, peace, forbearance, kindness, goodness, faithfulness, gentleness and self-control. Against such things there is no law.
GALATIANS 5:22, 23 NIV

I've been to quite a few cities, towns, and villages in my travels, but one of the most unusual places I've visited was a city in France called Mont Saint-Michel. The town is located on the north coast of France. The drive to get there took us through some beautiful parts of France, and when we finally arrived, we were able to appreciate how unique this place was. The little town sits about two thousand five hundred feet off the coast on a little island. When I was there, the way to get to the island was by driving or walking out on the long causeway. The interesting thing about this island is that at certain times of the day when there is high tide, most of the causeway is covered with water. This makes it quite important to have a plan before arriving!

When I first walked through the city walls, I felt like I had traveled back in time to the middle ages. Now, only about fifty people live there, and half of them are monks. Hundreds of years ago, more than a thousand people lived there. The center of the island has a tall, rocky hill, with a church tower built at the highest point. Even if you are miles away, the first thing you see is the church tower that overlooks the entire town.

As Christians we are like Mont Saint-Michel. Jesus is important in our lives—even when people see us from a distance, they should be able to know that we are Christians by the way we act and behave. When they are close, they should especially know that Jesus is number one in our lives. Does the way you act and talk let people around you know that you love Jesus? If not, what should you change?

Three Hundred Islets

But, as it is written,
"What no eye has seen, nor ear heard,
nor the heart of man imagined,
what God has prepared for those who love him"
1 CORINTHIANS 2:9, ESV

Recently I was in Nicaragua doing a speaking tour through a few of the larger cities with my family. Between two of the cities, a free day was scheduled to allow for a break. Our hosts were gracious enough to arrange a tour to some of the interesting places nearby. First, we visited an active volcano, smelling the sulfur as we stood at the edge of the crater. Next, they took us to the colonial city of Granada at the edge of the huge Lake Nicaragua, and we boarded a little pontoon boat that slowly went out into the lake. This was no ordinary lake; this huge lake has about three hundred tiny islets. As we cruised along we discovered something unusual about these little islands: many of them were inhabited by people and homes! Some islands were rustic, but many were very nicely developed with fancy docks and large spacious homes.

As we cruised around dozens of little islands, we found a little island that housed an Adventist church! We then went to an island where an elder of that church lived. The island was small, but there was a complete house built on it with large terraces for lounging around and even an in-ground pool! To our delight and surprise, there were several mango trees on this island, and the gracious hosts invited us in and gave us mangos to eat! This was definitely one of the most unusual neighborhoods I had ever visited. Naturally, there were no cars, no sidewalks, and no streets; everyone had to have some sort of water craft. It was like a city on water.

God is planning a city in heaven, and I guarantee you it will be like nothing you could ever imagine. You will have a place built specifically for you, everyone will be happy there, and the best part is that Jesus will be one of your neighbors!

Racing Toward the Ocean

For even when we were with you, we would give you this command: If anyone is not willing to work, let him not eat. For we hear that some among you walk in idleness, not busy at work, but busybodies. Now such persons we command and encourage in the Lord Jesus Christ to do their work quietly and to earn their own living.

2 THESSALONIANS 3:10–12, ESV

A few years ago I knew I had an upcoming trip to El Salvador, so I started to do some research about what I could see while I was there. After a little research I found out that there was a very special beach in El Salvador along the Pacific coast of the country where sea turtles came at certain times of the year to lay their eggs. I also read that this was a government-protected beach. Once in El Salvador, I arranged for a driver, and soon we were driving from the capital down to the coast. We drove right onto the beach and parked our car on the sand. I could see at least a couple of miles of the beach in both directions. There was not a single person in sight. No one. I thought this was unusual. *Were we at the wrong place?*

We walked toward the water, and about seventy-five feet from the beach we arrived at a little ten-by-ten foot grass hut. As we approached, a small elderly man came out and greeted us. He was there all alone. It turned out we did have the right beach. This elderly man was the one in charge of protecting the area, and he lived in this little hut during the months of the year that the eggs are laid until they hatched. He walked me a few feet away to the place where the turtles were hatching in the sand. Hundreds of baby turtles hatched every day, and I was thrilled that I got to cheer some on as they raced toward the ocean. The elderly man took seriously his responsibility to protect the eggs and make sure the baby turtles made it to the ocean.

Someday you will have a job. You may experience many different jobs. It's important that you take your responsibility seriously and always do your best. Don't be lazy or try to get out of doing your work. If you read today's verse you will see God is pretty serious about this.

A Mission of Love

"A new command I give you: Love one another. As I have loved you,
so you must love one another."
JOHN 13:34, NIV

A few years back, several families decided to organize a mission trip to Honduras. Of course, the enemy is not happy when we serve others, and he tried to create stumbling blocks for us. When our group of about twenty-five arrived at the airport in Chicago, our flight had been canceled for no apparent reason. As we waited for a resolution, we prayed often. God prevailed, and the next day our group was able to get safely to Honduras.

Most of the work took place at a daycare center in the city of Santa Barbara. Sadly, in some countries the poverty level is so high that parents go to work and leave their very young children at home all day to fend for themselves. The kids don't always stay home, and though it's hard to imagine a four-year-old wandering the streets looking for something to eat, that was the reality of the situation. This daycare gave the poorest parents a place for their kids to be safe while they worked. The daycare provided care and food and kept them off the streets till their parents could get them. The daycare existed as a ministry, and they did not charge for this service, so over time maintenance of the property had been neglected. Our group came to do a handful of things: paint, repair broken downspouts, patch the leaky roof, build new playground equipment, and clear out a rocky area. We also built a concrete wall around an exposed side of the property and spent lots of time playing with the kids, teaching Bible stories, clothing them, cleaning them, and simply loving them.

God loves everyone. He doesn't care what we have, or how we look. God values individuals, not things. Remember that no object in this world is more important than a human life. Remember that as you interact with people today!

Way Off the Beaten Path

*Therefore, since we have these promises, dear friends, let us
purify ourselves from everything that contaminates body
and spirit, perfecting holiness out of reverence for God.*
2 CORINTHIANS 7:1, NIV

Our mission trip to Honduras a few years back was a blessing to everyone on the team. We were exhausted and dirty but our spirits were soaring high as we completed the goals we had set out to accomplish during the trip. At the end of our time working there, we decided to take an afternoon off and visit a local waterfall called Pulhapanzak, located in the nearby rain forest. The road to get there proved to be a challenging drive over a mountain range on a small dirt road, but we finally made it. One of the local leaders came with us to guide the group in the rain forest.

From a distance we could hear the thundering sound of a huge waterfall. We parked and found a muddy path in the forest that led to the river several hundred feet downstream from the waterfalls. Our guide led us along the edge of the river on an old dirt path and over big boulders as we got closer and closer to the falls. To our surprise, we continued to get closer and closer to the falls, climbing over rocks and swimming through side pools till we were only fifteen feet from where the water crashed down on the rocks. There was a little sheltered area there, where a few people stayed while a handful of us continued. The water pounded us so hard at this point that we had to scramble over the last few rocks backwards because the water splashing up against the rocks would hit our faces and felt like hundreds of pinpricks. We finally arrived at a cave under the waterfall where the water reached our chest, and there were only a few inches above our head. When we came out, it felt like we had gone through a heavy wash cycle in a washing machine!

God expects clean bodies from His children. This means that we keep our bodies clean and pure, but it also means keeping our mind and spirit pure. We do this to honor God.

The Ultimate Fans

So, whether you eat or drink, or whatever you do, do all to the glory of God.
1 CORINTHIANS 10:31, ESV

During one of my visits to Chile, I asked my cousin what was involved in attending a professional soccer game. He told me that attending games in the National Stadium in Santiago was risky. Soccer fans around the world can get out of control when their team is losing, and he told me that things were especially unpredictable and possibly dangerous for the games played in the capital. I asked him if there were any other options for attending a soccer game, and he suggested we attend a game from a team located in the suburbs of the city where the stadium was smaller and the crowd less rowdy. Not sure what to expect, we arrived at the stadium about an hour before the game. As we went through the gate and into the stands I was shocked to see the entire stadium was already filled.

Not only was it filled, everyone was standing or jumping up and down and singing fight songs for the home team. Every few feet it seemed as though there were fans pounding on drums and blowing trumpets. For the next hour, the fans never let up, and when the game finally started, they continued, but with even more intensity! At the half, after almost two hours of singing, jumping and chanting, the fans in the audience finally took a break for a few minutes before the second half started. As you can imagine, by now we knew all their fight songs by memory and were singing along as well. Never in my life had I seen such passionate fans!

There's nothing wrong with being passionate about something, and our verse today tells us that whatever we do, do it heartily for God, not man. Honor God in the way you do everything— big things, little things, and especially the things you are passionate about.

Timing the Fossil Hunt

If any of you lacks wisdom, you should ask God, who gives
generously to all without finding fault, and it will be given to you.
JAMES 1:5, NIV

A few years back I spoke at a church in Santa Cruz, California. On Sabbath afternoon I had a few hours before my next presentation, and the family I was staying with offered me a tour of the area. Santa Cruz lies toward the north end of Monterey Bay, so we jumped in the car and drove south along the coast. We stopped by a little beach town called Capitola. The tide was out for a few hours, and we had the opportunity to explore some hard-to-reach parts of the coast that weren't accessible at high tide. We walked along the beach and saw many rocks and marine features. In one instance we saw a huge vertebra of a whale embedded in a rock. Farther down the beach we explored along the cliff face and found huge concentrations of fossils sticking out of the rock. It seemed as though the farther we went, the more fascinating things we discovered. We had to be careful though and keep track of the time when the tide would come in again. If we did not return in time, the tide would come in and we would be stranded on a beach against a jagged cliff. Not a good place to be stranded!

As we explored, we kept an eye on the clock to make sure we had time to get back off the beach before the tide came in. We timed it perfectly because just as we were reaching our exit point, the waves left us a few feet of dry land on which to escape. If we hadn't decided to come out at a certain time, we would have had a big problem.

We usually don't realize how many important "little" decisions we make every day. Sometimes the "little" decisions we make are huge, potentially impacting our lives. It is important to ask God for wisdom. Fortunately, our verse today reminds us that God is generous. Ask Him for wisdom today.

Pass It On

*He said to them, "Go into all the world and preach the gospel
to all creation. Whoever believes and is baptized will be saved,
but whoever does not believe will be condemned"*
MARK 16:15, 16, NIV

Merced, California is called the "Gateway to Yosemite" because the city is located in the central valley where much of the traffic entering Yosemite National Park crosses. During a trip to visit my parents, my brother and sister and I made a plan to go up to the Yosemite park on Sunday for a day hike. This was no ordinary day hike, though. Our goal was to climb one of the park's most famous spots, Half Dome, a huge granite rock that looks like a rock dome that's been split in half, with a sheer rock wall rising almost five thousand feet up from the valley floor. The hike from the valley was about thirteen miles long, so it was important that we start hiking before the sun rose that day. The first part of the hike would take us up to Vernal Falls. Next the trail proceeded through miles of backcountry as we circled around to approach Half Dome from the opposite side.

The closer we got, the bigger Half Dome looked. Soon we stood before this huge granite rock and saw the cable route we would need to take up a steep part of the rock. The final four-hundred-foot ascent was steep, going up the rock between two steel cables used as handholds. Carefully we proceeded up the steep slope, making sure we always had at least one hand on the cable. Sometimes a quick gust of wind would blow, and we'd hang on tight. We made it to the top and stood at the edge of the cliff wall, almost five thousand feet above Yosemite Valley! The view was incredible, and I felt as though I could see the whole world! I was reminded of the classic praise song, *Pass It On*. The second verse talks about wanting the whole world to know about the joy you find when you depend on God by shouting it from the mountaintop. Do you have joy in your heart? Let others see it; pass it on!

The Forest Fire

*"I will make them and the places surrounding my hill a blessing.
I will send down sowers in season; there will be showers of blessing."*
EZEKIEL 34:26, NIV

I recently traveled to the city of Bogotá, Colombia to speak at a series of events at several schools and a church. During my few days there, I stayed at the home of the conference president on the north side of the city, while most of the events I attended were to take place on the south side of the city. The traffic we'd encounter each day in this metropolitan area of more than thirteen million people seemed to increase every day. Along the entire eastern border of the city was a sharply rising mountain range.

On the first day of our drive to one of the schools, I suddenly noticed that the side of the mountain was on fire! The conference president was just as surprised as we drove past it, getting a good look at the huge plume of smoke rising from a section of woods on the side of the mountain overlooking the city center. On the second morning we drove by again and noticed that the fire was spreading fast. That evening as we drove home in the dark, we could see the actual fire blazing amongst the trees. On the third morning, the fire was clearly out of control and descending toward the city. At this time, we now saw multiple helicopters flying back and forth, each carrying a large container of water they would drop on the fire. Unfortunately their efforts seemed futile as the fire continued to spread out of control. The situation looked hopeless until suddenly, on the afternoon of the third day, something happened. A huge cloudy front moved in over the city, and within an hour an enormous downpour proceeded to soak the city. By evening, the forest fire was out. They were showers of blessing!

God loves to show His strength, and He loves to shower His blessings on His children. He doesn't do it to brag; He does it to comfort us during difficult times.

Cliff Dwellers

He replied, "Because the knowledge of the secrets of the kingdom of heaven has been given to you, but not to them."
MATTHEW 13:11, NIV

D riving through the southwestern part of the United States provides something new at practically every turn. A few years ago when I was driving across the southern part of Colorado, I stopped by one of the more unique national parks in the United States—Mesa Verde. The park sits up on a mesa, a big flat area on the top of the mountain. Amongst the flat areas at the top there were rolling hills and canyons that had eroded away. The reason this place became a national park is that in the late 1800s some explorers discovered the remains of an ancient Puebloan civilization that lived high up on these mesas, many hundreds of years ago. There were no nice roads back then, so how and why they chose that location is a bit of a mystery. Although the Puebloans lived on the flat surface areas of the mesa, this civilization has become a famous tourist destination because they also built cities into the side of the canyon cliff walls. Several tours were available allowing us to climb down ladders and narrow stairs to reach these unusual cities.

Historians estimate that the largest of these cliff cities once housed around one hundred people. Apparently these people really wanted to "get away." They were up on a high mesa that was hard to get to, and they built their cities on even harder-to-reach cliff walls. Many people have tried to figure out why, but the interesting thing about this civilization is that they left very little written history behind. Even more mysterious was why these cities were eventually abandoned.

There are many mysteries in the world, and it's exciting to try to solve them. God provides answers to some of life's mysteries. When we get to heaven, all of our questions will be answered. We will understand then, and we will not wish to change one thing that God has done in our lives.

JULY 3

Goosenecks Side Trip

He set the earth on its foundations;
it can never be moved.
PSALM 104:5, NIV

Have you ever been surprised by a surprise birthday party? You walk into a room, and suddenly the lights turn on or a bunch of people jump out from hiding and scream, "Surprise!"

Surprises are fun. A few years ago I was traveling through the southwest in an RV. As usual we were prepared with a list of places we wanted to see and visit. Some of the places were well-traveled national parks, while other places were far off the beaten path, where only a few visitors are willing to make the effort to get there. One particular day we planned to visit a place in southern Utah called Goosenecks Canyon. The problem was that we were racing against the setting sun, and as you can imagine, you don't race in an RV and win. When we finally arrived at Goosenecks Canyon, not only had the sun set but it was pitch dark, and there weren't any lights in the parking lot. The only reason we knew we had arrived was a little sign. We were miles from the nearest highway. Since we were in an RV, we decided to just stay there the night and see the canyon in the morning. I woke up the next morning and noticed that it was still dark, but a faint light was starting to appear on the horizon. I got up and got dressed and went outside. It was still too dark to see anything, but I walked to the edge of a cliff where there was a bench and sat down. What unfolded over the next half hour was like a surprise birthday party. As I sat there, the scenery before me seemed to change minute by minute as the sun came up over this incredible S-shaped canyon before me that was more than one thousand feet deep!

God causes the sun to rise and set. He keeps the earth spinning. God keeps your heart beating. It is comforting to know that God causes all good things to happen!

Celebrating Freedom

You, my brothers and sisters, were called to be free. But do not use your freedom to indulge the flesh; rather, serve one another humbly in love.
GALATIANS 5:13, NIV

The Fourth of July is a special day in the United States because it's Independence Day. In 1776 our first leaders decided they would create a new country in order to establish certain laws and liberties. Every year millions of Americans celebrate by gathering with friends, eating together, and watching fireworks at night. One Fourth of July several years ago we had about thirty people at our home to celebrate. In the evening we had our own little fireworks show. A few days or weeks beforehand, all the people who were planning to attend contributed a few dollars, which I put in a big pile and then bought as many fireworks as possible. Each year my brother-in-law and I go to the fireworks store and look for the best deals and the biggest bang for our buck, literally. As darkness fell, we gave the kids sparklers to start playing with while I and a couple of other brave guys went down to the far end of our property to set up our little fireworks show. I usually took an old piece of plywood to set as our base on the grass. We had flashlights and lighters, and one by one we unpackaged each of the fireworks and made sure each wick was ready to light. On this one night, as we were lighting our fireworks, someone accidently stepped on the plywood sheet, causing one of the fireworks we had just lit to fall down, directly pointing at our audience! The firework shot directly at the group, but we were blessed that no one was hurt. You can say they had never seen a firework so close in their lives!

Freedom usually comes with a price, and many people have given their lives so that we can have our freedom. We should be grateful that God has blessed us with freedom, but now we are reminded to use that freedom to bless and serve one another.

Conditioned to Pray

Very early in the morning, while it was still dark, Jesus got up,
left the house and went off to a solitary place, where he prayed.
MARK 1:35, NIV

I've been to the Grand Canyon at least a dozen times in my life. If you go at dawn or sunset, you are almost always guaranteed an amazing light show as the sun creates amazing shadows and colors on the canyon walls. During a filming trip a few years ago, we planned to film at the Grand Canyon, and our plan was to do a day hike down to the halfway point and back. We got all our gear, packed a lunch, and filled our Camelback water packs with water and headed off. The first hour or so was a steep drop down into the canyon through a series of steep switchbacks. After filming all the things we needed, we had lunch and soaked in the view and started to head back up toward the rim. The climb was not easy, but every once in a while as we hiked up we had to step off the trail to let a group of donkeys go by with riders on top. If you don't mind paying, you can travel into the canyon by donkey. It got me thinking about the donkey and how every day these donkeys make the arduous climb down and up out of the canyon with riders on top.

I learned two things from watching this. Number one, hiking up the canyon could be pretty difficult at times, but donkeys were available to help carry you up. Just the same, life can be very difficult at times, and God has offered to carry our burdens for us. Number two, I thought of how the donkeys do this climb practically every day and how that daily hike continuously kept them in perfect shape in order to do the climb. For us, there's also something we should be doing every day to condition us to have a strong relationship with God. When we spend time in devotions and prayer each day, it will help us be in perfect shape to deal with the problems life throws at us.

The Continental Crossing

If either of them falls down,
one can help the other up.
But pity anyone who falls
and has no one to help them up.
ECCLESIASTES 4:10, NIV

While I studied architecture at Andrews University in Michigan, each Christmas and summer I had to figure out how to get home to California where my parents lived. Most times I flew home. Four times I drove the thirty-two hours home. Three of those times I drove alone. One time I decided to take the bus home. It was cheaper than flying, but it was a rough way to travel since I had to sleep a couple of days on the bus. Sometimes I had to get up in the middle of the night to let the person sitting next to me on or off the bus.

One year I had an opportunity to go home by train. I had a friend at Andrews who lived in Fresno, which was only an hour or so from my parents' house. When I asked him how he was going to get home that summer, he told me he was going to take the train. That sounded interesting, so we decided to take the trip west together. His parents had already bought him a first-class ticket, which meant he would have an entire compartment to himself, so we decided to share it. From Michigan we took a train to Chicago, where we boarded a train that would take us all the way to Los Angeles. Our compartment was made for four people, so with only two of us traveling, there was plenty of space. There was a huge window that allowed us to look outside, plus a table that would fold away and beds that would fold out at night. Even though it took us two days to get home, it was by far the most memorable journey home ever.

The journey of life is rich because of the friendships we make along the way. When you have a hard day, a friend is there to help you make it through. In return, when your friend falls you can help them up. Don't take those friendships for granted. They are a blessing from God!

Stuck

*The plans of the diligent lead to profit
as surely as haste leads to poverty.*
PROVERBS 21:5, NIV

'm pretty sure everyone knows what a canyon is, but have you ever heard of a slot canyon? A slot canyon can be hundreds of feet deep but sometimes only a couple of feet wide. A few years ago while filming a video, we traveled to southern Utah to film a few scenes in a slot canyon. There were many slot canyons in the area, but we decided to search for one that would be far off the beaten path in order to film our scenes with minimal interruptions. After doing some research, we decided on a slot canyon that sounded exactly like what we wanted. The camera crew and I were traveling in a four-wheel-drive Jeep, so we weren't worried. We found the off-road trailhead and headed in. We had to drive about five miles off road, and as we drove farther into the desert, the ground became very sandy, like on a beach or dune. That's when the Jeep got stuck. Even with the four-by-four traction, the wheels dug deeper and deeper into the sand. Fortunately, we knew what we had to do, even though it sounded like a strange solution. We got out of the Jeep and let most of the air out of the four tires. It felt like we were sabotaging our own Jeep, but we knew that this was the solution when driving in very loose sand. After lowering the pressure of our tires to a mere 15 psi, we got back into the Jeep, and a moment later we were on our way. Soon we arrived at the slot canyon and spent the afternoon filming. This little adventure would not have been possible if we hadn't planned ahead and anticipated our problem with the sand so that we would know what to do. There was no phone signal where we were, so we wouldn't have been able to Google the solution.

Planning ahead is an important principle God wants us to have in life as it will help us be successful. But don't just plan ahead; ask God to be part of the process too!

Two-Thousand-Foot Trust

For he will command his angels concerning you
to guard you in all your ways.
PSALM *91:11, NIV*

During my college years I spent a year living and studying French in the town of Collonges-sous-Salève, France, right on the Swiss border next to Geneva. Right behind the college was an enormous, nearly two-thousand-foot rock face called the Salève. Each morning of the school year as I walked to class, I admired this huge rock face and was thankful I had the opportunity to study nearby. Of course, one of the best things about studying in France was the opportunity to make new friends from different parts of the world with different backgrounds and outlooks on life. After the first few weeks, I had made some new French friends, and they invited me to participate in a little adventure activity.

One Sunday morning we walked to the top of the Salève behind the school. After the vigorous walk, we were soon standing at the top of this enormous cliff face looking down over the campus and the city of Geneva in the distance. The view was spectacular! Over the next few minutes we scrambled over some rocks to the very edge of the cliff. Next, I was given a harness to put on—we would rappel down the face of the rock. Rappelling involves putting on a harness and tying into a rope line and then backing out over the edge of a cliff and slowly letting out the rope, allowing you to descend the rock face of the mountain.

As I prepared to climb off the cliff, I said a quick prayer, hoping that my guardian angel knew how to rock climb. I was only kidding myself, but I do that sometimes when I get nervous. I knew God's angels were always around me, and that brought me comfort and courage as I rappelled down the face of that huge cliff!

Cross Country

And let us consider how we may spur one another on toward love and good deeds, not giving up meeting together, as some are in the habit of doing, but encouraging one another—and all the more as you see the Day approaching.
HEBREWS 10:24, 25, NIV

I spent most of my childhood on the east coast, but most of our extended family lived in California, so each summer we'd take a cross-country trip from one coast to the other. Since we were not wealthy, we did our trips the "cheap" way. But each summer was a new adventure!

My father loved road trips, so each summer he would make sure our trip out west was different by taking a new route each time. One summer we drove to Florida first and then cut across the lower United States on Interstate 20; then, on the return trip, we came back through the north on Interstate 80. Sometimes we'd pull over on the side of the road for thirty minutes to watch a herd of bison cross the road. I would climb up on the roof and watch them go by, sometimes only a few feet away from our car. Sometimes we'd stop on the side of the road simply because we spotted an area densely packed with huge saguaro cactus. And we never missed the opportunity to explore a national park. Over the years our lodging improved and instead of sleeping the car, we would stop in campgrounds. My dad always tried to stop at a campground that had a pool so that my siblings and I could splash around for a few hours each evening to burn off energy.

We may have roughed it a little, but I have wonderful memories. Building memories is a special part of life. Some people wait around for something to happen, but I encourage you to go and build your own memories. I do that by having parties at my home as often as possible; those are some of my favorite memories in life. God put people in our life to bring us joy. I don't believe that objects bring us joy. God has given us friendships, and spending time with others is the best way to build memories. Just make sure your parties honor God!

I Made a Mistake

Brothers, I do not consider that I have made it my own. But one thing I do: forgetting what lies behind and straining forward to what lies ahead, I press on toward the goal for the prize of the upward call of God in Christ Jesus.
PHILIPPIANS 3:13, 14, ESV

During a video shoot, we drove to a wonderful national park in Utah called Bryce Canyon. It was the first time I had been there, so we drove around the rim looking at the various overlooks. After a while we found an overlook we wanted to explore. We parked and geared up and walked along the rim till we found the trailhead that would lead us down into these areas of erosion. The odd-looking eroded rocks are called hoodoos, which were formed from erosion caused by water. As we started making our way down we were amazed by the red, orange, and white colors of the rocks. Little by little we made our way down that day without realizing how high in elevation we had actually started from. The rim there was almost nine thousand feet above sea level!

We went down hundreds of feet in elevation till we were surrounded by the unusual hoodoos. Soon we were on our way back up to the car. The day was ending, so our next task was to drive back out of the park to the place where we had left our RV to stay the night. We were tired after a long day of hiking, so I was ready to hit the bed. Unfortunately, the night did not go very well. The heater in our RV wasn't working, but we decided to sleep just outside the park anyway, even though we were at more than eight thousand feet above sea level. This turned out to be a very bad decision as the temperatures at that elevation at night were still in the teens. We survived the rough night but regretted our decision to stay there.

We all make mistakes in life, but God does not want us to dwell in the past. Some people have a hard time letting go of past mistakes. We should learn from our mistakes and then look ahead to the future, applying what we've learned while forgetting the bad things from our past.

The Miracle Day

You are the God who performs miracles;
You display your power among the peoples.
PSALM 77:14, NIV

S ome people don't believe in miracles. I do. Something happened when I was about ten years old that removed any doubt in my mind about whether miracles happen or not. We lived in Massachusetts at the time. My mom and dad worked, and my mother also took in sewing projects to make a little extra money for our family. She made little dolls with incredible dresses using lace and sequins. On Sundays, my mom would take my sister and I to a nearby city where we would go door to door selling my mom's creations. One Sunday we stayed out late, and it was dark. On the way home, we stopped at a store in a plaza on the edge of town to buy more materials. We stayed so long that the store finally closed, and when we went to our car we noticed there were only one or two other cars left in the parking lot. Our car was parked way in the corner in the dark. When we got to our car we discovered we had a flat tire. None of us knew how to change the tire, and of course there were no cell phones back then. We poked around in the trunk trying to get the spare out, but it was hopeless.

It was late, it was dark, we were clueless, and we were alone. The situation seemed quite hopeless. That's when I quietly snuck to the front of the car, knelt down, and prayed a quick prayer for help. Less than ten seconds after I prayed, a car far away in the street suddenly turned off and came straight to us. A man got out and said he thought he recognized our car. None of us had ever seen this man before, nor did we understand how he could recognize our car in the dark.

In a few minutes he changed our tire and left. Let me tell you, God is listening. Sometimes He answers fast, sometimes slow. Sometimes He answers Yes and sometimes No. Since that day I never had a doubt that God can do miracles in our lives. Just ask.

My Zion Discovery

"Look at the birds of the air; they do not sow or reap or store away in barns, and yet your heavenly Father feeds them. Are you not much more valuable than they?"
MATTHEW 6:26, NIV

As a kid I went to the Grand Canyon several times but never to the North Rim of the canyon, because it was an extra two hundred miles to get there. When I grew up and had my own family, I decided to finally see the canyon from the North Rim. One of the advantages of driving around to the North Rim was that we were also close to another park, one that I had never been to—Zion National Park in southwest Utah.

Since we arrived in the summer, we had to use the shuttles to get around the park. The most prominent feature we noticed right away was Zion Canyon. As the bus proceeded into the park, the road led us into an amazing canyon about fifteen miles long and up to half a mile deep. The canyon walls have a reddish-tan color to them, and it seemed as though at each turn there was something new and exciting to see. As we walked around, we noticed a lot of people with binoculars. We wondered if there was something in particular they were trying to see. The shuttle stopped often, and each time we got off and saw what was there. We were amazed at the diversity of life zones there. I always thought it was only desert, but there were also woodlands, a coniferous forest, and riparian zones, which are basically the areas where river and land meet. As we explored, we finally figured out why so many people had binoculars with them. It turns out there were almost three hundred species of birds in the park!

There is a passage in the Bible about birds that I really like. It's our verse today. It tells us how valuable you are to God. If God is concerned about birds, imagine how much He's concerned for you—so much so that He was even willing to sacrifice His Son to save you! Thank Him today.

The Mighty Fortress

I will say of the LORD, "He is my refuge and my fortress,
My God, in whom I trust."
PSALM 91:2, NIV

A couple of years ago I traveled with my family to San Juan, Puerto Rico. The top thing on my list to see and do there was to go to the old city and visit the fortress that looked out over the ocean from a high bluff. I had seen many pictures of it before, and many friends had told me about this old historic structure. As is the case in many cities, our first challenge was to find a place to park. Once we parked, we walked a little way toward the fortress. The approach to the fortress was impressive. As you approach, there is a huge grassy clearing so that all you see at a distance are the big stone walls surrounding the fortress. As I walked toward the walls, I tried to imagine what it was like in the old days when people were inside the walls and attackers were on the outside trying to get in—there were no airplanes or helicopters in those days. If you wanted to get over or through ten-foot-thick walls of stone, it was not easy, especially when there was a deep moat surrounding the fortress. I'm pretty sure the people on the inside felt pretty safe, especially since the walls are still standing there today, hundreds of years later.

It reminded me of the old hymn, "A Mighty Fortress." Have you ever stopped and noticed the lyrics of that hymn? It says that God is a mighty fortress for us and that He will never fail us. It goes on to say that our enemy is strong and is trying to get us and that we should not trust in our own weak strength to win the battle. It says we should not fear because God will triumph and that His kingdom is forever! As I walked around the fortress that day and explored all the little secret areas, my mind thought about how awesome it was to be protected by God, the Mighty Fortress!

Mushrooms and Hoodoos

"Why do you call me, Lord, Lord, and do not do what I say? As for everyone who comes to me and hears my words and puts them into practice, I will show you what they are like. They are like a man building a house, who dug down deep and laid the foundation on rock. When a flood came, the torrent struck that house but could not shake it, because it was well built."
Luke 6:46–48, NIV

I love visiting Utah. I've driven through many, many times, and each time I go I look for a new place to explore. On one particular trip, I decided to visit a place called Goblin Valley State Park, near the middle of the state. A drive on a desert side road led us to the entrance of the park. The parking lot was about thirty feet above an unusual valley that I estimate was about a mile wide and a mile deep. As we stood there overlooking the valley we could see that this was a unique geological site filled with thousands of mushroom-shaped hoodoos. On the far side of the valley there were jagged cliffs that displayed many colorful layers of dirt that had been washed away. The layers here are unusual—some are harder and some are softer. Since the time of the flood, the way water and wind have eroded the rocks here is unusual because it left behind funny-looking hoodoos they call goblins. We walked down into the valley and started exploring the hoodoos. Most of them were about ten feet tall and ten feet around.

If you look closely at the hoodoos, you can see that the top part is made up of a harder stone, while the bottom part is a softer stone that eroded away faster than the stone at the top. This is why they look like mushrooms. As we walked around, we could tell that some of these hoodoos were delicate because they had a small base holding a larger top. Having a good foundation is important for those hoodoos. And it's also important when you build a house.

What's the foundation of your life? When the hard times come, will you be ready to weather the storm? Make God the foundation of your life. As your foundation He will be an unmovable rock that will be there to help you through the strongest storms life may throw at you.

Let Freedom Ring

*It is for freedom that Christ has set us free. Stand firm, then, and
do not let yourselves be burdened again by a yoke of slavery.*
GALATIANS 5:1, NIV

When I was about sixteen years old we lived in Allentown, Pennsylvania. One Sunday my parents decided to take a day trip into New York City. When I was a kid we used to go there often to visit family who lived in the Bronx. Eventually those family members moved to California, and we stopped our regular visits to New York. Now, at sixteen years old, it would actually be my first time going as a tourist, so I was very excited.

We only had one day, so we had to pick a couple of things we wanted to do and see. After crossing over the George Washington Bridge into the city, we went to the Empire State Building. We got tickets and rode the elevator to the observation deck. It's the tallest open-air deck in the city, so it was exciting. That week they were celebrating the fiftieth anniversary of the movie *King Kong*. In the movie, a giant ape climbs the Empire State Building, and to celebrate the anniversary they actually had a fifty-foot-tall inflatable ape up there on the deck.

Next, we traveled to the World Trade Center to see the Twin Towers and walk around the plaza at the bottom. Unfortunately, many years later, on September 11, 2001, terrorists destroyed the Twin Towers and killed thousands of innocent people. Our last stop that day was a visit to the Statue of Liberty. We went down to Battery Park and got ferry tickets to Liberty Island. After walking around the base for a while, our turn came to go inside the copper statue and climb the 354 steps of the circular staircase all the way up to the forehead. The space up there was a lot smaller than I thought, but it was exciting to look out through the crown at New York Harbor.

The Statue of Liberty is a symbol of freedom. When God created us, He proved His love by giving us freedom to choose. Of course, Satan wants to trick us into giving up our freedom and being slaves to sin. Ask God each morning to free you from Satan's temptations.

Unscientific Science

In the beginning God created the heavens and the earth.
GENESIS 1:1, NIV

When I was a kid we visited Washington, DC, a couple of times. I loved to visit the Smithsonian museums—my favorite was the Air and Space Museum, which is filled with displays and exhibits of our history of flight and space travel. Another favorite was the Natural History Museum, filled with exhibits of many unusual and interesting animals, areas filled with beautiful minerals, places to learn about other cultures, and a whole area on dinosaurs. As a little kid, I did not spend too much time reading the little signs at each exhibit. I just wanted to run around and see everything there was to see in the museum.

Almost forty years later I went back with my own kids to see all those cool museums I remembered as a kid. This time, I was much more interested in reading all the displays and learning about many wonderful things. Everything was great until we went into the Natural History Museum. As I made my way through the museum, I was shocked at the constant referral to evolution as the factual explanation of our past. Evolution is an idea that tries to explain how this world and universe came to be without a Creator. In other words, it's the idea that millions of complex creatures and life forms developed by themselves over billions of years.

Teaching that nothing created everything is clearly not scientific. The definition of science is knowledge gained from testing and observation, yet never in history has anyone proved through tests or observation that nothing created everything. Science actually shows us that the natural world around us is filled with incredibly complex design. The Bible offers the best explanation: in the beginning the Creator created the heavens and the earth and everything in them.

The Dark Path

In all your ways acknowledge him,
and he will make straight your paths.
PROVERBS 3:6, ESV

A few years after I graduated from college, some buddies and I from church started a little club called the Michigan Adventure Club. A small group of guys would go somewhere for a weekend and do something together. Each morning and evening we'd have worship, and we'd encourage and pray for each other. One of the last trips we took was a weekend bicycle trek across the Kal-Haven Trail. This is a wonderful bike trail that goes between the cities of Kalamazoo and South Haven in Michigan. Most of the thirty-three-mile trail is an old abandoned railroad track, and it cuts through some of the loveliest backcountry areas in Michigan. Add to this that we purposefully planned our trip at the end of October when the autumn leaf color changes were in full bloom. On Sunday morning we got up and got our bikes ready and started our trek toward South Haven. We weren't in a hurry; we had all day to cover thirty-three miles, and we wanted to take our time and enjoy everything along the way. But our day didn't quite go as planned.

Since the trail was so beautiful, we constantly stopped along the way to soak in nature, take pictures, relax, and talk. That's when we suddenly realized that the sun was starting to set and we had only traveled about twenty miles. We started biking faster, but soon the sun set and it became pitch dark. Biking through the middle of the deep woods in the dark was quite a challenge; we couldn't see where we were going, and we struggled to be sure there weren't obstacles in our path. We finally made it to our campsite almost two hours after the sun had set.

There are times in life when it will seem like our path is dark. We don't want to make the wrong decision, so what do we do? Start by making sure you intentionally keep God in the center of everything. If He's involved in everything you do, He will bring light to your dark path!

The Real Father

*"And do not call anyone on earth 'father,' for you have
one Father, and he is in heaven."*
MATTHEW 23:9, NIV

During my years in university studying architecture, I took a few History of Architecture classes. In these classes, the majority of time is spent learning about amazing structures in amazing places all over the world. When I got to visit Rome as a college student, I was excited to visit St. Peter's Basilica, which has one of the largest and tallest domes in the world. The basilica, or church, is located within the walls of Vatican City, an independent city-state where the Catholic popes have lived for hundreds of years. The day we visited St. Peter's happened to be a Sunday, which is the day the pope traditionally comes out and blesses the thousands of people who congregate in the plaza. This particular trip was taken in 1990, and it was Pope John Paul II who stood at an opening overlooking the masses. I remember standing in the plaza, surprised and confused at the reaction of the people to seeing this man. I remember thinking to myself, "These people seem to think he is some sort of god!" I couldn't help but remember that to God, all men and women are created equal in His sight. Personally, I choose to honor and glorify only the true God in heaven who created me and not a substitute or representative.

As I finally got a chance to explore the amazing structure, I discovered that there was a staircase that led all the way to the top of the dome. I bought a ticket and started climbing. Little did I know that it would take more than 550 steps to climb to the top, but the view was worth it! Still, I couldn't stop thinking of the way people reacted to seeing the pope. The word *pope* means "father," and we're warned in the Bible that there is to be no earthly substitute for our Father in heaven. Make sure your worship and praises are always directed to our one true Father in heaven, who is the Creator and the only One who can answer your prayers.

Arlington Cemetery

Keep your heart with all vigilance,
for from it flow the springs of life.
PROVERBS 4:23, ESV

During a field trip to Washington, DC, we went to an unusual place one day—Arlington National Cemetery. If you've never been there, you're probably wondering why we would take kids to a cemetery as part of a field trip. We were curious too, until we finally got there. This cemetery is a United States military cemetery in Arlington, Virginia, just across the Potomac River from Washington, DC. This huge cemetery is where soldiers have been buried, beginning with those from the American Civil War. There are about four hundred thousand soldiers who have been buried in Arlington. Most of the graves are identical—simple, small white tombstones.

There are two places that I distinctly remember from my visit to Arlington. First of all, we were taken to where President John F. Kennedy is buried. It's easy to remember because there is a little flame there that never stops burning. The other memorable place we visited was the Tomb of the Unknowns. This is where an unknown soldier from each of the previous U.S. wars is buried and honored and guarded by army soldiers. The guards are there every single day of the year, and they guard the tomb twenty-four hours a day no matter what the weather is like. If you are home in the middle of a snowy blizzard, just think, there is a soldier there right then, guarding that tomb, and one has been guarding it nonstop since 1937. It's impressive to think that at all times from 1937 until now, there has always been a guard there.

God wants us to guard our hearts and our minds. Satan is constantly looking for ways to lie to you about God. God only wants what is good for us, while Satan only wants to destroy us. Ask God today to help you protect your heart and mind from Satan's attacks.

The Floating Village

Welcome people into your home and don't grumble about it.
1 PETER 4:9, CEV

My family and I recently spent a twenty-four-hour "home stay" with a wonderful family. We first flew to Juliaca, Peru, about 12,500 feet above sea level near the Bolivian border. From there we took a taxi about forty-five minutes south to a town called Puno, on the edge of Lake Titicaca. We were dropped off at the edge of the lake where a little wooden motorboat waited for us.

We boarded, pushed off from the shoreline, and slowly proceeded to make our way out into Lake Titicaca. For the first fifteen minutes we made our way through a ten-foot-wide channel with reeds on either side. Soon we came out into a larger opening and realized we had arrived at one of the most unusual villages on the planet. Right there on Lake Titicaca we were now surrounded by dozens of handmade floating islands where a people group called the Uros live. The larger islands had up to ten families living on them, while smaller islands only had two or three families. Our little boat finally arrived at the island where we would be staying for the next twenty-four hours. Our hosts made us feel welcome right away. During our stay they provided meals and showed us how they fish. They also showed us how they harvest the totora reed, which they use to make their island, huts, and boats—and even food!

The islands are anchored so they won't float away, and there is no plumbing or electricity or Internet on these islands. Generations of the Uros people have lived this way in solitude for centuries. It was an amazing experience to stay there. A day later we were sad to leave our host family and continue on our journey, but we will never forget the wonderful hospitality shown to us by that family. There are many verses in the Bible where God encourages us to be hospitable. I really like today's verse because it's about as plain as it gets!

Foiled by Flies

Let no corrupting talk come out of your mouths, but only such as is good for building up, as fits the occasion, that it may give grace to those who hear.
EPHESIANS 4:29, ESV

In Australia, Ayers Rock, called Uluru by the aborigines, is famous because it is thought to be the largest single solid rock in the known world. It's big and it's red and it's visible from miles away. As we approached it, we stopped at several points to take pictures. The views were amazing, but we noticed there were thousands of annoying flies all over the place. These were not your ordinary houseflies; these were the kind that bite. We'd take our picture and quickly jump back in the car to escape the flies. When we finally arrived at Uluru, we found even more flies!

Our plan that day was to climb Uluru, but in those first few minutes outside, we were so annoyed by the flies that we jumped back in our car. My wife and I sat there wondering what we should do next. We decided to drive around Uluru, a loop that allowed us to have a nice view of the rock from multiple angles. Soon we were faced with the same question again, *what next?* We stepped outside again, and in a few moments we were attacked by the flies. At this point we knew we would not be able to tolerate hiking up this rock with flies attacking us every step of the way. We were quite disappointed because we had driven two days through the Australian desert in order to spend time hiking on the Uluru. We ended up settling for just taking a few pictures at Uluru and wishing we had brought mosquito nets on the trip.

It amazed me that a fly could ruin our visit. I'd compare that to bad language. If I'm having a conversation with someone and suddenly they use cuss words, or use God's name in vain, those tiny words start to ruin the whole conversation. Watch what comes out of your mouth. Don't let little, inappropriate words ruin what you say.

A Killer Tour

I urge, then, first of all, that petitions, prayers,
intercession and thanksgiving be made for all people.
1 TIMOTHY 2:1, NIV

A few years ago I was in Washington filming a video, and part of our plan was to take a whale-watching trip to see orcas, also known as killer whales. Humans have tried for years to train them to do tricks in parks, but unfortunately every once in a while when you put orcas and humans in such close contact with each other, bad things can happen. For our tour, there would be no close contact. As a matter of fact, it was one of the rules. We took a small boat that could carry about eight to ten people from a small village on the coast of Puget Sound. We chugged along for almost forty-five minutes to the place where pods of orcas usually swam that time of year. Sure enough, after a short while we found two distinct pods swimming along. We stopped the boat, and from about fifty to one hundred feet or so we were able to see the orcas swimming along with their pods. We saw several little ones that seemed very playful, breaching and slapping the water with their tails. Then something unexpected happened.

As we stood on the back part of the boat looking out over the water, from behind the boat we suddenly saw a dark shadow approaching us in the water. We could clearly see that an orca was coming toward us. We were standing right at the edge of the boat railing when this massive creature passed right next to us, probably six to eight feet away from us!

Pods consist of a very tight and loyal community of whales. Animals were not created with the capacity to pray for each other, but humans were. We can practice being unselfish by making it a habit to pray on behalf of others in our "pod"—that is what intercessory prayer is. Think of someone near you who could use your prayers, and ask God to be near them today!

Two Step, One Step, Slide

Then, because so many people were coming and going that they did not even have a chance to eat, he said to them, "Come with me by yourselves to a quiet place and get some rest."

MARK 6:31, NIV

During a trip to Chile to visit my father's family, my wife and I toured the countryside to see some of the nearby natural features. It turned out that we were staying only a couple of miles from an active volcano! When most people hear that they are near an active volcano, they usually go in the opposite direction, but not us—we drove up into the mountains to get closer to the volcano. As we drove up the mountain, we started seeing little clues that we were approaching an active volcano. The first thing we saw was an occasional steam vent, where small puffs of steam were escaping from the ground. Farther up, we came across a huge hotel resort that offered hot springs baths that customers could bathe in. We continued driving higher and higher till the road finally ended. We couldn't actually see the entire mountain because it was covered by a cloud, but we could see up far enough to see a huge slope of pumice with scattered boulders and steam vents. It looked like a landscape from another planet. We decided to climb up a bit, just to see how far we could go. Walking in pumice is not easy. The loose volcanic material gives way easily. For every two steps we took up it seemed that we would slide down one. This made hiking up the mountain very difficult. Soon we had hiked up so far we couldn't see where we had left the car behind. After a while, the group didn't want to hike anymore, but I continued alone for another hour or so. When I finally stopped my family was way below me and I felt completely alone on the mountain. I clearly remember thinking how quiet and peaceful it felt up on that mountain.

Even Jesus needed time alone sometimes. God created the Sabbath so that we could have some time alone with Him. Look for opportunities to be alone with His Word. Listen to what the Holy Spirit has to say today.

Dunes and Pits

But now, O LORD, you are our Father;
we are the clay, and you are our potter;
we are all the work of your hand.
ISAIAH 64:8, ESV

I love summer. The kids are out of school, and almost every weekend we go to the beach. Now wait a moment; you know that I live in Michigan, which is almost a thousand miles from the ocean! How could I go to the beach every weekend? I live about ten minutes from Lake Michigan, which has some of the nicest beaches in the United States, with miles of wide, powdery sand beaches, tall dunes, and wonderful lighthouses. I've had friends tell me those aren't beaches, but I looked in the encyclopedia, and I confirmed that a beach is the sandy edge of an ocean, sea, river, or lake.

There's one particular beach we go to almost every weekend called Warren Dunes State Park. We bring our chairs, umbrellas, a canopy, and munchies to the beach. Right behind the beach there is an enormous 240-foot-tall dune that is super fun to climb and run back down. Just up the beach there is a stream that runs through the middle of the park and empties into Lake Michigan. The stream winds its way inland through a shallow ravine until you reach what is locally called "the clay pits"—layers of light gray clay in the walls of the ravine. People love to come to this spot and grab a handful of clay to make funny shapes with it or smear it all over their face and body, then wash it off at the beach.

My favorite clay mentioned in the Bible is found in our verse for today. It says that we are each wonderful works of God by saying we are the clay and God is the potter who has carefully molded us. Next time you create something out of clay or putty or even Lego blocks, think of God who created you and loves you.

Midnight Adventure

*Be still before the L*ORD *and wait patiently for him.*
PSALM 37:7, ESV

A few years ago while I was filming a video series, the script called for a handful of scenes to be shot in a cave. I decided to contact a few of the cave tour companies in central California to see if they would allow us to film in their caves after hours. I found one near Placerville, California. Everything was set up for us to arrive and film in one month. A week before the shoot date, I called the manager again, and she assured me that everything was in order for our visit. The day finally came, and my film crew and I arrived at the cave about half an hour before our designated time. We went into the office and asked to see the manager to let her know we were there.

I will never forget what happened next. She looked us in the eye and out of nowhere said, "Sorry, I changed my mind; you can't film here." We all sat there in shock as she offered us no explanation why we would not be allowed to film there. As we left the office, we felt rejected, but I had reminded our crew several times during the project that the enemy was working hard to stop us from producing videos for kids that give glory to God the Creator. We also prayed and remembered that we had asked God that His will be done, not ours. The next day we continued filming in a different location, but by noon we encountered someone who offered to take us to go film that night in a wild cave nearby. In the end, we were able to shoot a caving scene that was much better than we had originally hoped. I'm so glad we trusted God, because He ended up having a better plan for the video! God has an answer to all your problems. But we must learn to be patient and trusting as we wait for His answer.

A Brush With Revolution

Yes, and those who decide to please Christ Jesus by living godly lives will suffer at the hands of those who hate him.
2 TIMOTHY 3:12, TLB

It's said that the Cuban Revolution started on July 26, 1953, when Fidel Castro, his brother Raul, and about 160 other rebels attacked the Moncada army barracks in Santiago, Cuba. The attack was a failure; almost a hundred fighters died, and the Castro brothers were captured and jailed. My father was in Santiago that day, working as a colporteur. He stayed with some church members that night and remembers hearing bullets hitting the roof of the house where he was staying. The next morning he took a bus from Santiago, leaving the city.

Just outside the city limits, the bus was stopped by the military. The Cuban army was looking for rebel soldiers trying to escape the failed attack. When the bus stopped, everyone had to get off the bus while the soldiers inspected the bus and looked over the passengers. Suddenly a soldier pointed at my father and said, "Take this man inside for questioning!" My father was shocked and terrified as they dragged him and put him in a jail cell. For twenty-four hours he was held and repeatedly questioned. They were convinced he was one of the rebels. During the questioning he finally figured out why he was being held—it was because of his belt. My father was a Pathfinder Master Guide, and he was wearing a Pathfinder belt that looked very similar to the belts the rebels wore. He finally convinced them that he was not a rebel, that he was a student at the Adventist college there in Cuba, and that he was working to earn money for school.

At the end of time, things will get worse. People will be openly persecuted for being a Christian. As you get older, you will encounter people who will challenge your faith. Stay faithful, because God promises that the Holy Spirit will tell us what to do and say in those difficult situations.

The Big Jump

Those who know your name trust in you,
for you, Lord, have never forsaken those who seek you.
PSALM 9:10, NIV

I was once filming a video series that called for a bungee jump scene. I had never gone bungee jumping before, so I was excited for the new experience. Part of my job was to find locations to film our scenes, and it seemed as though most of the places that offered a bungee jump were either off a bridge or from a tall crane. For the video I knew the crane wouldn't look very nice, so I looked around for a bridge over a nice canyon. I finally found a company that hiked up to an abandoned bridge over a canyon in California for their bungee jumps, but shortly after, I stumbled upon another company in Northern California that sounded even better! I called them and made all the arrangements.

The first half of our hike was mostly uphill on a well-worn path, but soon our guide took us completely off the path and even deeper into the forest. Soon we arrived at a tall grove of redwood trees. Next, I put on my harness while the guide prepared jumar gear for me. Jumar gear is used when you want to just climb up a rope. The first order of business was for me to climb up a rope almost two hundred feet to the top of a redwood tree. Once at the top there was a taut steel cable spanning between that tree and another tree next to it, plus another rope about five feet above the cable to hang on to. The bungee cord was attached to me, and my guide told me to move out to the middle of the cable between the two trees and jump. I did exactly as he said.

My trip to the redwoods would have been useless if I had not been willing to trust the guide and jump out of the tree. There are times when God asks us to do something that doesn't make sense. Perhaps He is testing us to see if we are willing to trust Him in all things even if they don't make sense at the time. That is trust. Will you trust God today?

What's in Your Suitcase?

The twelve gates were twelve pearls, each gate made of a single pearl.
The great street of the city was of gold, as pure as transparent glass.
REVELATION 21:21, NIV

During a family road trip to California, we drove to a place near Placerville, California, to visit a gold mine. Back in the 1800s, the United States experienced a gold rush that drew thousands of people west to see if they could strike gold in California and get rich quick. Reports came out of California about people supposedly finding gold just lying around on the ground! They heard stories about people who went out to California, claimed a spot in the hills with a stream and a pan, and they found gold.

People in that time were obsessed with finding gold—in many cases risking everything they had for a chance at finding gold. For many of them the story did not end well. Visiting the gold mine was a reminder for me of how desperate people were to find those little gold rocks. After getting our tickets, we followed the path to a cave opening. A large wooden door was built to keep people out, but it was open now for tourists to come in and visit. It was a self-guided tour, so we got to explore the mine at our own pace. We walked in and went down a 350-foot corridor that had been carved out of solid rock. Along the ceiling were lights that allowed people to see as they walked deeper and deeper into the mine. At one point we could see remnants of the old tracks and carts that would carry tons and tons of rock out of the cave as the miners dug for gold.

The Bible says that in heaven the streets will be made of gold. I once heard a joke about a man who loved his gold so much that he wanted to take a suitcase full of it to heaven. When he arrived at the gate, the angel didn't understand why he wanted to bring pavement to heaven! Don't get caught up in loving gold or silver. True happiness can be found by loving God and following His commandments!

Going Up

"For I know the plans I have for you," declares the Lord, *"plans to prosper you and not to harm you, plans to give you hope and a future."*
Jeremiah 29:11, NIV

When I was a child, we drove through St. Louis many times, and each time we looked in awe as we drove past one of the most famous monuments built by humans, the St. Louis Arch. As a child I knew people could ride up an elevator to the top of the arch, but I never got the opportunity to go up. I told myself that someday I would return and go to the top. It was a goal I never forgot. When the opportunity came for my family to drive through St. Louis, I made plans to take my family to the top of the arch. We found some parking and walked to the base of one of the legs of the arch. There were elevators in each leg and a whole underground area for tourists to explore, with a museum, a documentary to watch, and a gift shop. We found the ticketing booth, got our tickets, and went to the line to take the elevator up. Each elevator was a pod that looked like a giant egg. These were not ordinary elevators, though. Since the arch was curved, the elevators were created in a special way to adjust to the angle as they climbed higher and higher. At the bottom, the elevator shaft was almost vertical, but by the time it neared the top, the elevator pod had adjusted to be traveling almost horizontally. When it stopped, we got out and walked a few more feet to the very top of the arch where there were a few small windows allowing visitors to look hundreds of feet down to the ground.

Life is can be very unpredictable. Sometimes we move to a new city or sometimes our family situation changes. Sometimes we have to change schools or make new friends. Making adjustments reminds me of that elevator we rode in. As the situation around it changed, the elevator adjusted to the new direction. Even though we will have to experience changes, ask God to help you adjust to those changes. Cling to God's promise of a special plan for your future.

Shaky Ground

When the centurion and those with him who were guarding Jesus saw the earthquake and all that had happened, they were terrified, and exclaimed, "Surely he was the Son of God!"
MATTHEW 27:54, NIV

The first summer I spent in Southern California with my parents was interesting because every week I went to work and church—never seeing a nearby sight. At the end of the summer I went back to school in Michigan, but I soon returned for Christmas break. As soon as I got home I was shocked to see what I had missed all summer—a mountain practically in my back yard! Because of poor air quality that summer, I had never noticed that there was a mountain a couple of miles away from my house! It had been hidden by smog. Several years later, I returned and was happy to see that the quality of the air had slowly improved.

That first summer, I had another experience that was a bit shocking too. I worked as an intern in an architecture office in a town called Redlands. I had only been at work for about thirty minutes when something happened that I had never experienced before. As I sat at my desk working, I suddenly felt a strange sensation as if everything around me was moving. I looked up and I looked around, then I looked out the window right next to me. It's hard to explain what I felt and saw, but it looked like the ground was moving like a wave. I then realized I was experiencing an earthquake—my first earthquake! It only lasted about forty-five seconds, but it was an unusual experience. When my father was a boy living in Chile, he survived two earthquakes, but those were massive, and tens of thousands of people lost their lives.

The Bible talks about earthquakes in several places. When Jesus died there was an earthquake, and when He rose from the dead there was another earthquake. The Bible tells us that earthquakes will be signs that Jesus' return is soon. We don't need to be afraid, because the Creator of the earth can protect us even from earthquakes.

Find the Tiny Ledge

Make me to know your ways, O Lord;
teach me your paths.
Lead me in your truth and teach me,
for you are the God of my salvation;
for you I wait all the day long.
Psalm 25:4, 5, ESV

Last summer I visited a natural landmark in the northeast corner of Wyoming called Devils Tower. First of all, I have to tell you that I'm not very excited about the name that was given to this monument because it doesn't belong to the devil; it belongs to the One who created the world. I was there to shoot a video for a TV show. We drove to an outfitter about five miles from the monument, where I met a man who would take us rock climbing on the monument.

At the shop, we were fitted for three important pieces of gear: a helmet, a harness, and climbing shoes. Next, we drove to the monument and walked along the base to a spot where our guide told us we would climb. We went over a few climbing rules and got our gear on. All of our filming would happen along the first pitch, or section, of the monument. My job was simple; all I had to do was climb up about sixty feet while the cameras rolled. As I started to climb, I discovered that there were sections of the rock face that had small ledges I could grip, but there were some that didn't. At times I would be climbing along and hanging off the side of the rock, looking all over the place for the tiniest ledge I could use to climb higher. Sometimes I felt like giving up because I just couldn't find a spot to grab. That's when I would hear the voice of the guide telling me to look up or to the side for a place I could grab on to.

In life we will arrive at spots that seem impossible to get past. This is when we must carefully listen for God. Sometimes He speaks directly to us, but other times He speaks to us through His Word or other people. Pay attention, and only listen to godly influences today!

Surrounded by Needles

Speak up for those who cannot speak for themselves,
for the rights of all who are destitute.
Speak up and judge fairly;
defend the rights of the poor and needy.
PROVERBS 31:8, 9, NIV

In the southwest corner of South Dakota there is a wonderful place called the Black Hills National Forest. The surrounding area is flat prairie lands, but in this corner of the state, hills covered with trees rise up and, from a distance, look black, thus earning the name "black hills," from the Native Americans who lived there. As we drove our car west toward the Black Hills we could see what looked like a huge, dark mound rising from the flat prairies. Soon we were driving into the Black Hills and into Custer State Park.

In the park, we drove along a loop and saw many wonderful things, including bison that casually walked across the road in front of us. There was one section of the loop we were looking forward to visiting—the Needles Highway. The road went high up into the black hills to an area of granite mountain peaks that look like pointy spires standing tall and rising up out of the mountain. It was obvious that a massive effort had gone into building the road that weaved in and around these amazing vertical rock formations. In one part, the road cut right between two of these narrow spires just wide enough to get a car through. There was also a trail we wanted to hike—the Cathedral Spires Trail. We parked the car and followed the trail up through a forested area for about twenty minutes. It eventually led to a little valley surrounded by a bunch of rock formations standing tall around us.

Did you know God has asked us to stand tall too? He wants us to stand up for others who can't stand up for themselves. He wants us to defend the poor and needy and those who are misjudged. Pray that God will give you the courage to stand tall today!

Glowing Water

"You are the light of the world. A city set on a hill cannot be hidden."
Matthew 5:14, ESV

Puerto Rico is home to a very unusual natural phenomenon. There are three separate places on the island that are referred to as "bio bays." No, "bio" doesn't refer to biology; it refers to bioluminescence—light produced by living creatures, like fireflies or, as in this case, creatures that live in the water. A few years ago I went with my family to one of the bio bays in the town of La Parguera. When we got there it was well after sunset, and we made arrangements to take a boat ride into the bay. Soon the boat headed out into the bay, stopping when the boat entered a clearing. There was no moon that evening, and it was pitch dark. The captain had a bucket with him, and he proceeded to scoop a bucketful of water out of the bay and brought it into our boat as we huddled around it. He agitated the water in the bucket with his hand, and the water started to glow!

The microscopic plankton in the water made its own light! He said that whenever the water is stirred or agitated, the little creatures light up for a few moments. Then he told us that if anyone wanted to experience a unique way of appreciating the bay, we could jump in the water and the creatures would glow all around us as we swam around in the water. Swimming in the ocean in pitch darkness sounded a little creepy, but we decided to jump in the water anyway. We created huge swirls of light in the water as we splashed around in the bio bay.

Even though the plankton is extremely small, it makes a big difference in the darkness. The same is true for us. Even if it's only you telling others about Jesus, you can make a big difference wherever you go. Imagine how much light we can bring to the world when all of God's children share their light with the world!

The Discovery

The Lord is my light and my salvation;
whom shall I fear?
The Lord is the stronghold of my life;
of whom shall I be afraid?
Psalm 27:1, ESV

I recently bought a house to fix up and sell. Behind the house was a densely wooded area and a sloping ravine that went down to a creek on the property. On the side of the hill was an old wooden door. I turned on the light on my phone and looked inside. About eight feet in was a concrete wall, but to the left there was a narrow opening in the wall. I slowly walked toward the opening and shone my flashlight through it. There was another small room with concrete walls, but at the end of the wall I noticed another door. I walked to the back and opened the door.

I was shocked to find a Cold War bomb shelter! It extended about another twenty feet into the side of the hill. There was an old-fashioned water pump at the end, and a crank device, which I assumed was to pump fresh air into the space—it was very humid and musty—and there were six cots hanging from the ceiling. During the 1950s and 1960s, a lot of people in the United States built bomb shelters, fearing that a nuclear bomb would be detonated. The shelters were usually stocked with supplies, food, and batteries to survive for a while.

Back in the 1950s, people were scared of things we don't really fear today such as nuclear war and radiation. That doesn't mean we don't live in fear anymore; we just have different kinds of fears. Satan considers it one of his most important jobs to put fear in people, but God says we should hand our fears over to Him so we can be at peace. Our verse today is one of the most famous verses in the Bible about having God near us so we don't have to worry about our fears. I'm so happy I have God's promises to help me deal with the things I fear. What are things that you fear? Claim God's promise today, and let your fears go!

Tough Days Ahead

"But I tell you, love your enemies and pray for those who persecute you."
MATTHEW 5:44, NIV

As a college student I was able to travel to Amsterdam in the Netherlands, where I was able to visit the Anne Frank House. Anne was born in Germany to a Jewish family, but when she was a couple of years old, Hitler became the leader of Germany. Many families fled Germany, and when she was only four, her family fled to Amsterdam. Five years later, World War II began. The Franks considered fleeing again but then decided to stay. The following year, Germany invaded the Netherlands. Soon, Jews were rounded up and taken to concentration camps. But Anne's father had a plan. They built a hideout in the building next to his place of work. The door to their tiny hideout was hidden behind a bookcase. They had to be very quiet as they hid, fearing for their lives. On her thirteenth birthday, Anne got a diary as a gift and spent hours writing about her life in hiding and other thoughts about her life and her feelings. Her family lived in hiding for almost two years. But on August 4, 1944, the Germans discovered their hideout and sent everyone to concentration camps. Sadly, about six months later Anne died in the camp from a disease. Her mother and sister also died; only her father survived the camp. After the war, her father found Anne's diary, and two years later it was published and became a popular book throughout the world.

As our family toured her secret hideout, we imagined what it would be like to be persecuted. The challenge I have for you will be hard, but the words come directly from Jesus. Read today's Bible verse and pray for the strength to follow it. With God's help, you can do it.

The Big Dig

All Scripture is God-breathed and is useful for teaching, rebuking,
correcting and training in righteousness, so that the servant of
God may be thoroughly equipped for every good work.
2 TIMOTHY 3:16, 17, NIV

When I was a kid, I enjoyed digging holes. I'm sure my dad didn't appreciate it when I dug holes in the yard, but I was always fascinated with what I might find. Maybe a treasure chest? Gold and silver? Ancient scrolls and maps? I never found any of those things in my yard, but after I grew up I got to go on a special dig in Wyoming—we were digging for dinosaur bones!

The dig site is in a very remote part of Wyoming that required me to ride dozens of miles on dirt roads, passing countless cow fences and rolling hills. When I reached the dig site, I talked to the leaders and soon found myself at one of the quarries where people from all over the country had come to dig up dinosaur bones. The exciting part about this dig was that the bones were in what they called a "graded bed." That means larger bones were toward the bottom of the layer, medium bones in the middle, and smaller bones were at the top of the layer. This is exciting because this means that hundreds of these creatures were killed in a water-related event, and then their bodies were washed to this spot as a big jumbled mess until all their bones settled to the bottom in order from small to large.

In Genesis, the Bible talks about a giant global flood that killed millions of living things on our planet. In Wyoming I saw how thousands of creatures were killed by a huge water catastrophe and how their bodies were buried in that place. Nature provides a lot of evidence that a global flood once ravaged our planet. It builds my faith to know that nature and science confirm the historical accounts we read about in the Bible.

Canary Black Sand

*He heals the brokenhearted
and binds up their wounds.*
PSALM 147:3, NIV

Not too long ago I had the opportunity to travel with my family to the island of Tenerife, one of the Canary Islands off the northwestern coast of Africa in the Atlantic Ocean. The islands are part of Spain, and part of my mother's family came from there in the early 1900s. What made the trip extra special was that we accompanied my elderly parents.

From the United States we flew to Madrid, Spain, and then from Madrid we took a flight to Tenerife. We rented a car for the next week and enjoyed exploring the island. The middle of the island has a gigantic volcano, towering twelve thousand feet above sea level. This volcano has been erupting on and off for the past several hundred years. Along the northern coast of the island we stopped to enjoy white sandy beaches. A few hours later we drove along the south side of the island and made a startling discovery. The sand on this beach was jet black! We pulled over and got out and walked down to the beach to make sure there wasn't something funny going on. Sure enough, the grains of sand were as black as the night. The black sand formed when a large lava flow entered the ocean and made contact with water. When it cooled rapidly, the lava shattered into sand-size pieces!

You will probably experience days in your life where you feel as though you've been shattered into little pieces. Life in a sinful world is not easy for anyone. Maybe a friend has betrayed your trust, or perhaps your family life is going through some difficult moments. Everyone goes through these shattering times, but God has promised to heal our broken hearts when we come to Him. If your heart is broken today, spend time telling God about it. He will bring you healing comfort.

Hot City

*I know your deeds, that you are neither cold nor hot. I wish you were
either one or the other! So, because you are lukewarm—neither
hot nor cold—I am about to spit you out of my mouth.*
REVELATION 3:15, 16, NIV

Driving through Wyoming is pretty fun; every part of the state has something new and exciting to discover. In the middle of the state, I found myself driving into a city called Thermopolis. The name of this city is quite unusual, but the name hints at what is going on in this small town. The name is made up of "therm," which means "hot," and "polis," which means "city." Hot city. The town claims to be the home of the largest hot springs in the world. I drove into a part of the town that has been set aside to preserve some of these interesting features.

First, I visited a place called Big Spring, where hundreds of gallons of hot water come out every hour. As I stood at the edge of the spring and looked down, I noticed that the water coming up looked super clean but also super hot. I read it was coming out at a constant 135 degrees Fahrenheit. I definitely did not want to fall in! I followed the stream of hot water downstream, and it led to a series of mineral platforms created from the flowing mineral hot springs. Around the corner I found a series of boardwalks built on top of the mineral terraces, allowing us to explore and get some close-up looks at the terraces. Nearby I saw an unusual dome-shaped building; the sign said it was hot-spring baths that were open to the public. I put on my swimsuit and went to check it out. Wow, it was hot!

I reflected on the fact that the water was heated up a mile or two below the surface of the earth. Fortunately, the people running the place cooled the water down to 104 degrees so I could get in! The Bible is clear that God wants us to be hot for Him. It's not good enough to be lukewarm, because lukewarm is half cold and half hot. Our verse today is a blunt reminder that lukewarm is not good enough. Choose to be completely hot for God today!

Faithful and Predictable

*But the Lord is faithful, and he will strengthen you
and protect you from the evil one.*
2 THESSALONIANS 3:3, NIV

Yellowstone National Park sits on a super volcano. As you can imagine, a super volcano is a very large volcano. The park sits in the caldera where the lava used to be. Once you enter the park you will see a variety of interesting animals including bison, bears, elk, wolves, and more. A geyser, like Old Faithful, happens when water from the surface drains deep below the surface and comes in contact with hot volcanic rocks. The water is super heated, and it comes blasting back up to the surface, where it is thrown high into the air for a short period of time.

As I approached the geyser area, I immediately noticed something different. As I looked across the valley, I saw dozens of steam vents. That's when I knew that not too far down below me there was a lot of volcanic activity going on. There were elevated wooden boardwalks that we were required to stay on, and they took me to the different geyser vents. Some geysers I could get really close to, while with others, the boardwalk makes sure you can't get too close in order to keep visitors safe.

Soon a large crowd formed at the most famous geyser, Old Faithful. Millions of people come each year to see this geyser erupt because it is so consistent. Most geysers are a little unpredictable; some only erupt once or twice a day or less. But Old Faithful got its name because every hour or two it faithfully erupts.

God is also faithful, and He has given us many signs that He created us and that He can be trusted. Satan is anxious to make us fall, but God promises to strengthen and protect us if we trust in Him! Will you trust Him today?

Isolated Island

For you know very well that the day of the Lord will come like a thief in the night.
1 THESSALONIANS 5:2, NIV

I enjoy living in Michigan. One year I decided to take a camping/hiking trip with some friends to a place called North Manitou Island located in the northern part of Lake Michigan. The interesting thing about visiting North Manitou is that no one lives there. It's not very big, only about eight miles long and about four miles wide. While there, you are free to hike and explore the island, which includes woodlands, swampy areas, beaches, and dunes. A boat service takes visitors to the island twice a week, on Fridays and Sundays. In other words, you can either visit the island from Friday to Sunday—a weekend—or go Sunday and stay all week till the next boat comes on Friday.

We could only go for the weekend, so our plan was to take the boat out on Friday and come back on Sunday in time for the new workweek. It was important to make sure we'd be back at the dock on time on Sunday. We had one chance to get off the island on Sunday, and if we were not there on time, the boat would leave and we would be forced to stay on the island another five days. This would be a big problem, since we had responsibilities at home, not to mention we only brought food and supplies for a couple of days. As much as we enjoyed the island, when Sunday came, we were ready when the boat returned to get us.

Someday, Jesus is coming back to save us from this sinful world. No one knows when that day will be; the Bible compares it to a thief in the night because you never know when they will show up. That's why we need to be ready every single day. Don't risk missing out on getting to our real home, heaven! Ask Jesus to be part of your life every day!

The Destructive Disconnect

I meditate on your precepts
and consider your ways.
I delight in your decrees;
I will not neglect your word.
PSALM 119:15, 16, NIV

The Chilean government says there are 123 active volcanoes in the country! Once, we decided to go visit one of the most active volcanoes in Chile—Osorno, which has erupted eleven times since 1575! In the winter there's a big ski area on Osorno, but it was closed when we visited during the summer. We found out that tourists could ride the chairlift to the top just to look around, and we decided to go.

First of all we were equipped with heavy snow pants and big coats. The chairlift had open-air chairs, and it would take almost an hour to get to the top. The view from the top was spectacular. It was a clear day, and we could see miles and miles of lakes, other volcanoes, and mountains all around us. As we rode the chairlift down, my youngest son, who was only about two years old, dropped his pacifier. It had been attached to his coat by a little strap, but somehow it disconnected and fell, never to be seen again. To this day, we often comment and laugh about his pacifier, because that one event caused him to stop the habit of using a pacifier.

Everyone has bad habits. Maybe we eat between meals or spend too much time engrossed in electronics. Perhaps you are always arguing with your parents or siblings. God wants to help us break bad habits. Our verse today says we should meditate on God's "precepts." Precepts are principles or guidelines that steer our behavior. When we stay close to God and focus on His will for us, He will help us stop our destructive habits.

The Harness and the Wire

I will instruct you and teach you in the way you should go;
I will counsel you with my eye upon you.
PSALM 32:8, ESV

After visiting the summit of the volcano Osorno, we decided to explore the areas around the base of the volcano. As we drove around the base of the mountain we discovered a zip-line adventure park. In those days, there were no zip-line parks in North America; I had only seen them in Central and South American countries. We found out they were open and that there would be no problem taking the boys on the zip-line adventure tour even though they were only four and two years old. The woman working there took us around the corner to a room filled with ropes and cables and harnesses and other gear. She proceeded to outfit each one of us with a harness, including a small harness for my two-year-old! It was a funny sight to see them with their little harnesses and helmets, but they seemed to enjoy adventure.

Our guide taught us a few basic rules to follow, and then a truck drove us hundreds of feet up a bumpy mountain road and dropped us off with our guides. There was a tree there that had a long cable attached to it on one end, and a couple of hundred feet downhill the other end of the cable was attached to another tree. Our harnesses were tied into a long wire, and we would remain connected for the next couple of hours as we came down twelve different cable lines from treetop to treetop down the side of that volcano. One of the professional guides went "tandem" with the boys.

I'm glad our guide taught us about this adventure before we started. It made things a lot easier. Although the guides were only qualified to teach us how to safely zip line, I'm glad that God exists in all other locations. He has promised to help us know the best and safest way to go about life. That's a promise from God, and it's our verse for today. Claim that promise today!

King of the Canyon

Be alert and of sober mind. Your enemy the devil prowls around like a roaring lion looking for someone to devour.
1 PETER 5:8, NIV

The western part of the United States seems to have an endless variety of national parks to explore. I recently went to King's Canyon, located in central California, just south of Yosemite National Park. Getting into the park included an amazing drive up mountains and through canyons, but once you arrive in the heart of the canyon, it's quite an amazing view.

As we drove down into the canyon, we discovered that the road went all the way to the bottom of the canyon, where there was a river flowing. We were told that there had been a lot of rainfall recently and that the river was exceptionally full of water. As we pulled over in several spots, it was always amazing to hear the thundering sound of the water. One of the places I stopped had a trail that led up to a beautiful waterfall. The trail ended almost right under the waterfall. Although I could have gotten even closer, I didn't want to get soaked since I didn't have a change of clothes in the car. As it was, the mist was doing a pretty good job soaking me already. I walked along the river at several points and reflected on how bad it would be if I accidently slipped into the water. It would be very hard to get back out of it, because it was moving very quickly and violently through the canyon.

Sin is like that sometimes. You think you can just put one foot in and nothing will happen, but sin is deceptive and sneaky—you have to pay attention. Satan is anxious to get you to fall into sin, and he will try to convince you that some things are "small sins." Don't be fooled into thinking there are small sins. All sins will hurt us and take us further away from God. I'm so grateful that Jesus died on the cross to get rid of all my sins. He did the same for you. Thank Him today!

Green Everywhere

However, if you do not obey the LORD your God and do not carefully
follow all his commands and decrees I am giving you today,
all these curses will come on you and overtake you.
DEUTERONOMY 28:15, NIV

The lower forty-eight states have only one temperate rain forest zone, located in Olympic National Park, in the state of Washington. Tropical rain forests are hot and filled with tons of living things, and a temperate rain forest also has an amazing amount of living things, but the temperature is cooler. During a trip to the Pacific Northwest, I decided to make a point of driving out to Olympic Peninsula to one of these temperate rain forest areas. I found a trail that did a nice loop into the rain forest, allowing us to get deep into the rain forest.

As we drove, the ecosystem began to look more and more like a temperate rain forest. Soon we found the trailhead and parked and started walking in. Within the first hundred feet it felt like we were swallowed up by the rain forest. There were no noises of cars or traffic. The tree canopy above us darkened the forest floor. The vegetation growing was thick and green. The forest floor was filled with huge carpets of moss and enormous fern gardens. Mosses of various types hung from the tree branches and covered the trunks of trees that were hundreds of years old. Being in there was like being in another world. Even the air felt different from breathing "regular" air not found in a rain forest.

There was something pure and earthy about this place that made me wonder what the Garden of Eden was like. Was it hot and steamy like a tropical rain forest, or was it cool and comfortable like a temperate rain forest? Either way, we can be sure that the real Garden of Eden was much, much better than anything we have on our planet today. It's unfortunate that Adam and Eve disobeyed God. Fortunately, someday God will recreate the earth to be how it was when He originally made it. I can't wait! In the meantime, choose to obey God.

Holes of the Yucatan

But the LORD said to Samuel, "Do not look on his appearance or on the height of his stature, because I have rejected him. For the LORD sees not as man sees: man looks on the outward appearance, but the LORD looks on the heart."

1 SAMUEL 16:7, ESV

The terrain in the Yucatán Peninsula of Mexico is very flat, but it contains a lot of karst rock in the ground, which is rock that dissolves easily. Because of this, the countryside is filled with sinkholes—underground caves where the roof has caved in. In Mexico these sinkholes are called cenotes.

We rented a car and drove off following our map to where the cenotes were. It was almost impossible to spot the sinkholes. Arriving at one, we saw that the hole was probably one hundred feet across. When we got to the edge we looked down and saw there was water at the bottom—about one hundred feet below us. We walked around the corner to a staircase carved into the ground, leading visitors all the way down to a little platform at the edge of the water. A posted sign reminded us not to be deceived by appearances—the water in this cenote was actually two hundred feet deep! Since we had brought our swimsuits, we made our way to the upper platform and jumped in!

Appearances can be deceiving. I never would have guessed that the water was two hundred feet deep, and I almost didn't find that cenote hidden in the jungle either. We often make conclusions about people based on their appearances. We see what they're doing or saying or how they dress, and we end up judging people unfairly. God doesn't want us to fall into the trap of deciding what a person is like until you spend some time getting to know them. If today you see someone who is often misjudged, make a point of trying to get to know their heart.

Total Darkness

Your word is a lamp for my feet,
a light on my path.
PSALM 119:105, NIV

Have you ever been to Mount St. Helens in Washington? Mount St. Helens is a volcano that had a massive eruption on May 18, 1980. It left a huge crater on the top and many other fascinating features to explore. On one particular trip we decided to visit the south side of the mountain, where we could explore some lava tubes. The hike took a while, but it finally led to a place on the side of the mountain where there was a depression in the ground. At the bottom of the sunken area was a small hole barely big enough to fit a person. There was also a metal ladder to help you get down into the lava tube.

At some time in the past when lava flowed during an eruption, the paths were covered up, and the lava flowed down the mountain through tunnels. When the flowing lava stopped, the tunnels remained, empty and ready to be explored. This particular lava tube could be followed down the side of Mount St. Helens for a couple of miles. There were no fancy sidewalks, no electricity, and no maps. In many areas of the tunnel, the ceiling had caved in, so you had to be ready to scramble over twenty-foot-tall piles of rock. And if I turned my light off, it was a kind of darkness that can only be experienced in a cave. It really made me appreciate my flashlight, because being in a place like that without light would have been awful.

There will be dark and difficult times during the hike of life. God gave us the Bible to guide us and to be a light for our path. I'm so happy to have the Lord as the Guide in my life. He has a light that will never go out. Will you invite Him to be your Guide today?

Obstacles

Therefore let us stop passing judgment on one another. Instead, make up your mind not to put any stumbling block or obstacle in the way of a brother or sister.
Romans 14:13, NIV

During a trip to Oregon recently, I decided to look for a nice trail to hike. After a little searching, I found the perfect trail to hike at the base of Mount Hood. I got all the necessary gear together and drove to the trailhead. Soon, I was happily on my way up the trail. This wasn't a sidewalk, and I had to keep my eye on the trail so as not to trip over roots or rocks. After a short while, the trail joined up with a brisk river. I had seen a trail map and knew that later on, the trail crossed over to the other side of the river. The farther up I got, the rougher and faster the river got, and the more rocks blocked the path. I started wondering if crossing over to the other side of the river would be dangerous. Finally, I came around a corner and saw the crossing—a huge log that spanned the river. It was so big that the park service had actually built rustic rails on either side of the log so you could hold on as you walked across. Soon the hiking started to get very steep, and it seemed as though I were walking in a canyon with the river rushing by below me. Finally I came around the corner and saw it, a beautiful waterfall thundering over a 150-foot-tall lava cliff! The going was still difficult as I scampered over huge boulders and climbed up the side of the waterfall to an overhang behind the sheet of falling water.

There were plenty of obstacles during my hike that could have tripped me up. For us as Christians, the Bible tells us something that should be obvious. We are not to try to trip up our brothers and sisters by judging them during their Christian hike. When we quickly judge each other, we tend to get it wrong. God knows the heart, so let Him judge. Our job is to love.

Banyan Branches

We must support people like them, so that we can
take part in what they are doing to spread the truth.
3 JOHN 8, CEV

While working on a film project on the island of Maui in Hawaii, part of our filming required us to hike a trail that had a variety of fascinating things to see on it. The trailhead started near the southeastern coast of Maui and went up into the mountains, directly into the heart of the island. We started on the trail knowing that the majority of this hike would be uphill. The trail was filled with all kinds of vegetation and animal life making noises in the tropical rain forest. Soon we came to our first natural feature, a huge banyan tree—an amazing tree whose central trunk is made up of dozens of vertical trunks and roots that make up a huge, complex tangle and that work together to support the tree. In certain parts of the tree trunk, you can actually climb between the vertical roots that make up the huge trunk. Equally as fascinating, the branches of this tree extend to create an incredibly wide but low canopy cover. In many cases the branches extend horizontally away from the tree trunk for dozens of feet, sometimes swooping low enough for a person to jump on the branch. The branches almost seem to defy gravity.

The intriguing thing about these branches is that they get a little bit of help from some special additional roots called aerial roots that are far from the trunk. As the branches extend away from the tree, these special roots reach down to the ground and establish additional columns of support so that the branches can continue to extend outward. Without the support of the aerial roots the branches would not be able to extend so far.

There are many people, churches, and ministries dedicated to spreading the truth. We should do our part to help support the work they do. Just as the aerial roots help the banyan tree branches reach farther, when we work together we can reach further and further out to spread the good news about Jesus.

Speedy Grass

And so, from the day we heard, we have not ceased to pray for you, asking that you may be filled with the knowledge of his will in all spiritual wisdom and understanding, so as to walk in a manner worthy of the Lord, fully pleasing to him, bearing fruit in every good work and increasing in the knowledge of God.
Colossians 1:9, 10, ESV

After climbing around the banyan tree in Maui, we continued hiking higher and higher into the rain forest. Soon we walked along a high ridge looking down over a valley we had just crossed. Then, after crossing a wooden bridge where there was a small waterfall, we suddenly arrived at the next fascinating part of the hike, an enormous bamboo forest right at the edge of the river.

Immediately upon entering the bamboo forest we were enveloped in darkness, even though it was the middle of the afternoon. Bamboo is a grass, but this grass can grow up to one hundred feet tall. At the top of the shoot are tufts of foliage, and since the bamboo shoots grow so close together, the foliage creates a dense canopy that blots out much of the sunlight. It created a mysterious feeling down below where we were. The bamboo also grows very close together, not like in a rain forest where there is some space between the trees. Bamboo is quite fascinating. The shoots are incredibly strong and are often cut and used for many different purposes. In some countries I've even seen construction job sites using scaffolding made from bamboo. Pound for pound, it is said to be stronger than steel! One of the most amazing things about bamboo is how quickly it grows. Certain types of bamboo have been known to grow up to three feet in one day!

Can you imagine if people grew that fast? There is one part of us that would be wonderful to grow quickly in, and that's spiritual growth. Open your heart to God today and ask Him to help you grow spiritually. Our verse today says that as you grow, you will bear fruits of the spirit and your knowledge of God will grow!

Four Hundred Feet of Water

"You will seek me and find me when you seek me with all your heart."
JEREMIAH 29:13, NIV

After exploring the bamboo forest in Maui, we continued our hike higher and higher up the mountain path. The higher we went, the thicker and denser the rain forest became. There are actually four distinct parts of the rain forest. At the very top is the emergent layer. These trees are taller than the surrounding trees. Below that is the canopy layer. These are the rest of the tall treetops that create a shady covering for the forest floor below. Below that is the understory layer; this is from the canopy down. Finally there's the forest floor.

As I walked through the rain forest, it was fun to observe the different types of plants and creatures that live in each habitat. For example, some creatures spend their entire lives in their layer, never coming down to the forest floor or exploring the treetops. As we walked, we followed a stream upward that started getting bigger and bigger. Soon it had become a roaring river, and up ahead we could see that there was an enormous cliff wall. Soon, a four-hundred-foot-tall cliff towering above us came into view, and we were able to see where the water of this river came from. Moments later a four-hundred-foot-tall waterfall came fully into view. We crawled over some rocks to get a little closer to where the water fell into a pool at the bottom. As we approached the base of the waterfall, a fine mist enveloped us, and we stood there looking up in amazement.

It took total commitment for me to get to the waterfall. Without being willing to sacrifice and go through struggles, I never would have experienced it. The same is true when you get to know God. Our Bible verse today reminds us that if you seek God with all your heart you will discover the beauty of who He is. Will you seek God today with all your heart?

The Long Hike

*Pray for us. We are sure that we have a clear conscience
and desire to live honorably in every way.*
HEBREWS 13:18, NIV

few years ago a group of my buddies and I planned a hiking trip to Manistee National Forest in Michigan, a forested part of the state that was set aside for people to enjoy and explore. Before the hike, we spent time reading about the many trails available for hiking. We finally found a loop that sounded like the perfect trail. It was about twenty-eight miles long, and it would take us through a variety of different ecosystems. Once we chose the trail we would hike, we began to plan the trip. We had to decide which weekend was the best—one that would not be too hot, too cold, or too crowded. Next we started planning and making a list of things we would need to take. We figured out how many tents to bring, how much food to carry, how much water we would drink, the right kind of clothes and shoes we would need; and we created a list of other helpful objects we would bring such as flashlights, bug spray, and a portable stove.

Soon the weekend came, and we packed our things in a car and drove four hours north to the trailhead. The trailhead was actually quite deep in the Manistee National Forest, and we finally found the designated parking area where we would leave the car for the weekend. There was a sign with the instructions for paying our fee—five dollars for each person hiking—and a slot where we could insert the money. No one was there; it was just an isolated trailhead. And soon our two-day hike was underway. There was no electricity, no phone signal, no sign of civilization; we thoroughly enjoyed disconnecting from normal life and spending two days hiking and camping in the forest.

Since no one was there to charge us, we probably could have gotten away with not paying the fee, but that would have been dishonest. When we intentionally choose to live like Christ, it means we always choose to do the right thing, even when no one else is around.

Warm Waters

Then God said, "Let Us make man in Our image, according to Our likeness; and let them rule over the fish of the sea and over the birds of the sky and over the cattle and over all the earth, and over every creeping thing that creeps on the earth."
GENESIS 1:26, NASB

As I've traveled around, I've discovered that no matter where you go there is always something unique and interesting to see and enjoy. A few years back I went to Florida to record some videos. On this particular trip I decided that I would swim with manatees—large mammals that live in the ocean and are often called sea cows. They are extremely docile and even friendly, but seeing one requires planning because manatees like warm water. For the majority of the year, they spend their time swimming along the eastern seaboard as far north as Massachusetts! When winter comes, hundreds of manatees go to Florida, where warm spring waters come out from under ground and flow into the ocean. There are many places in Florida where they congregate during the winter, so it's a great way to see them. Most places in Florida do not allow visitors to get in the water with manatees, but it's allowed near Crystal River.

During this trip, it would be the perfect time to view them, so I found a boat that would take me to see them. The boat captain was very knowledgeable at finding the spots where they swam, plus he was extra careful as he steered his boat to make sure we didn't hit any of them. Soon we found a group of manatees, and I carefully slipped into the water with my mask and snorkel and had a wonderful face-to-face experience with these wonderful creatures.

The Bible says animals were given to us to rule over, but that doesn't mean we are to be cruel or mean to them. God asks us to be good stewards, or managers, over all the creatures on the earth.

Return to the Falls

*Dishonest money dwindles away,
but whoever gathers money little by little makes it grow.*
PROVERBS 13:11, NIV

S everal times during my childhood we visited Niagara Falls on the border between New York and Ontario. We loved going as a family because during the day we'd visit the falls and at night we'd stay at a nearby campground and play board games or swim in the pool. There are lots of amazing activities to do at the falls, but as a kid I wasn't able to do any of them because they cost a lot of money. My parents taught me to be patient, and I told myself that someday I would save some money and go back. When I grew up, I did exactly that.

First on my list was to ride a boat called *Maid of the Mist,* which got pretty close to where the falls were crashing down. They gave us rain ponchos but we got soaked anyway; it was great. On the Canadian side we then went to the Journey Behind the Falls, where we took an elevator down into the rock, walked through a long tunnel, and came out behind one of the falls. The highlight for me was the Cave of the Winds on the American side. We took an elevator down to a tunnel that emerged near the rocks where the water from the falls came crashing down. Each year the park workers erect a long boardwalk that leads visitors right to the base where the water crashes onto the rocks. It's called the Hurricane Deck because the water crashing down onto the deck feels like you're standing in the middle of a hurricane. It was an intense experience! I had to wait twenty years to enjoy this experience, but I learned a valuable lesson in being patient and saving money.

Some people try different questionable methods to get rich quick, but the Bible says it's important to be honest and patient in our work, and little by little we will be able to save up for something special. Don't risk getting in trouble because you refused to be patient. Be honest and pure in everything you do, especially in dealing with money.

The Hike

But whose delight is in the law of the LORD,
And who meditates on his law day and night.
PSALM 1:2, NIV

When I was in high school I once took a camping trip with a couple of buddies to hike a small portion of the Appalachian Trail in Pennsylvania. The Appalachian Trail stretches from Maine to Georgia along the ridges of many long mountain ranges for about two thousand two hundred miles. We planned to hike a few miles and have fun camping and exploring the area. I didn't have much gear, but I was able to assemble a few basic things I would need for the excursion such as a sleeping bag, some food, and some water. The weather forecast looked clear, so we didn't even take a tent.

Soon we were on our way, climbing up the mountain to the ridge, enjoying nature and some amazing views. After a few miles of hiking we started to look for a good place to make camp. We came across a little lake and decided this was the perfect place to stop for the night. Since we didn't have a tent, we just had to find a reasonably smooth area of ground where we could lay out our sleeping bags right under the stars. Once we made camp, we took a quick swim in the lake and then ate some food. It started to get dark, and we decided to gather some wood to make a small fire. As darkness settled in, we sat around the fire and talked and shared stories.

Later, when we lay back in our sleeping bags, we were amazed by the star show in the sky that night. Because of our location, the sky was extremely dark and the stars looked particularly bright that night as we stared into the sky till sleepiness overtook us. Before falling asleep, I spent some quiet time talking to God. Sometimes it's in the quiet places that you can hear God the loudest. Find time each day to spend quiet time alone with God.

Marine Encounters

Those who guard their mouths and their tongues
keep themselves from calamity.
PROVERBS 21:23, NIV

Near San Diego, California there is a place called La Jolla—a great place to kayak in the ocean. I rented a kayak and headed to the beach and started paddling out. There were big waves coming in that day, and it took a little effort to get my kayak past the waves. To the right were miles of beach, but to the left was a neat-looking cliff wall, so I went toward the cliff wall. The cliff wall looked amazing, with rocks that looked as though waves had beaten them for thousands of years. That's when I decided that I would jump off my kayak and see what was in the water. I had my snorkeling mask with me, so with one hand holding on to my kayak, I started snorkeling to see what I could find. A few minutes later I spotted something that got my attention. I was snorkeling in water that was about eight to ten feet deep, and just below me I saw two leopard sharks swimming. They were both about five to six feet long. I knew leopard sharks were harmless, so I proceeded to follow them in the water. Fortunately, they were not in a hurry, so I was able to follow them for about five minutes till I couldn't keep up anymore.

Once back in my kayak, I heard something in the distance that sounded like barking. I started paddling farther along the cliff wall and went around the corner. As I came around the corner I encountered a tiny rock outcrop that was filled with sea lions! They were all barking and making a bunch of very loud noise. I moved closer to them and started barking too. They didn't seem concerned about my imitation barking and kept on making noise.

Sometimes even people make too much noise. They often open their mouths and say way too much before thinking about what they're saying. Oftentimes they hurt someone or they get themselves in trouble. Be wise and ask God to help you guard your mouth and tongue from calamity!

The First Pitch

He replied, "Because you have so little faith. Truly I tell you, if you have faith as small as a mustard seed, you can say to this mountain, 'Move from here to there,' and it will move. Nothing will be impossible for you."
MATTHEW 17:20, NIV

A few years ago I needed a film scene where I was climbing a rock, so we went to one of the most famous rock-climbing spots in North America, El Capitan, a three-thousand-foot vertical rock in Yosemite National Park. Arriving at the park, we hiked a little way up to where the actual rock face began. Our goal was to climb and shoot on the first pitch, or the first section of the rock wall. The first thing we did was to get our special climbing shoes on that would help us grip the cracks in the rock wall. Next, we strapped on our harnesses and got all the camera equipment ready.

Our guide went up first. He climbed a few feet and then connected a rope to the rock wall using a carabiner and a cam—small but important pieces of gear. As he climbed, one of the camera crew was belaying him, which means they held the other end of the rope. If he slipped and lost his grip, we would not let him fall. Every few feet he installed another cam and carabiner and tied his rope in higher and higher. Once he reached the top of that section of rope, it was my turn to follow. Now my harness was tied into the rope, cams, and carabiners. If for some reason I slipped, they would hold me up. I had never climbed an actual rock wall before, and little by little I climbed my way up, having faith in the guide, in the rope, cams, and carabiners. Even though cams and carabiners are small, their role is incredibly important.

In an airplane, a tiny computer is responsible for making sure things run properly. Pulling out one important part from a car will render it completely useless. Small things can have big impacts, and our Bible verse today proves it, because even if you only have faith the size of a mustard seed, you can do big things. That goes for you too! Even if you are young, God can do big things through you today!

Dark Ocean Waters

Because he himself suffered when he was tempted,
he is able to help those who are being tempted.
HEBREWS 2:18, NIV

I hadn't been to Key West, Florida since I was a kid, so I was excited to return. One of the neat things I experienced while I was there was a trip out into the open sea on a large catamaran. We got our tickets and boarded the catamaran that took us many miles out. First, we went to one of the nicest reefs in the Keys. The tour operator provided us with masks, snorkels, and fins so that we could explore the reef, but this particular time was a little different. As the boat traveled out into the open sea, the tour operator informed us that the place we would be snorkeling was great but potentially dangerous.

As we arrived at the spot, they proceeded to point out an area in the distance where the color of the water was noticeably darker. The guide explained to us that the darker water was the edge of a deep ocean trench. He told us that we could swim out to explore but to not snorkel close to the area where the trench was. An ocean trench is a spot where the ocean floor suddenly drops hundreds or even thousands of feet into a deep trench. He warned us not to fall into the temptation of getting too close.

Sometimes we see something that we know is bad for us, and instead of running in the opposite direction we find ourselves trying to see how close we can get. One of Satan's tactics is to tempt us with things that look good but are ruthlessly destructive. Don't give in to temptation, because nothing good will come of it if you do. Stay as far away from temptation as possible and call on Jesus for help. Our Bible verse today reminds us that Jesus was also tempted, so He knows how hard it is, and He has promised to help us if we trust Him.

Jump Off the Cliff

Be imitators of me, as I am of Christ.
1 CORINTHIANS 11:1, ESV

When I was invited to go speak in Bermuda, I was quite excited to visit the little island in the middle of the Atlantic Ocean. After my speaking duties, I stayed a few extra days with my family.

At one beach we found a sand castle competition going on. We saw a bunch of amazing things built out of sand and the various prizes. Another beach had pink sand! But one of our favorites was a beach on the north point of the island that had some large rock cliffs out about fifty feet from the beach, plus a bunch of nice shallow reefs to explore. We ended up going to this beach twice because we enjoyed it so much. While there, we noticed that people swam out to the cliffs and scampered up the cliff face by a little path that we hadn't noticed before. Once at the top, they would jump down into the water in one area were the water was deepest. The cliff looked to be about twenty-five feet tall, and it looked pretty safe, so we decided to copy them. For the next few hours my boys and I repeatedly climbed the cliff and jumped into the beautiful ocean water.

When we copy people, we must make sure they are good role models. Some of the role models our society offers us are actually horrible role models. Some of the sports figures, actors, and celebrity figures often display bad attitudes, hurtful actions, and inappropriate behaviors. Not sure who to copy? Try Jesus. After all, that's what it means to be a Christian, a copier of Christ!

The Darkest Swim

Be strong and courageous. Do not be afraid or terrified because of them, for the LORD your God goes with you; he will never leave you nor forsake you.
DEUTERONOMY 31:6, NIV

While visiting Bermuda with my family, we spent some time exploring a few different beaches. In fact, the island is so small that no matter where we stayed, we were always within walking distance of a beach.

On one of the days, a local pastor told me he was going to take us swimming at a unique place. Soon he arrived along with his family, and we all piled into his car and headed out. About ten minutes later, we stopped and parked the car in a parking lot that appeared to belong to a hotel or resort. Apparently the spot we were going to was open to the public, because we walked to the back of the main building and through some gardens to a cave opening. We went into the cave and down a set of stairs to a place where the cave suddenly got a lot bigger. This was no ordinary cave, though, because the bottom of it was filled with water. Along the edge there were some areas where people could walk, but the majority of the cave bottom was filled with water. A couple of lights lit the cave so we could see through crystal-clear water to the bottom of the cave down below. At the deepest part it seemed to be around twenty feet deep. The edges of the cave lake were very dark, and we couldn't see what was below the surface. I jumped in the water all alone at first and swam around. I have to admit, at first it was creepy swimming around the edges where I couldn't see what was under me.

In life we will have to face some times when we are afraid of unknowns. No one knows the future except God, but our Bible verse reminds us to be strong and courageous, because God will be with you every step of the way!

The Big Buddha

"So in everything, do to others what you would have them do to you, for this sums up the Law and the Prophets."
MATTHEW 7:12, NIV

Our world is a very diverse place. Whenever I travel, I must keep a very open mind because there may be things that are very special and sacred to some that may not be to me. It's also a great opportunity to learn about other cultures in order to understand how different people around the world think and view life. During a trip to Asia, my wife and I spent a few days in Hong Kong. There were several things on our list to see and do, but one of the things I didn't want to miss was a visit to the "Big Buddha," one of the largest Buddha statues in the world. The challenging part was the location. This statue was in a very hard-to-reach place because it was built next to a very secluded monastery.

First, from Hong Kong we took a ferry to a small island. Next, we found a local bus that would take us up a winding road up the mountain. The bus finally arrived at the top and dropped us off at the bottom of an enormous staircase. We started climbing, and 268 steps later we made it to the top. There were a lot of people there who had made long pilgrimages to see this statue of bronze and to honor this person they consider to be holy. At the top we were treated with an amazing close-up view of this enormous 112-foot-tall statue and also an incredible view of the island and the surrounding ocean.

During our whole time there, we did our best to show respect to the people and the place, since we knew it was a special place of worship to them, even though Buddha was just a man. I worship a God who is the Creator of the universe and all the things in it. God is the master of all and worthy of our worship every day. We are still to treat others with respect and love, but when it's time to worship, I'm thrilled to be a child of the living God of the universe!

Victoria's Peak

Do not forget to show hospitality to strangers, for by so doing some people have shown hospitality to angels without knowing it.
HEBREWS 13:2, NIV

Getting to Hong Kong from my home in Michigan was quite an ordeal. It started with a two-hour drive to the airport in Chicago. After that, we took a four-hour flight to San Francisco. In San Francisco we boarded another plane and flew another fifteen hours to Hong Kong. Between all the stops and layovers, we traveled for almost an entire day. Over the years, whenever I had looked at pictures of the city of Hong Kong, it seemed as though they were always taken from a very high hilltop overlooking the city. The pictures looked down on hundreds of skyscrapers on both sides of Victoria Harbor between Hong Kong and Kowloon.

When we arrived at the Hong Kong airport, we took a train to Kowloon. From there we needed to cross the harbor in order to get to Hong Kong. There were basically two ways across: you could take a taxi or bus through a tunnel under the harbor, or you could go the more traditional way, by boat. We decided to cross the harbor by boat. Next, we took a bus all the way up to the overlook, which was called Victoria's Peak, and admired the view. It was amazing to look down over this compact city and realize that there were more than seven million people crowded into the streets below us.

There are a lot of people in the world, and most are strangers to us. When we're little we're taught that we should not talk to strangers. That's because it's very important to keep kids safe. But as you slowly become an adult, that rule won't apply as much anymore. God has asked us to show kindness and hospitality to strangers while always exercising common sense and wisdom as we do it. In the meantime, why don't we practice kindness and hospitality to everyone else we do know?

Buddha's Rotten Food

"Do not turn to idols or make metal gods for yourselves. I am the LORD your God."
LEVITICUS 19:4, NIV

Hong Kong is a very diverse city. One of the first places we visited was Aberdeen Harbor, on the other side of Hong Kong Island. Because Hong Kong is surrounded by water, travel by water is a very popular way of getting around. One of the most traditional modes of transportation is a boat called a sampan, a wooden boat available in various sizes. Some are as big as houseboats; some only fit a few people. Once in Aberdeen, we found a man with a sampan to take us for a ride though the harbor, where there were hundreds of unique houseboats parked in what is locally called the floating village. Nearby we found a Buddhist temple where people came by the hundreds to worship and pray. The temple was old and richly decorated with statues and candles. In one area of the temple I noticed that people brought bags of food to the temple and set it there for their stone idols. I was curious to see what would happen to the food. Would it later be taken and given to the poor? I knew the idol wasn't going to use it! Then I noticed that half of the food sitting around was already rotten.

The Buddhists left food in order to honor Buddha, who died a couple thousand years ago, but I find so much more joy in honoring a living God who wants to spend meaningful time with us. God has asked us not to allow things to become idols in our hearts and minds. We often get distracted with many things that come into our world, but we must ask God to help us stay focused on Him and make our relationship with Him priority number one. Pay attention today to how you spend your time and energy. Do you have some idols you may not have known about? Ask God to help you not let those things absorb all your attention!

247

Geared Up, Tied In

For it is by grace you have been saved, through faith—
and this is not from yourselves, it is the gift of God.
EPHESIANS 2:8, NIV

While filming a video in Maui, we drove along the northern shore where we entered an amazing rainforest. Soon we arrived at our destination, and we got our gear and microphones ready and met the guide who would outfit us. We proceeded to put on harnesses, helmets, and special shoes. Our guide checked all our equipment and gear and announced that we were ready to go. He led us to a path that immediately went into the incredibly dense rainforest—so dense that after ten or fifteen steps you couldn't see where you had just been. We went up and down several slopes, and then suddenly we came out into an opening with a view in all directions. It looked as though we were up on a high bluff.

Our guide then took us to the edge of a cliff and showed us where we would be rappelling down. When you rappel, your harness is connected to a rope, and the rope is connected to another person who makes sure you descend safely. That person is called a belayer. I backed out over the edge of the cliff and made my way down backward. At the bottom of the cliff was a waterfall! Our next rappel would be down the face of the waterfall. This was a little harder because you couldn't quite see where you were stepping since the cliff wall was covered with a rush of falling water. Even though I couldn't see where I was stepping, nor could I see my belayer, I backed my way down the waterfall as water pounded me. It was an intense experience, but I was happy knowing that my belayer was there to make sure I didn't fall.

In life, God is the best belayer. As our Creator, He's very interested in protecting us and keeping us safe. He is the only one we can truly count on in every situation we may go through to never let us fall. More than anything, He wants each of us to be saved.

Surprised in Idaho

Command them to do good, to be rich in good deeds,
and to be generous and willing to share.
1 TIMOTHY 6:18, NIV

I have had the chance to visit several of the most famous waterfalls in the world, including Angel Falls in Venezuela, Victoria Falls in Africa, and Iguaçu Falls on the border of Argentina and Brazil. Not long ago, I got to visit another waterfall that completely surprised me. I was planning a cross-country road trip through the United States when I learned about a waterfall I had never even heard of before. At first I didn't think much of it because I had already seen Niagara Falls, the most visited falls in the United States. I had also visited several different waterfalls in Yosemite National Park, which also draw lots of tourists. I thought I had seen most of the larger waterfalls in the United States, but I was wrong.

The falls I discovered were in Twin Falls, Idaho. When I saw pictures of the waterfalls, I knew this was a place we had to visit. As we neared the waterfalls that day I was excited with anticipation. We parked and got out, and there before me was Shoshone Falls, one of the most impressive waterfalls I have ever seen! My first thought was, "Why don't more people know about this place?" The waterfalls are taller than Niagara Falls, and there aren't any of the annoying touristy distractions you see at Niagara. There are some trails along the sides of the canyon that allowed us to get an amazing view of this impressive waterfall from several different angles. Now, anytime someone asks about waterfalls, I never forget to share what I know about an awesome, lesser-known waterfall in North America, Shoshone Falls.

We've been taught since we were little that we are to share with others. This doesn't only include sharing about special places; it also includes sharing your time serving others, and of course, sharing your things with those in need. God will bless your generosity!

A View From Above

Every good and perfect gift is from above, coming down from the Father of the heavenly lights, who does not change like shifting shadows.
JAMES 1:17, NIV

If you have ever driven though South Dakota going east to west, it's a very long drive full of seemingly endless prairie grasses. Eventually you see the entrance to a unique national park called Badlands National Park. This strange name was given to the park by some early explorers who said these lands were bad because they were difficult to cross. At this point in the state, a higher plateau drops to a lower one by way of a series of amazing canyons. The canyons are filled with trails and paths you can explore. Unlike the Grand Canyon, where the rock layers are very hard, the Badlands canyons are constantly changing because they are not made of rock; they are made from a packed mud that erodes easily when it rains.

As we explored the park, we noticed that every once in a while we would see a small helicopter flying overhead. We concluded that somewhere nearby, someone was offering helicopter tours over the Badlands. Sure enough, as we exited the park we saw a company offering helicopter tours, so we pulled over. We filled out the necessary forms and paid. A few minutes later we walked toward the small helicopter that fit a maximum of three people. Moments later we lifted off and zoomed off toward the Badlands. The view of the Badlands from the sky was amazing. The canyons extended for miles and miles, where we could now clearly see how waters receded and eroded the amazing canyons.

As the earth slowly erodes and changes little by little, I'm reminded that God doesn't change. He is the same yesterday, today, and tomorrow. He's consistent and reliable; you can always count on Him. Lean on Him today!

An Unexpected Encounter

And God is able to bless you abundantly, so that in all things at all times,
having all that you need, you will abound in every good work.
2 CORINTHIANS 9:8, NIV

One summer when my boys were small we did a road trip to Yellowstone National Park in Wyoming. Once you enter the park, the main road is a giant loop that takes you to many incredible natural wonders. There are areas with petrified wood, areas with hot springs, mud pots, geysers, and fumaroles. There are canyons, lakes, prairies, mountains, and forests. It is impressive how many natural wonders could exist in one place!

As we drove around the park, one of the things we always watched for was a bunch of cars stopped on the side of the road. This usually meant there was some wildlife nearby to view. Sometimes we saw a huge elk a few feet from the road, chomping on grass. Other times, we'd see a handful of bison in a meadow grazing or even walking across the road. One time we saw a family of wolves walking down the road! We followed them for a few minutes until they took off into the woods. Our most memorable animal encounter took us by surprise. We were pulled over at a rest area when suddenly we saw a mother black bear with two cubs about two hundred feet away. As the bears neared, a few more people gathered. Before we knew it, we were back in our cars because the bear family came right into the parking lot and walked past us! As they went by, the cubs played around as they followed their mother back into the woods on the other side of the parking lot. What a gift it was to experience this!

God loves blessing us in so many different ways. Sometimes it's something as simple as this bear experience we would never forget. God even knows how to bless us with things we would have never even asked for. I wonder what blessings God has in store for you today.

SEPTEMBER 5

A Salty Place

By the first day of the first month of Noah's six hundred and first year, the water had dried up from the earth. Noah then removed the covering from the ark and saw that the surface of the ground was dry.
GENESIS 8:13, NIV

When I was a kid we used to take a lot of cross-country road trips from the east coast, where I grew up, to the west coast where a lot of my relatives lived. Driving through Utah was always one of the most scenic parts of our drive. I especially remember many times driving past the huge salt lake just west of Salt Lake City. The lake wasn't all completely a lake. A big part of it was a smooth, dry lake bottom where salt had accumulated when the lake dried up. As a kid I had no idea why all this salt was sitting there at such a high elevation; I just remember being amazed when we'd pull over to the side of the road and we'd stand on the lake to take a picture. My dad would have us touch the surface of the white salt and taste it. Wow, it was salty!

Many years later, I came back through that area, but this time I was the dad and my family was traveling with me. I learned about a place where we could drive out onto the salt flats. It was fun to drive as fast as you wanted, and since there was no road, you could drive in any direction. During our time there, we also stopped so that my family could taste the salt and also ask me why there is a huge salty ocean there, thousands of feet above sea level.

The Bible says that a few thousand years ago, a global Flood ravaged the planet and all the dry land was covered with water. Later, the water retreated and the land dried up. It would make sense to see huge areas of the planet that once were covered with water, even at the highest elevations! I love seeing how often the Bible seems to perfectly match with the things we see in nature. That is why I trust the Bible and I know it's the Word of God.

Backcountry Waterfall

Search me, God, and know my heart;
test me and know my anxious thoughts.
PSALM 139:23, NIV

On a recent trip to Puerto Rico, I spent the weekend speaking in three different churches on the island. To my surprise, the kind folks who invited me to come told me that on Sunday we would take a trip and do something fun in a place called El Yunque National Forest—in a part of the rain forest that only locals knew about. That morning, we got up early and took off in the car toward the rain forest. Soon we were driving through a heavy jungle higher and higher into the mountains. In order to get to this place, we had to leave the usual road and travel on rough side roads. Soon we arrived at a place where a bunch of cars were parked and knew the rest of the way we'd have to go on foot. About a mile in, the path started getting incredibly muddy, and we had to climb over logs and scramble up and down muddy slopes in order to continue forward. Soon, at a distance I could to hear the deep thunder of water falling. A few minutes later we were at an incredible location in the rain forest where a river flowed down a series of huge rock piles, creating a bunch of neat waterfalls and pools where about fifty locals were swimming, playing, and jumping into the water. There was even a huge rock where you could climb and jump in and a rope you could swing on and drop into the deepest part of the pool. My hosts that day knew the kind of excursion I would really enjoy, so they planned this outing with me in mind, and as far as I'm concerned, they nailed it because I had the greatest time there with them!

No one knows you better than God. He created you special and unique, and He knows the desires of your heart and the things that worry you. That's why God is the best and most trustworthy friend there is. Spend some quiet time with Him today.

Island Driving Adventure

*Anyone who lives on milk, being still an infant, is not acquainted with
the teaching about righteousness. But solid food is for the mature, who
by constant use have trained themselves to distinguish good from evil.*
HEBREWS 5:13, 14, NIV

When my wife and I got married, we took a cruise to the Bahamas for our honeymoon. Each day the boat stopped on a different island. One day we spent the day at a beach, another day we spent exploring an island we had stopped at. At one of our stops we decided to rent a scooter big enough to carry both of us, in order to see more of the island. With helmets on, we left to explore the island. There was one challenge that made the day a little more interesting—they drive on the left side of the road. Of course, North Americans drive on the right, but there are a handful of countries in the world where people drive on the left, such as the United Kingdom, Australia, several African nations, and of course, the Bahamas.

Naturally, I was extra careful driving around the island. I was amazed at how habits form and we get so used to things being a certain way, and then we have to change—it's hard. My instinct was to be on one side of the road, but now this had to change. Adapting to the new situation was important, otherwise we could get hurt. Interestingly, by the end of the day I was getting used to driving on the left.

Habits are formed when you do something often. Some habits are good and some are bad. Do you need to break a bad habit? Do you want to add a good new habit? Check out our Bible verse today. It says babies are in the habit of drinking only milk. But as they grow and mature, little by little they will form new habits, such as eating solid food. It's the same for us. Try to stop your bad habit, but substitute it with a new good one and pray that God will help you to be consistent. Before you know it, your new habit will feel natural!

A Week of Nothing

And God blessed them, saying, "Be fruitful and multiply,
and fill the waters in the seas, and let birds multiply on the earth."
GENESIS 1:22, NKJV

Almost every trip I take has a goal or mission. Sometimes I'm traveling because I was invited to speak somewhere, other times I travel to film different parts of the world. Occasionally I'm traveling because I need to attend a special meeting or event. At times my family gets to come with me, which makes the trip so much better. Once, my wife and I took a trip to do nothing. We went to a Mexican island called Cozumel, just off the Yucatan Peninsula. For one of the first times ever, we booked a hotel right on the beach and stayed there for a week. It was strange at first, since I was not used to "resting vacations."

Having the opportunity to travel is a blessing even if it's to work, so I would never complain, but this time in Cozumel stood out as one of the only resting vacations we've ever taken. I took a book and a music player and nothing else. Every morning after breakfast we went down to the waterfront and sat in a chair till lunch. After lunch we'd go back and sit there again till supper. Our first day there, I discovered a beautiful reef only a few feet away in the water, and each day I went snorkeling. Every day I looked forward to that peaceful time in the water surrounded by colorful fish and diverse coral creatures. During those seven days I estimate that I spent twenty hours in the water exploring the reef and all of God's amazing creations.

The ocean teems with living things. God took the time to create the creatures of the sea, so it would make sense to study and appreciate them whenever you get a chance. We're usually surrounded by nature, so today I challenge you to think of God every time you see something in nature. Go out and enjoy and appreciate all of it!

The Fangoree

*Then I will give you rain in its season, the land shall yield
its produce, and the trees of the field shall yield their fruit.*
LEVITICUS 26:4, NKJV

O nce or twice a year I get the privilege of speaking at a Pathfinder or
Adventurer camporee in different parts of the world. Each place is unique
and has many wonderful people. One time I got to speak at an Adventurer
camporee in Massachusetts, where I grew up. It was great to be able to return
after so many years. Another time I went to a camporee on the Caribbean
island of Puerto Rico. When I was a baby, our family lived in Puerto Rico for
a short time, and my father told me about the place where I would be going
for the camporee.

Each year the camporee took place in the rain forest up in the central
mountains of the island. When I landed in San Juan, I rented a car and drove
to the camporee site. The weather in San Juan was hot, but as we started
driving up into the mountains, the weather started to change to the more
typical tropical rain forest weather—humid. By the time we arrived at camp
it was an all-out downpour. I started hoping the storm would pass through
quickly. That was not the case. When we arrived on Friday it was raining,
and by the time we left Sunday morning it was still raining. You might think
this put a damper on the event, but that was not the case—our Puerto Rican
brothers and sisters are some of the most joyful people I've ever met. They
could not care less about the rain and never stopped smiling, laughing, and
enjoying every moment at the camporee. They even nicknamed it the "fan-
goree," which is like saying "the muddy camporee."

Seeing rain shows us how God waters the earth and makes things grow.
May that be a reminder that only God can cause the rain to fall. Have a
positive attitude when it rains, and feel at peace because God knows what
He's doing.

The Imitation Game

Therefore be imitators of God as dear children. And walk in love, as Christ also has loved us and given Himself for us, an offering and a sacrifice to God for a sweet-smelling aroma.
EPHESIANS 5:1, 2, NKJV

Part of my work is producing videos of me exploring amazing natural locations. Recently, I was approached by a producer from the North American Division about helping in a video they were producing where they recreated scenes and told stories based on the Adventist pioneers. Because of my looks, I was asked to play the part of a pioneer called Joseph Bates, who lived in the 1800s. I got my lines several weeks in advance, and I memorized them. A costume from that time was prepared for me, including glasses and fake sideburns that had to be glued onto my face. If you've ever seen a picture of Joseph Bates, there was one other prominent and obvious feature on his face we had to deal with. He had a large mole on his cheek, so a fake mole prosthetic was made and glued to my face as well. Next, a makeup artist started to put a bunch of makeup on my face, especially around the mole to help it to blend in with my face. Our call time soon approached, and we were ready to record the scenes.

We filmed in Battle Creek, Michigan, at the historic Adventist Village where Ellen White once lived. The cameras and lights were in place, and I spent the rest of the day pretending to be Joseph Bates. There are no video or audio recordings of Joseph Bates, so it was hard trying to figure out how to copy him. I read all about him and did my best to be as I imagined he was.

I thought about how many people are role models: actors, sports figures, models, politicians. Unfortunately, many of them are terrible role models, and sadly, they are copied and admired by millions of people. Christians, on the other hand, should have only one role model—Jesus. He is the ultimate role model. Go out and be like Jesus today!

SEPTEMBER 11

Ground Zero

For God so loved the world that he gave his one and only Son,
that whoever believes in him shall not perish but have eternal life.
JOHN 3:16, NIV

On September 11, 2001, terrorists attacked the Twin Towers in New York City and brought them crashing down to the ground with thousands of people trapped inside. A separate attack that day targeted the Pentagon building in Washington, DC. Another attack was thwarted when brave people on a hijacked airplane over Pennsylvania forced the plane to crash before letting the terrorists hurt more people. Many brave firefighters also died trying to save people in the buildings as they burned. That day was a dark day in the history of the United States. The people who died were mourned, the structures were rebuilt, and the government worked to find the people responsible for the attacks.

It took me a long time to soak it all in. I had a friend in one of the towers that day, but she was one of the fortunate people on the lower floors who was able to escape before the building collapsed. As I talked to my wife about all this, we decided to take a weekend and go to New York City and Washington, DC, to visit the places that were attacked. I felt this would give us the closure necessary to deal with what had happened. A few months after September 11, we drove from Michigan to Washington, then on to New York, where I had booked a room in a hotel. Our room was on the fifteenth floor with a direct view of Ground Zero. It was shocking to look down at the huge mess as people worked around the clock to carefully sift and remove the debris. After a while, my wife went to bed, but I stayed up till almost 2:00 A.M., sitting by the window, crying and looking out over the ruins.

The sacrifices people made that day are similar to the sacrifice Jesus made to save humanity. Our verse today is the most famous verse in the Bible and a reminder of God's amazing sacrifice.

The Big Pile of Sand

"Go, gather all the Jews who are present in Shushan, and fast for me; neither eat nor drink for three days, night or day. My maids and I will fast likewise. And so I will go to the king, which is against the law; and if I perish, I perish!"
ESTHER 4:16, NKJV

One time when I was driving through Colorado, we stopped at a very interesting place called Great Sand Dunes National Park and Preserve. Strangely enough, nestled right up against the mountains in the southern part of the state were the largest piles of sand I had ever seen. I used to imagine sand dunes in dry deserts or coastal areas, but this place was neither. We drove through the entrance and discovered there was a bunch of off-road trails for people driving four-wheel-drive vehicles. Fortunately, I was driving my Jeep Wrangler. We enjoyed crossing loose, sandy areas, forested areas, and even streams that were about three feet deep, finally arriving at the base of one of the largest dunes.

The climb was incredibly difficult; it seemed as though for every three steps I took, I slid about two steps back. I had purposely found the steepest dune I could find, and when I finally made it to a little ridge and sat down, I was exhausted! Once I had caught my breath, I pulled out the thing I had dragged all the way up there. My snowboard! I had read that it was possible to use a snowboard on a sand dune as long as it was steep. I had never tried this before, but I put my board on and stood up. I took a deep breath and quickly started sliding down the face of the dune. Miraculously, I made it all the way down without falling. Of course, I didn't try any fancy moves. I just wanted to make it down in one piece, and I did!

In the Bible, Queen Esther was anxious for her people to make it to the next year in one piece. She had faith and risked herself to save her people, regardless of what happened to her. She said, "If I perish, I perish." Doing God's will is more important than anything else.

A Real Handy Man

Why, you do not even know what will happen tomorrow. What is your life?
You are a mist that appears for a little while and then vanishes. Instead,
you ought to say, "If it is the Lord's will, we will live and do this and that."
JAMES 4:14, 15, NIV

Driving through Cuba, we arrived at Holguín, a city on the eastern side of the island. Our host took us down a small street, and we stopped at the base of a large hill. Right in front of us was a huge staircase leading to the top of the hill where there was a lookout over the entire city and beyond, called the Hill of the Cross. Our host dropped us off to climb these famous stairs and told us that he would meet us at the top so we wouldn't have to walk all the way down. Before leaving, he mentioned that there were 458 steps to get to the top! This seemed like a fun activity and a great way for our boys to spend some extra energy, so we started climbing.

As we were climbing up the stairs we encountered a man coming down the steps. This was no regular descent; he was coming down walking on his hands! He quietly passed us and continued toward the bottom. We were amazed and impressed, because simply walking on your hands seems hard to do. But he was climbing down the 458 steps on his hands! What we saw next shocked us. When he got to the bottom, without pausing a moment, he turned around and started climbing the steps, still on his hands! Before we made it to the top, he had passed us and was coming back down again!

The Bible talks about another strong man named Samson. Samson fell to temptation, which led to sin, but in the end, God still used Samson to do His will. Everyone is guilty of sin, but that doesn't mean God doesn't have a plan for us anymore; He does! Ask God for forgiveness each day and how He wants you to accomplish His will.

Catching the Big Wave

Then He arose and rebuked the wind, and said to the sea, "Peace, be still!"
And the wind ceased and there was a great calm.
MARK 4:39, NKJV

The first time I went to Hawaii with my family, we spent a day visiting the North Shore of Oahu. Oahu is the Hawaiian island that holds the capital, Honolulu. One of the places we didn't want to miss was the North Shore, which is famous for one thing—surfing the big waves! I didn't know much about surfing, but it seemed like an exciting sport. I definitely wanted to watch some of these brave guys and girls catching a wave. Since those beaches were well known for having huge waves, I expected to see big waves, but when we arrived at one particular beach called The Pipeline, I was shocked at how *huge* these waves were.

There were about half a dozen guys surfing that day, and I assumed they were either the bravest people on the island, or the craziest. As I watched in amazement, I decided to try to estimate how tall the waves were. I took out my camera and looked at some of the photos and compared the estimated six-foot-tall guys against the waves, and I determined that the waves were between twenty-five and thirty feet tall! Besides the impressive size of these waves, the sound these waves made when they crashed was a deafening thunder. A couple of hours later, we were several miles down at a beach with much smaller waves, where I decided to try boogie boarding. It was fun, and I thought to myself, "Maybe someday I'll learn how to surf."

Can you imagine if I had tried to surf those huge waves? Not good. In the Bible we read the story about when Jesus and His disciples were on a boat during a violent storm with huge waves. The disciples panicked. They thought they were toast. For a moment they forgot Who was napping on the boat, but our verse today reminds us what happened. God's power can be seen when nature obeys the Creator! Jesus is in your boat now; call on Him today!

Cowabunga, Dude

I can do all things through him who strengthens me.
PHILIPPIANS 4:13, ESV

About ten years passed between my first and second visits to Hawaii. The second time, I came with a goal: I wanted to try surfing! I found several instructors who offered surfing classes, so I signed up.

My goal was simple: If I could get up on the board, ride a wave in and successfully lie back down on the board without falling off, I would accept that as having successfully surfed. When I got there, I was happy to see that the waves were small that day. This would make learning to surf a lot easier and increase my chances of successfully catching a wave. I was given a board, and we spent the first twenty minutes learning the basic moves of surfing. When you are first trying to catch a wave, you're paddling on your tummy, but at the right moment, you must quickly pop up on your feet, balance yourself with your arms, and hopefully ride the wave all the way in. Soon it was time to grab our boards and head into the water. I'm sure you know what happened. I would catch a wave, pop up for a second or two, and then wipe out. I was exhausted from falling and paddling back out to the spot where we could catch waves, but I persisted through the pain because I wasn't going to give up. After about fifteen exhausting attempts, I got up on the board and I rode it all the way in without falling! When I noticed the wave was dying off, I lay back down on the board. I had done it!

Do you have any goals? Good goals require work and persistence to accomplish. Some can be accomplished quickly, but others can take years. Don't be discouraged! Ask God to be part of your journey because when God is with you, He will lift you up and give you strength when you need it!

Prison Break

Everyone who sins breaks the law; in fact, sin is lawlessness.
1 JOHN 3:4, NIV

My sister lives in the San Francisco Bay area, so one year while visiting her we decided to take a day trip into the city to visit a few places. First we visited Fisherman's Wharf, where there are many unique shops and restaurants by the waterfront. Toward the back of this area is a place where sea lions often congregate around piers and lie in the sun—often making a lot of noise with their barking. We then decided to ride the famous trolley cars that slowly make their way up and down the hilly streets of San Francisco. Our last stop that day was to visit a famous island in the bay called Alcatraz—one of the most famous prisons in the world. It closed back in 1963, but for many years it was known as one of the hardest prisons to escape from.

As we approached the island by boat, we could already see the tall walls and fences that surround parts of the island. Over the next couple of hours we toured different parts of the prison as well as the concrete yard where inmates were allowed to go out and get fresh air. Everywhere we went, there were fences and bars and barbed wire. The prison cells looked tiny and very uncomfortable. It made me think of sin, because sin is also like a prison. Even though sinning my not lead to you being put in prison, it does something worse. It separates us from God. Luckily, Jesus is there to forgive us every time we ask. I'm sure the prisoners in Alcatraz wished they could have been freed simply by asking for forgiveness.

Muhammad the Goofa Boy

So God, who knows the heart, acknowledged them by giving
them the Holy Spirit, just as He did to us.
ACTS 15:8, NKJV

After graduating from university, I didn't have to start work for a couple of months, so I decided to go to Jordan and participate in a summer archeological dig. The place we would be digging had never been excavated before. Our team arrived, and the staff archeologists assigned the spots where we would be digging. They created "squares" that were about ten feet by ten feet, where we would dig each day. Our job was to carefully dig out the dirt in our square, being careful to look for anything out of the ordinary. Local teenagers were hired to spend the day helping us remove the dirt from our area. The dirt was placed into a container called a *goofa*, and our local helpers would take the container and dump the dirt on a wire screen. They shook the screen until all the dirt passed through. This was to make sure we didn't miss any important objects during the dig. The goofa boy assigned to our square was called Muhammed, and even though we couldn't understand each other, during the course of the summer, we became friends. That's kind of strange considering we never got to have a real conversation with each other. Once in a while when a translator came by, he would translate a few comments between us, but most of the time we just joked around, smiled a lot, were kind to each other, and sat together during breaks and snack time.

The reason I'm sharing this story is that Mohammed was a devout Muslim. Will Mohammed be saved? No one knows except God, because God is the only one who knows what is in the heart of every person. It is not our place to even try to guess if someone will be saved or not. God knows what's in my heart, just as He knows Muhammad's heart. Our job is not to judge, it's to be a witness to the world.

Adventures at Camp

Let everyone be subject to the governing authorities, for there is
no authority except that which God has established. The authorities
that exist have been established by God.
ROMANS 13:1, NIV

Each year for the past several years I've been thrilled to spend a week as camp pastor at a summer camp. My two boys get to participate in the many wonderful camp activities, they make lifelong friends, and they learn from a bunch of really great camp leaders and staff. Each time I go, I discover something new. A couple of years ago when I was there, I spent some time exploring along a wooden boardwalk that goes all the way around the lake. Another year, I came across a little beach area near my cabin, where I watched a turtle come up the sandy beach, dig a hole in the sand, and lay her eggs. Another year, a staff member took me to a lookout, deep in the woods, made for bird watching. With his help, I was able to spot a wonderful variety of birds I wouldn't have seen without his help. My favorite moment was when he pointed out a huge nest in the top of a tree. The nest was huge—at least four feet across and about seven or eight feet tall! I thought to myself, "Wow, that is one big bird!" To my delight, he told me that it was the nest of a pair of bald eagles. A little while later, we spotted the eagles flying high over the camp.

Since the bald eagle is the national bird of the United States, I felt very patriotic watching them fly around. The business of running a country sometimes gets ugly, though. As you get older, you will notice that politics often brings out the worst in people. It is our responsibility to do our best to choose good leaders to lead the country we live in, but regardless of who ends up elected, God says we are to respect and honor the governing authorities. It's impossible to have an election where 100 percent are happy with the results; our duty is not to complain and criticize but to accept and respect the authorities that have been established.

Go With God's Plan

And we know that all things work together for good to those who love God, to those who are the called according to His purpose.
ROMANS 8:28, NKJV

There are hundreds of locations all over the world that contain preserved dinosaur footprints in hardened mud or clay. During a film shoot, I was supposed to explore a dinosaur track site. As I searched for a location, I discovered that the southeast corner of Colorado has one of the best dinosaur track sites in North America. I researched what it would take to get there, what the terrain looks like, and how hard it is to reach the tracks. When I did the calculations, I discovered it would require driving four hours into the wilderness. After arriving, we would have to continue on foot through a desert canyon for several more miles. It was not an easy place to get to, but I was determined to select some of the best scenic locations in North America for this video series!

Besides the eight-hour round-trip drive, it would take us another six hours hiking to and from the track site, plus time there to film scenes—we were in for a fifteen-hour workday! After driving four hours, we made it to the parking area only to discover that there was an uncontrolled brush fire nearby and the entire area was off-limits! At this point we realized our entire day was lost, and we'd lose another day trying to shoot these scenes elsewhere. A couple of weeks later, we finally shot the scenes at another track site in Wyoming.

At first I was disappointed that we weren't able to film those scenes in Colorado and found myself wishing the fire hadn't happened. When we ask God to be in control of our lives, we don't have to worry, because the Bible says that all things work together for those who love God. I may never fully know why that Colorado location never worked out, but I have decided to trust that God was working things out. Will you let Him work things out for you today?

A Mammoth-Size Pit

"Watch and pray so that you will not fall into temptation.
The spirit is willing, but the flesh is weak."
MATTHEW 26:41, NIV

Several years ago I was driving through the southwest corner of South Dakota shooting some scenes in the Black Hills. Millions of people flock to the other big attraction in the area, Mount Rushmore, but forget to enjoy the amazing natural beauties of the Black Hills. As we drove, we discovered amazing scenic drives with plenty of bison and other creatures freely roaming around. Some of the coolest rock formations in the country—called needles—cover the rolling hills. These needles are huge, pointy rock formations that dot the mountainsides, allowing tourists to drive through and even under some of these rocks.

Since we finished recording early, I was anxious to drive to a place nearby called Mammoth Site. As you can imagine from the name, this was an attraction that had to do with those big, extinct elephant cousins, woolly mammoths. We arrived and paid the entry and took the initial little tour in the museum, which eventually led to a very fascinating part of the attraction—the actual mammoth skeletons still in the ground. Years ago, a pit was discovered in this location, where various creatures had fallen in and died, including mammoths. As the scientists started digging deeper, they were very surprised to find that the deeper they went, the more mammoths they found. Dozens of mammoths had fallen into that pit and died.

Satan's goal is to get us to fall into the pit of temptation. He uses every method he can to tempt us; each day we must pray and ask God to deliver us from falling into Satan's traps. Since he's a clever enemy, you must be especially careful in areas you might be weak in. Satan will specifically try to get you to trip up in those areas, so avoid getting anywhere near those temptations—at all costs! Daily closeness to God is the best way to avoid falling to temptation.

The Fault Line Flight

For if they fall, one will lift up his companion.
But woe to him who is alone when he falls,
For he has no one to help him up.
ECCLESIASTES 4:10, NKJV

A few years ago I was involved in a filming project that required us to charter a small airplane in Bakersfield, California. We arrived early in the morning just before the sun rose in order to prepare and discuss the plan with our pilot. Next, we went over the script and discussed at which moment during the flight we'd record our lines. Finally, we were ready to fly. We went through all the necessary preflight checks, and soon we were on the runway taking off.

For this particular segment, we were going to fly to the Carrizo Plain, a desert place where we could observe the San Andreas Fault—a giant crack in the surface of the earth caused by the movement of earth's tectonic plates. This one runs hundreds of miles across California. In order to get there, we had to fly for about fifteen minutes over the agricultural plains of central California. Next, we needed to cross a small mountain range. After passing the range we were now officially flying over the Carrizo Plain. A few minutes later we found ourselves looking down at an amazing sight. The fault line looks like a giant crack in the earth that runs as far into the distance as the eye can see!

Just as cracks have formed in the earth, sometimes cracks form between friends. Trust is the glue that keeps friendships strong, and if you are not careful and break the trust between you and a friend, it can be very hard to regain that trust. Since you can't control others, your job is to simply be the best and most loyal and trustworthy friend you can be, and pray that God blesses your friendships. Treasure and protect your friendships; they are given by God. Otherwise you may find yourself without friends.

Untouched Beauty

"Are not two sparrows sold for a penny? And not one of them will fall to the ground apart from your Father. . . . Fear not, therefore; you are of more value than many sparrows."
MATTHEW 10:29, 31, ESV

One time I decided to take my family to the island of Culebra, off the eastern coast of Puerto Rico. We drove to the city of Fajardo on the northeast corner of the island, because that is where we would be able to catch a ferry that traveled to Culebra several times a day. The island is about twenty miles away from the coast and about halfway between Puerto Rico and the British Virgin Islands.

Once we arrived in the little port town, we asked around for the best beach, and everyone pointed us to the same place, so we headed in that direction. When we got there, the suggestions appeared to be right—the beach was very beautiful! It was located in a safe little bay with white sand, palm trees, a cool breeze, and wonderful views. We played in the surf and in the sand and eventually decided to take a walk down the beach. A local told us that most people only go about a half mile to where the beach ends, but if we were to climb over a bunch of rocks, the beach would continue around the corner for a while through a very isolated and seemingly deserted part of the island. We took his advice and set off to the end of the beach and climbed over the rocks. Soon we were on another beautiful beach, and we were the only people as far as we could see. We walked and collected shells. Since very few people visited this beach, we found incredibly beautiful shells untouched all over the beach. My youngest son even found a big conch shell half-buried in the sand! He brought the conch home and proudly displays it in his room.

God reminds us in today's verse that we are worth a lot to God. It says even the little sparrows that are sold for pennies are worth a lot to God. Start every day knowing that you are way more valuable than sparrows to God!

The Hottest Day Ever

*I long to dwell in your tent forever
and take refuge in the shelter of your wings.*
PSALM 61:4, NIV

A few years ago, my family took a road trip that brought us to Death Valley, California. It's one of the hottest places on earth, and we were not disappointed. As we approached the valley from Nevada, it was ninety-eight degrees, and we thought it was toasty. Fortunately, our car had air conditioning, so we only appreciated the heat when we stopped. As we approached Death Valley, the first thing we noticed was that we drove down into the valley—below sea level. When we finally made it to the bottom, the landscape seemed to be completely void of plant or animal life. We finally found a spot to stop and opened the car doors. Kapow! We couldn't believe how hot it was—114 degrees!

We stayed in the valley for several hours, exploring, and every time we went from one place to the other, we enjoyed cooling off in the car for a few minutes. Then all of a sudden the air conditioning stopped working! The inside of the car started to heat up. You know how, when you leave a car parked in the sun, it usually gets hotter inside the car than outside? Well, we were getting cooked in the car as we drove along! I finally pulled over and told the family that we needed to pray about this. Our road trip would last another eight or nine days, and we wanted to continue our trip with air conditioning! We prayed and moved on. You probably won't be surprised to learn that our air conditioning suddenly started working again!

The Bible says that the best shelter is under God's wings. Just as birds use their wings to protect and shade their young, there's always room for you under God's protective wings, even in 114-degree heat! God doesn't force us to be there; it's a choice we're each given. I hope today that you choose to take shelter under God's protective wings.

The Ghost Town

When you ask, you do not receive, because you ask with wrong motives, that you may spend what you get on your pleasures.
JAMES 4:3, NIV

During our trip to Death Valley in California, we learned that there was also a nearby ghost town in Nevada called Rhyolite. In the early 1900s, the economy in the town started to change and caused people to leave, until eventually the entire town was completely abandoned. At its peak in 1907, there were almost five thousand people living in this town, and many buildings lined the streets. The town had sprung up to serve and support the mines and the gold rush, but it didn't last. By 1920 it was pretty much empty.

When we arrived, no one else was in the town. Only a handful of the ruined buildings were left. In some buildings, all that was left were a few of the exterior walls such as the bank, which was originally built with stone blocks. Other buildings were more complete, such as the train station, but I was amazed to think that a little more than one hundred years ago, almost five thousand people lived there, and now there was not a single soul. Up the street about a mile away were a mine and mill that employed many people from the town. Over the years, movie companies have used the town for some of their backgrounds, but today this town serves no purpose except as a look back through history. The buildings were there, and piped water and electricity had even been brought to the town, but the most important thing was missing—people.

Sometimes we put way too much value in material things, and we pray to God asking for material things we think will bring us happiness, but true joy can be found when we serve and pray for others. God warns us in the Bible that we sometimes ask for things but don't receive them because we have selfish motives in our hearts. Ask God today to help us not be selfish in how we pray. Make your requests the kind of requests that honor God, not you.

X Marks the Spot

My son, keep my words,
and treasure my commands within you.
PROVERBS 7:1, NKJV

Driving cross-country provides an opportunity to see a lot of interesting things. Perhaps you've visited a famous national park such as Yellowstone National Park. Or have you ever visited a famous national monument such as the St. Louis Arch? During one of our recent road trips, we stopped at a place called Four Corners located in the Colorado Plateau. There were no famous parks, monuments, or attractions. You're probably wondering why this place even exists.

Four Corners is the only place in the United States where four state borders touch each other in one spot. The states are Utah, Arizona, Colorado, and New Mexico. Canada also has a Four Corners, where the Northwest Territories, Saskatchewan, Manitoba, and Nunavut meet, but that spot is hundreds of miles from the nearest road or railway and very hard to reach. When you get to Four Corners in the United States, there is a large concrete area laid out on the ground with a big inscribed circle. In the middle of the circle is a giant "X" creating the four quadrants, each one representing one state. Of course, the fun thing to do is to try to stand exactly in the middle of the "X" so you can say that parts of your body are in four different states at the same time. Maybe it would be fun to call a friend, and when they ask you where you are, you could respond by saying, "I'm in Arizona, New Mexico, Colorado, and Utah!" That would really confuse them. It was a unique place to visit, since X marked the spot.

In many treasure-hunting stories, X marks the spot. Our verse today says that God's commands are a treasure we should keep close. We sometimes think God's commands are rules that prevent us from doing things, but God's commands were given to make you happy and keep you safe. That's something to be thankful for!

My African Safari

But one of the elders said to me, "Do not weep. Behold, the Lion of the tribe of Judah, the Root of David, has prevailed to open the scroll and to loose its seven seals."
REVELATION 5:5, NKJV

During our time in Africa, we drove through one of the most famous animal reserves, Kruger National Park in South Africa. We immediately saw many different creatures wandering around such as baboons, impala, zebras, wildebeest, and giraffes. There were several other animals we were even more excited to see such as hippos and rhinos, but more than anything we were anxious to see lions.

A reserve is nothing like going to a zoo in North America. In a zoo, the animals are in an enclosure, and they really have nowhere to go, nowhere to hide. At a reserve, there are hundreds of square miles where the creatures can roam. That is very good for them, but for us, finding them required patience and good eyesight! Toward the end of our day we were beginning to get concerned because we still hadn't spotted any lions. Then suddenly up ahead we saw two or three cars stopped in the middle of the road. Our hopes were high as we slowed down and stopped to see if we could see what they were looking at. To our shock and surprise, calmly walking down the middle of the road was a full-grown lioness with four lion cubs following her. We were so excited! I pulled out my camera to start taking pictures. Little by little they got closer. At first I thought they were just trying to cross the road, but they were actually walking along the road toward us. A few moments later, the lion family walked within four feet of our car! I never dreamed we would get so close to a lion!

Our verse today refers to Jesus as the Lion of Judah. Seeing those powerful lions in Africa brought to life images of how powerful Jesus is and what He's done to save us and deliver us from sin. What a blessing it is to have such a powerful protector looking out for us today!

Stuck in the Jungle

"Therefore I say to you, whatever things you ask when you pray, believe that you receive them, and you will have them."
MARK 11:24, NKJV

A few years ago I went on a unique mission trip with my church to Honduras. Our group had older folks, middle-aged adults, college kids, high school kids, and about six elementary kids. During our time there, we moved around in a big yellow school bus. On Sabbath afternoon, we decided to take the group up a mountain to an overlook in the jungle. When we arrived, we explored some ruins, and a local man gave us a few stalks of sugar cane to try.

When it was time to return, the only way out was to back the bus several hundred feet to a place where it could turn around. It had rained heavily earlier that morning, so there was a lot of slick mud on the dirt road. As the bus began to back down the small jungle road, it started to slip in the mud. As the wheels spun, it only slid farther into the jungle. Soon the front tires of our bus were two feet deep in mud. Everyone got off the bus, trying to figure out what we should do. The men decided to try pushing the bus, but our efforts seemed to make things worse. The bus slid deeper off the road and even started tilting into the jungle. We were miles away from the nearest town, and the situation seemed completely hopeless. That's when an older woman in our group suddenly said, "We should have prayed right away!" Our group grasped hands and prayed right there in the muddy jungle. The men decided to try pushing again, but this time the bus came right out of the mud! It was one of the fastest answered-prayer miracles I had ever experienced.

The power of prayer is real. Since God made you and loves you, He's always ready and willing to hear about your concerns; it doesn't matter if they're big or small.

The Cost of the Canal

*And God will wipe away every tear from their eyes; there shall be
no more death, nor sorrow, nor crying. There shall be no
more pain, for the former things have passed away.*
REVELATION 21:4, NKJV

After completing all my speaking responsibilities in the country of Panama, I was very excited when the leaders offered to take us sightseeing for a day. Can you guess what was on the top of my list? You're right if you guessed the Panama Canal. We parked at the Miraflores Locks near the Pacific Ocean.

The Panama Canal is one of the most impressive engineering projects undertaken during a time when a lot of the dirt still had to be moved by hand. Because of the various challenges of working in the jungle, I learned that the number of people who died during construction was horrifying— over twenty-five thousand people! A building at the locks serves as a museum, and over the next few hours, we went through the museum exhibits and eventually finished at the top floor of the building that had a large viewing platform overlooking the locks in both directions. From a distance we could see the enormous oil tankers approaching and entering the locks. The locks would then close, and, depending on which direction they were going, the canal would either fill up with water or the water would be drained out, thereby raising or lowering the ship a little at a time. This would be repeated multiple times during the six to eight hours it took to cross from one ocean to the other. We stayed there quite a while, watching three or four ships pass completely through the Miraflores Locks. The entire time the thought in the back of my mind was how many people had died to build this place.

Every day all over the world, people die because of war, sickness, conflict, or old age. It's very sad, but I'm encouraged to know that God will return one day soon and take us to a place where there will be no more death, no more crying, and no more pain. I can't wait for that day!

An Explosive Experience

A hot-tempered man stirs up strife,
but he who is slow to anger quiets contention.
PROVERBS 15:18, ESV

Our trek through Costa Rica led us to the north-central part of the country on a mountain road filled with huge potholes. Driving on this rarely visited road through the rain forest brought us face to face with amazing mountain ranges, old trees, birds, and countless coatis—little curious mammals similar to lemurs that scurried around the road as the occasional car went by. The long drive eventually led us to an overlook of our destination, Arenal Volcano. There are many volcanoes on our planet, but this one is unique.

First, it's a perfectly conical-shaped volcano, with steep sides and a point on the top. Second, it's a very active volcano. During the day you can see puffs of billowing smoke coming from the top of the volcano, and every once in a while we could hear a low rumble. That evening, we went to a restaurant to eat, and there was an outside terrace that provided an amazing view of the volcano. As the sun began to set, we finally discovered what the low rumbling sounds were. In the dark, we could now see bright, glowing volcanic rock spewing out of the volcano's peak. These huge chunks of lava tumbled down the mountain and created the low rumble.

It made me think that some people are often like volcanoes because they are hot-tempered and blow up all the time. Whenever you see them, a low rumble of complaints and negativity seems to follow. Wherever they go, they seem to stir people up and create conflict. God gives us the power to overcome bad habits. Satan wants you to think you can't, but God can help you if you ask Him to be part of every moment of your life. Ask God today to help you remove your bad habits and replace them with good ones!

The Unexpected Encounter

"And this gospel of the kingdom will be preached in all the world as a witness to all the nations, and then the end will come."
MATTHEW 24:14, NKJV

Before us were the great pyramids of Giza, just outside of Cairo, Egypt. Getting there had been an adventure, but now a new adventure waited. A man walked up to my friends and me, and with his broken English, asked us if we wanted to take a camel tour of the pyramids. This sounded like a very good idea. He prepared four camels for us and tied them all together in a long row with ropes between each camel. Soon we headed off into the desert. He said the best view of the pyramids was from behind and that our plan was to go deep into the desert and come around and to see the pyramids from a high ridge. An hour later we hadn't seen another living soul for some time, and we were happy to be getting the full desert-camel experience. Then at a distance we saw a man with a donkey coming toward us. Eventually this small, elderly man stopped and started talking to our guide. The guide pointed him to come back to talk to us, and he did, but we didn't understand a single word. He was selling something, so he finally reached into a big bag tied onto the donkey and pulled out was he was selling. We were quite shocked to find him selling Coca-Cola products in the middle of the desert. We were more amazed that it was cold! It really made me appreciate how hard that company was working to take its products to every corner of the world.

As Christians we also have something that we're trying to take to every corner of the world: the good news about Jesus. That's when it hit me that our message is much more important than Coca-Cola, yet I had to ask myself if I was working as hard as Coca-Cola to spread the news about Jesus. In order for this to work, we need to do our part to spread the word about Jesus. Your part in this work is very important. Will you share Jesus with someone today?

My Graceful Fall

For a righteous man may fall seven times
And rise again,
But the wicked shall fall by calamity.
PROVERBS 24:16, NKJV

As we rode our camels through the Egyptian desert, the camels stopped near the pyramids to get a drink of water. During part of this break, some of the camels peed on the sand. I know that sounds disgusting, but it is part of normal animal life. A few minutes later, my camel and the camel in front of me started to fight with each other. They started bumping each other and nibbling at each other, and at one point as they were jockeying for position, the rope between my camel and the front camel swung around and started to push me off my camel! Camels are pretty tall, and I was sitting at least seven feet off the ground. I really did not want to get knocked off my camel. It didn't matter, though, because a few moments later I fell to the ground.

Fortunately, the ground was sandy and soft. Unfortunately, I landed on the spot where one of the camels had just peed. The hot desert sand had absorbed the majority of it already, but I was grossed out. My friends made sure I was OK, but once they saw I was fine, it was hard to resist the humor of what had happened. They joked and teased as I got back on my camel, and I laughed along with them.

Sometimes things happen in our lives that are simply part of life, but sometimes we take them way too seriously. There will be many moments in life when we need to brush off the bad things, move along, and not dwell on them, thinking it's the end of the world. Satan will do everything he can to trip us up. God says when we fall, we are to get up again, repent, and ask for forgiveness, then dust ourselves off and continue on our way. Don't dwell on the bad times or your sins. Put them behind you!

The Small Pyramid

But he said, "Blessed rather are those who hear the word of God and keep it!"
LUKE 11:28, ESV

As we rode our camels through the Egyptian desert, we finally arrived at a ridge behind and above the great pyramids of Giza. It truly was a magnificent view. Right in front of us were the three large pyramids, and in the background, the sprawling city of Cairo. We got off our camels, and our guide took some pictures of us. As we continued our way toward the pyramids, we noticed something we hadn't seen before. Although there were three very large pyramids in this complex, we hadn't realized that there were several other smaller ones surrounding them. As we approached the pyramids from the desert side, we particularly noticed a series of three smaller pyramids that seemed to be isolated from the reach of most tourists.

Our guide stopped our caravan of camels and we dismounted. He then turned to us and said, "Go climb," pointing to one of the smaller pyramids. We had heard that no one was allowed to climb the three larger pyramids, but we didn't know anything about these smaller ones. We looked at each other, then looked at the small pyramid and decided to go for it. Pyramids, made up of large solid blocks of stone about waist high, are quite easy to climb. We proceeded to climb, one block at a time, till we reached the top. It was quite exciting to be up there, and we stayed there for a few minutes soaking in the view.

God will never ask us to do things that will hurt us, but He does encourage us to always obey Him because He has wonderful things in store for us. Sometimes they may seem difficult or impossible to do, but God promises to bless us when we listen and obey Him. In order to hear Him, you have to first listen. When you spend time in prayer, don't forget to also spend quiet time listening for God's voice. If you are patient, you will hear Him.

The Biggest Tomb

"And everyone who has left houses or brothers or sisters or father
or mother or wife or children or lands, for My name's sake,
shall receive a hundredfold, and inherit eternal life."
MATTHEW 19:29, NKJV

After our adventure climbing one of the small pyramids, we remounted our camels and continued toward the larger pyramids around the corner. When we arrived, we discovered there were tunnels we could take to the center of the pyramid. First we had to climb the outside of the pyramid up to the entrance. As you entered, the passageway went downhill for a small distance, then uphill for a small distance. The whole time, we had to be either squatting or crawling on our hands and knees. Finally we reached a large room called the Grand Gallery that also continued to lead us uphill. At the top of this large room we finally reached the King's Chamber, where the pharaoh had been laid to rest. At this point we were at the very center of the pyramid.

As we explored these rooms, we discovered they were mostly empty, but in the King's Chamber there was one thing—a giant sarcophagus, or big box carved out of stone, where the pharaoh's mummified body was originally placed. The whole experience was cool and creepy all at the same time, but we were curious about all the contents originally in these rooms. Our guide told us that many of them could be seen in the Egyptian Museum. The next day we went to the museum and were amazed at all the ancient Egyptian artifacts collected there. We were extra thrilled when we entered the part of the museum that held many of the contents from the tomb of one of the most famous pharaohs, King Tut, including his beautiful burial mask.

These pharaohs were very wealthy with earthly treasures, but God is offering you so much more. Not only does He offer us protection while we are on this world but He also offers us eternal life with Him in heaven! The question is, will you accept it?

The Incredible Victoria Falls

And he showed me a pure river of water of life, clear as crystal, proceeding from the throne of God and of the Lamb. In the middle of its street, and on either side of the river, was the tree of life, which bore twelve fruits, each tree yielding its fruit every month. The leaves of the tree were for the healing of the nations.
REVELATION 22:1, 2, NKJV

As my wife and I drove through the southern part of the African continent, there was one place I really wanted to visit—Victoria Falls. After driving through the Kalahari Desert, my excitement mounted as signs confirmed that we were approaching Victoria Falls. Before arriving at the falls we had to pull over and see the tree with the largest trunk in the world—it was about seventy-five feet around the base! Just off in the background we glimpsed the Zambezi River, which widens to more than a mile before plunging over the falls. The sound of the falls grew much louder as we got closer. Clearly, something huge was up ahead.

When we got there it was breathtaking. At this point, the entire river falls into a gorge, creating a mile-wide sheet of falling water more than 350 feet tall. It was impressive. On the opposite side of the gorge was a long hiking trail that allows you to hike across the full length of the waterfalls. At the midpoint, you can look in each direction and not see the end of the falls, all you see is waterfalls as far as the eye can see. As you can imagine, the sound of a mile of falling water is quite loud.

The interesting thing is that the area immediately around the falls is a lush rain forest because of the never-ending mist in the air. But once you drive a mile or two away from the falls, you are back in the dry desert again. This incredibly lush place reminded me of the river of life and the tree of life mentioned in our verse today in Revelation. Heaven is a special place, and I'm excited to be a child of God because I want to be in that number someday. Don't you?

Walking on Walls

Let no corrupt word proceed out of your mouth, but what is good for necessary edification, that it may impart grace to the hearers.
EPHESIANS 4:29, NKJV

During my visit to Jerusalem, I had one full day to explore the city. I knew of several things I wanted to do that day before returning to Jordan the next morning to resume work at the archeological dig site. Throughout my life I have been taught various Bible stories, many of which took place in Jerusalem. Of course, the city was destroyed and rebuilt over the years, but this was still Jerusalem. Tall walls surrounded the old city, and one of the places on the top of my list to visit was called the Wailing Wall. I had read that one could walk along the ramparts of the city walls and eventually arrive at the Wailing Wall. On average the walls are about forty feet tall and about eight feet thick. I was reminded of how, during biblical times, huge walls provided protection from attack for the citizens of the city. They relied on the walls, and I'm sure every day they walked past them they were grateful for their presence.

In Jerusalem, I was able to locate one of the stairways and follow it to the top of the walls. On the outside is the expansive, modern city of Jerusalem; the inside contains the ancient city streets and buildings. It really made me think of how different the world is.

People used to be able to hide behind city walls and no one could hurt them, but now it's very easy to hurt people. One of the easiest ways is with the words you say or type. It has especially become way too easy for people to make comments on social media because you don't have to say it directly to them. Be careful of the things you post or say to people. Before saying anything, think and ask yourself, "Will this comment serve to build someone up or tear them down?" As a worst-case scenario, if you can't think of anything good to say, the best idea is to just not say anything at all.

The Borrowed Kippah

*Now I saw a new heaven and a new earth, for the first heaven
and the first earth had passed away. Also there was no more sea.
Then I, John, saw the holy city, New Jerusalem, coming down out of
heaven from God, prepared as a bride adorned for her husband.*
REVELATION 21:1, 2, NKJV

In Jerusalem, I finally stood in front of the impressive Wailing Wall, a portion of the foundation of the original temple built by King Herod. King Herod was famously known in the Bible as the king who tried to be sneaky about trying to convince the wise men to tell him where Jesus was. Jewish men are required to cover their head during prayer, and it was required for me so that I could visit the wall. The problem is I didn't have a kippah, but fortunately I was provided with a paper version that was attached to my hair with a bobby pin. As I walked toward the wall, my moment of awe was interrupted when the wind blew and the paper kippah flew off my head. I was quite embarrassed that I had to run after it. I sure didn't want to be disrespectful of their traditions, so I managed to quickly catch up to the kippah and put it back on my head. I held it there with my hand for the remainder of my visit. I did finally make it right up to the wall.

Apparently, Jewish people come here with prayers written on tiny pieces of paper and try to smash them into the cracks between the giant stones in the wall. While doing this, they speak loud prayers and sometimes wails of supplication. I sat there in my chair for several minutes taking it all in. It occurred to me that I was happy that I could talk to God anytime and anywhere. Jewish people love God, but they don't believe Jesus is the Messiah. God is offering the world a place in the heavenly city for those who love and accept Jesus' sacrifice. We have been tasked to teach Jews and all the people of the world about Jesus so that they can have a chance to live in that heavenly city. Do you know what the name of that city is? See today's verse!

Three in One Place

After these things I looked, and behold, a great multitude which no one could number, of all nations, tribes, peoples, and tongues, standing before the throne and before the Lamb, clothed with white robes, with palm branches in their hands, and crying out with a loud voice, saying, "Salvation belongs to our God who sits on the throne, and to the Lamb!"
REVELATION 7:9, 10, NKJV

Before leaving Jerusalem I wanted to visit the Dome of the Rock. This is one of the most important religious locations for three major world religions: Islam, Judaism, and Christianity. Visiting the Dome of the Rock requires preparation. Because it was summer, I was wearing shorts, but I knew that if I wanted to visit the Dome of the Rock, I would not be allowed in with shorts. Near the entrance I stopped, opened my daypack, and pulled out a pair of pants to wear over my shorts. Naturally, I felt funny putting on pants in the middle of the street.

At the entrance there is an area where visitors can borrow the appropriate clothes to wear in order to be allowed to enter. Men have to wear pants, and women have to wear a long dress and a head covering. Finally, I was allowed into the area surrounding the Dome of the Rock and proceeded to go to the spot where a temple stood. The temple was old, but not from Bible times; it was built in the seventh century. Muslims believe this was the spot where, according to tradition, the prophet Muhammad ascended to heaven. For Jews and Christians, they believe it is the location where Abraham almost sacrificed his son, Isaac. For Christians, it is believed to be the location where the original temple was built. Getting into the compound required thorough security screening. Up until 1967, only Muslims were allowed to visit; even while I was there I was not allowed to bring any non-Muslim artifacts or books on site, nor was I allowed to pray there.

The way we dress says a lot. In most cultures, special attire is expected at school or in an office. When we go to worship in God's house, we should dress in a way that shows respect to God. Besides, God says He will have special clothing prepared for you in heaven!

The Unusual Train Ride

For there is one God and one Mediator between
God and men, the Man Christ Jesus.
1 Timothy 2:5, NKJV

Scandinavia is a region of northern Europe that includes Sweden, Norway, and Denmark. We first took a train from central Europe to Denmark, and from Denmark we crossed the Oresund Strait to Sweden. I had assumed the train would go as far as it could go in Denmark and that we would have to get off the train, get on a ferry, cross the Oresund Strait, then board another train and continue our voyage north into Sweden. I was surprised to find the plan was quite different. When the train reached as far as it could go in Denmark, our train car, which was destined for Sweden, was disconnected from the string of train cars, and our particular train car was pushed onto a special ferry designed to carry train cars, along with trucks, cars, and people. Next, the ferry crossed the strait into Sweden, and once again our train car was pushed off the ferry and reconnected to another string of train cars that was waiting for us. Finally, we took off again and continued north. The whole thing happened without us barely noticing what was going on.

One of my friends didn't even wake up during the whole process! When he woke up the following morning as the train continued north, he asked, "Are we still in Denmark?" We told him everything that had happened while he slept. Back in 2000, a bridge was finally built over the strait between Denmark and Sweden. It's one of the longest bridges in Europe now, but before the bridge was built, the way we crossed was the most common way to get across to Sweden.

The Bible says that Jesus is like a bridge between us and God. Our verse today uses the word *mediator*, which means He is a negotiator or a middleman who speaks on our behalf and fights for us. He went as far as dying and taking our punishment in order to save us. Thank you, Jesus!

The Dark Day

*There will be no more night. They will not need the light of
a lamp or the light of the sun, for the Lord God will give
them light. And they will reign for ever and ever.*
REVELATION 22:5, NIV

Our train arrived in Stockholm, Sweden around 6:30 A.M. A few of us had not slept well on the train, so we were pretty tired when we got off the train. It was pitch dark at 7:00 A.M, and we figured lots of sights wouldn't be open yet, so we decided to just hang out in the train station for an hour or so and take a nap. One hour later we looked outside. Even though we figured things would be opening soon, it was still pretty dark, and we didn't feel like heading out quite yet. We decided to wait a while longer. We found something to snack on and dozed on the train station benches, but when we walked outside, it was still mostly dark. We looked at each other and looked at our watches. That was odd. One of my friends wondered, "Is this a different time zone?" No, it was the same time there as in the rest of central Europe. Our watches were right; it was the middle of the morning and it was still very dark. We went back into the train station to wait a little more to see what would happen.

Eventually we figured out that the sun was never going to fully come up that day. We realized that because we were at such a northerly location, the days were much shorter. By late morning the sun popped out, but it never fully climbed to the top of the sky. It hovered over the horizon like a sunset for several hours, and then by 3:00 P.M. it was dark again. It was fun imagining this place in the middle of the summer because the opposite would happen. The sun would come up around 3:00 A.M. and it would set around 10:00 P.M.!

We'd be in trouble if we didn't have the sun. Someday in heaven we won't need a sun and there won't even be night anymore. The Bible says that God Himself will be the provider of light! I can't wait for that day, how about you?

Fjords of Forgiveness

Come now, let us reason together, says the LORD:
though your sins are like scarlet,
they shall be as white as snow;
though they are red like crimson,
they shall become like wool.
ISAIAH 1:18, ESV

When we left Stockholm and traveled to Oslo, Norway, we particularly enjoyed walking up to the ski park where the Olympics took place in 1952. There was plenty of snow on the ground, and a giant ski jump overlooked the city and served as a reminder that the greatest winter Olympians had once gathered there. The following day we decided to travel to the western edge of Norway to a city called Bergen. The interesting thing about this train ride was that in order to get to the city of Bergen, we had to travel through some of the most incredible mountain passes and ranges. On our way to Bergen we even took a little side tram north, to a little village called Flåm, tucked deep into the mountains and fjords of Norway. Very few people lived in this little town, and they were very friendly as we four American strangers wandered into their little town to get the feel of an authentic Norwegian mountain village.

We eventually made it to Bergen on the edge of the frigid North Sea, next to the majestic mountains. Getting there required us to adapt to the conditions in Norway, but the effort was well worth it. During our entire time in Norway, we saw snow everywhere we went. Did you know snow is mentioned in the Bible too? When God wanted to tell us about forgiveness, He used snow as an example. He said that even though our sins were red like the colors scarlet and crimson, when God forgives, our sins will be washed away and will be as white as snow. Getting forgiveness from God allows us to live without guilt as we continue to try to live as Jesus did. Do you need forgiveness from God today? The only one you need to talk to is God.

Journey Through South Germany

"And just as you want men to do to you, you also do to them likewise."
LUKE 6:31, NKJV

My wife and I decided to visit the Romantic Road in the south of Germany. Don't worry, I won't get all mushy on you—the road is not actually romantic, either. The reason they call it the Romantic Road is that there is a string of cute, romantic towns and castles in this part of Germany. Today, it's well known as a tourist attraction. Fortunately, my wife and I went during the month of October when tourism is at a low. The other advantage for going in October was that this part of the country was in full autumn colors. It was beautiful! We joined the Romantic Road in a town called Dinkelsbühl, a beautiful little town at about the midway point. From there we headed south. Each town was unique and had its own personality. Each village we visited felt as though we were entering the Middle Ages. Because of the historic value, these towns have made a lot of effort to preserve the old-world feeling. Some cities have a large cathedral in the center, with plazas and shops and cobblestone streets. Others have beautiful castles overlooking the town. Several towns have a large wall that surrounds the center of the town, which was put there to protect the villagers in the old days.

In some villages we had to park outside of the city walls and walk in to visit and explore. I learned something as I visited those towns. People loved that their history was being visited and celebrated. People take pride in their history. One way to show love and kindness to people is by honoring and respecting their history. Since we all come from somewhere different, it's important to be respectful of each other's differences and backgrounds. I'm sure you've heard of the golden rule in the Bible. It's a simple rule you can use to show respect to every single person around you. Read it; it's the verse for today.

OCTOBER 12

The Castle Visit

"In My Father's house are many mansions; if it were not so, I would have told you. I go to prepare a place for you. And if I go and prepare a place for you, I will come again and receive you to Myself; that where I am, there you may be also."
JOHN 14:2, 3, NKJV

Yesterday I shared with you our trek down the Romantic Road in Germany. At the very southern point of Germany, before entering Austria, is the last town on the romantic road—Füssen. Near Füssen, a beautiful castle is nestled in the Bavarian mountains. The Neuschwanstein Castle is in the rugged foothills of the mountains. It took us awhile, but we hiked up to the castle. This castle was built in the 1800s, making it one of the newest castles in Germany. It is also well known for being the castle that inspired the design of Sleeping Beauty castle in Disneyland, with the soaring towers, high-peaked roofs, and fairy-tale look. Inside, there's a magnificent ballroom, impressive bedrooms, and long halls filled with art and tapestries and huge chandeliers. The castle was built by King Ludwig II, but he died before it was finished. Six months later it became a museum, which means no one has ever really lived in it except for King Ludwig, who slept there eleven times while it was under construction.

After seeing the castle, we discovered that there was a trail that continued even higher into the mountains behind the castle. We were told to follow the path to a narrow bridge over a deep ravine, so up the mountain we trekked. Sure enough, a long bridge spanned a ravine, high above the castle. From the center of the bridge we enjoyed a fantastic view of the castle down below, complete with a couple of lakes and mountains in the background. It was picture perfect!

This place reminded me of the place God is building for us in heaven. The main difference—the most beautiful castles and palaces here on earth can't compare to the place in heaven God is preparing for us! I can't wait!

Canyon to the Treasury

Therefore comfort each other and edify one another, just as you also are doing.
1 THESSALONIANS 5:11, NKJV

While in Jordan I traveled to the ancient ruins of Petra, a desert civilization that was likely formed before the time of Jesus. About fifteen hundred years ago, it was abandoned and forgotten. The location of the city is in a unique canyon setting. We arrived on a bus, and we were dropped off at the entrance. The first thing we had to do was walk down through a long, narrow slot canyon. A slot canyon is a very narrow canyon, sometimes only a few feet wide, but is often a hundred feet tall or more. It is formed when rushing water cuts through the soft sandstone or limestone rock.

After hiking through the slot canyon with my friends for a little while, we suddenly saw a sliver of one of the ancient structures ahead of us. We continued walking until we walked into an opening, where we could see that an elaborate structure had been carved out into the rock. It was called the Treasury, and it is the most famous building in Petra. The treasury is a huge structure, almost 130 feet tall. It's one of the few structures in the world that was carved out of something instead of being built up with materials. Though actually a tomb, one legend says it was called the Treasury because bandits hid their loot in a stone vase carved into the second level. They say locals would come and try to shoot at the vase, hoping to break it and spill out the treasure. In reality, the vase is solid sandstone, but today you can still see all the damage from bullets!

This place made me realize you can build something by building it up or cutting or chiseling it out of something. True friendships are those that help build each other up. Bad friendships are ones that rely on chiseling or cutting each other down. Avoid those friendships; they will cause you pain.

The Intense Desert Climb

"No one is holy like the LORD,
For there is none besides You,
Nor is there any rock like our God."
1 SAMUEL 2:2, NKJV

After marveling over the Treasury in Petra for a while, we moved on, since there is a lot more to see in this amazing place. Fortunately, the friend who was traveling with me was a student studying archaeology, so he knew lot of things about this place. We walked down into a valley where there were countless caves and structures cut out from the rock. He then suggested we should hike up to another amazing structure called the Monastery, which was very similar to the Treasury. He said the hike was long and challenging but that it would be worth it; he added that the Monastery was probably twice as big as the Treasury and also chiseled out of rock. I was already impressed by the size of the Treasury; I couldn't start to imagine how huge and imposing the Monastery would be.

Sure enough, the journey was long and dangerous as we went up the narrow, steep path. At some points we walked along tall cliffs in temperatures that climbed above one hundred degrees. When we got there, the Monastery was truly incredible. It was also carved out of the rock, but it was done in such a way that we were able to climb to the top, 165 feet high! This was by far the largest monument in Petra, and it amazed me that it was still in such great shape after two thousand years. That's because it was made out of rock.

Rocks are solid, which is why God is compared to a rock many times in the Bible. It says God is my rock and my refuge, my fortress and my foundation. Have you ever sung "Rock of Ages" in church? All these are reminders that God is strong and we can lean on Him and always count on Him for strength.

Geared Up on Mt. Hood

Wise friends make you wise,
but you hurt yourself
by going around with fools.
PROVERBS 13:20, CEV

Mount Hood is one of my favorite destinations for outdoor hikes and activities. On one occasion, when I was invited to speak at a church in Portland, Oregon, I booked my return flight a day later in order to have time to make a quick trip to the mountain. The pastor who had invited me to speak at the church was a good friend and agreed to visit Mount Hood with me. I wanted to do something a little different and learned that a fun way to see Mount Hood is by snowshoeing. My friend was up for the challenge, so we made our plans and found a place to rent gear. Soon we arrived at the base of Mount Hood, a place called Government Camp, where we'd rent our gear.

Now there are two things you need to understand about Mount Hood. First of all, it has a bunch of glaciers on it, so there is always a snowy trail somewhere on the mountain, no matter what time of year it is. Second, I had not brought any winter gear with me, so we not only had to rent the snowshoes, we also had to rent boots, coats, and snow pants. We drove up to the highest spot we could reach, parked, and geared up. Over the next several hours, we trudged up the mountain at a slow, even pace. Sometimes we'd have to rest a little. Other times it got so steep that we had to stop to rest every few minutes. The higher we got, the more amazing the view was. For my friend and I, it was an amazing experience to share together.

Friends are a blessing from God, and you should be smart about who you decide to have as friends. Some friends will bring you down and actually make your life miserable. Avoid having these kinds of friends. Select friends who will bring joy to your life. The message from today's Bible verse is as clear as it comes.

An Unforgettable Swim

"Fear not, for I am with you;
Be not dismayed, for I am your God.
I will strengthen you,
Yes, I will help you,
I will uphold you with My righteous right hand."
ISAIAH 41:10, NKJV

While in Hawaii on the island of Oahu, I drove to a marina on the North Shore, where there was a company that offered people a chance to swim with sharks. Yes, you read that correctly, sharks. Don't worry, though; everything involved in this adventure was very safe.

After a short briefing, the boat took off and went about five miles out into the Pacific Ocean. Soon we arrived at the location where the boat would lower a large aluminum cage into the water. The top of the cage was open and had air tanks to keep it afloat. At this time, I was given the thumbs up to enter the cage. I checked all my gear and put my snorkel and mask on tightly. I climbed over the edge of the boat and down into the cage. Once I was in the cage, the boat disconnected the ropes holding the cage against the boat, and the cage started to slowly drift away from the boat. The cage extended down into the water about ten feet. I stuck my face under the water and looked around. We were told the ocean in this spot was several hundred feet deep. That's when I noticed that up from the depths of the ocean came a shark—then a second, a third, and a fourth. For the next twenty minutes, four sharks circled the cage over and over. They seemed curious but not aggressive. One of them was a very large female shark, about thirteen feet long. A few times the sharks passed within a foot or two of the cage, and I got a very close look into the face of a shark and his many rows of teeth. It was scary, but I felt safe and protected.

Our verse today is a reminder that there are times that we will feel fearful. I'm happy God said to not worry because He is with us and will always help us. Ask Him to be with you today.

Geared Up to Almost Fly

Stand therefore, having girded your waist with truth, having put on the breastplate of righteousness, and having shod your feet with the preparation of the gospel of peace; above all, taking the shield of faith with which you will be able to quench all the fiery darts of the wicked one. And take the helmet of salvation, and the sword of the Spirit, which is the word of God.
EPHESIANS 6:14–17, NKJV

While traveling through Denver, Colorado, a few years ago, we stopped by an indoor skydiving place. Indoor skydiving involves entering a large, vertical air tunnel that's about forty feet tall. The walls are made of glass, and the floor is a steel-mesh grill. Under the mesh was one of the largest fans I had ever seen. It was the size of the entire floor! The fan under the floor blows air upward, strong enough to make a person hover. First, they made us watch a video. Although it looks simple, standing above a giant fan while it makes you hover is actually a lot harder than you think. We then practiced a couple of moves, and the instructor showed us some hand signs we'd use. As the video showed us, you have to be perfectly in control of the position of your body; otherwise, the giant fan under your feet can flip you or slam you against the glass walls.

After watching the video, we went to get dressed with the proper gear—a special jumpsuit, a helmet, goggles, and special shoes. The jumpsuit was a little baggy to help catch the wind and hold up the skydiver. After getting all geared up, we got in line. The instructor was there with us the whole time in case we got into trouble, but when my turn came I was able to hover in a stable way and not smash into the walls. Toward the end of my second flight, the instructor joined me and grabbed my jumpsuit and told the fan operator to crank the fan up. We suddenly flew up twenty feet high and did circles and spins; it was a great experience.

Many sports require that we wear special gear to help protect us. God invites us to also wear special gear every day to protect us from Satan's temptations. Check out today's verse for a list of that special gear!

Hope in the Darkness of Humanity

Therefore, if anyone is in Christ, he is a new creation; old things have passed away; behold, all things have become new.
2 CORINTHIANS 5:17, NKJV

One of the most memorable places I've visited has stuck in my memory for terrible reasons. Out of respect for history we decided to visit a German concentration camp in Dachau, Germany, near Munich. During World War II our world witnessed one of the lowest points in human history when the Nazis, led by Hitler, captured and imprisoned millions of Jewish people. The concentration camp I visited was one of many different camps the Nazis set up during the war. Regularly, trains filled with Jewish people would arrive at the camps, where they would be held. By the time the war was over and the Nazis were defeated, millions of Jews had been killed at these camps. Just thinking about this broke my heart.

Even today, it's sad to see terrorists hurting innocent people and claiming it was Allah or God who has told them to do it. Walking around that concentration camp that day was one of the saddest, most somber days I remember, but it made me look to the Bible to find hope. Many terrible things happen when countries decide to declare war against each other, and usually the root of the problem has to do with power.

The sad part is that history repeats itself, and terrible leaders continue to come into power, bringing humanity some of its darkest moments. My challenge to you as you grow up is to be the kind of person or leader who imitates Jesus. His actions clearly showed that love is the most important thing. Each day we should ask God to come into our lives. He will change us and make us new and more like Christ.

One Big Dig

Then God blessed them, and God said to them, "Be fruitful and multiply; fill the earth and subdue it; have dominion over the fish of the sea, over the birds of the air, and over every living thing that moves on the earth."
GENESIS 1:28, NKJV

I recently visited a coal mine in Wyoming. It was an open coal mine. That means it opened on the surface, not underground in caves. It was fascinating to see how this company got coal out of the ground. Enormous excavating machines were used to dig the coal out of the ground; then huge hauling trucks were filled up, and the coal was dumped and crushed to the right size and loaded onto a long line of waiting train cars. The trains would then cart the coal away to be used around the country. This happens twenty-four hours a day. There were several neat lookout points, and one of the highlights of our tour was to check out the huge hauling trucks close up. They were colossal! The tires alone were ten feet tall and could carry almost three hundred tons of coal! I walked all the way around one truck in amazement. It was the size of a small house.

One of the fascinating things about the mine is what they do when a spot runs out of coal. They don't just leave the massive hole there—they fill it back in with dirt. Next, they plant the original types of grasses and trees found in that area across the new surface. During the tour we were shown huge fields. We were told that years ago those fields were deep mines, but now it looked as though nothing had ever happened there. I was very impressed at how much effort they made to return nature as close as possible to its original state after removing the valuable coal.

At creation, God gave humans dominion over our world. It doesn't mean we are free to destroy it. We have been given power and control over it for our benefit. It would make sense to do our best to protect it. We should always do our best to properly manage the things that God has given us.

Surrounded by Reptiles

*"But I tell you, love your enemies and
pray for those who persecute you."*
MATTHEW 5:44, NIV

While in Costa Rica we decided to visit one of the many wonderful national parks in the country, a place called Palo Verde National Park. We were interested in taking one of the unique tours available at the park that highlighted the living creatures found in the wetland areas. We got our tickets and walked down a long, rickety dock to a small boat. Since we had traveled to Costa Rica during the off-season, we had the entire boat to ourselves, along with the driver and a guide.

There are three very distinct things I remember about the ninety minutes we spent on that boat—lots of birds, monkeys, and reptiles. Costa Rica is famous for its bird-watching tours, and monkeys seem to be in practically every tree, but I was surprised by all the reptiles we encountered. As we passed near the shorelines, there was no shortage of little lizards darting around on the branches and fallen tree trunks. Above us, some trees were often crowded with several large iguanas that were at least five feet long. Lastly, in the water all around us there were dozens of crocodiles swimming in the river and basking on the shore. Some of them were big, too! Of course we made sure to keep all of our hands and feet safely on the inside of the boat at all times! The crocodiles were the kings of this jungle!

Being a bully is not cool, but many times bullies are that way because they are hurting on the inside. They won't show it on the outside, so instead they feel that have to put others down around them so they can feel better. A couple of things for you to consider: Don't seek revenge, and don't ignore the problem. Ask for help. Lastly, and this may seem strange, pray for the bully. Remember, the real enemy is Satan.

Trains, Planes, and Taxis

Let him have all your worries and cares, for he is always thinking about you and watching everything that concerns you.

1 PETER 5:7, TLB

I got off the airplane that morning at the Hong Kong airport and took the express tram into the bustling city of Hong Kong. I arrived at the metro station where we exited and quickly got a taxi and asked the driver to take us to the train station in Kowloon, which was on the other side of the city. Our taxi dropped us off in time to catch our train, which would take us a few hours into the mainland of China, to a large city called Guangzhou. A few hours later, we arrived at the train station in Guangzhou. We went outside and immediately boarded a taxi, and I asked the driver to take me to the airport in that city. Forty-five minutes later, we were dropped off at the airport, just in time to catch our flight to a city called Guilin, which was several hours' of flying into the Chinese mainland. After arriving, we exited the airport and found a taxi, showing the driver the name of the hotel we were going to. Our driver took us into the city and dropped us off at our hotel. We got checked in, and soon we were back on the street again, looking for another taxi. Airport taxi drivers could speak a little English, but the regular city taxi drivers couldn't speak a single word of English. They would stop, we'd try to tell them where we wanted to go, but they didn't understand.

In the last few hours we had been on two airplanes, two trains, and we were looking to ride our fourth taxi. It was quite frustrating to get so far and then get stuck. Getting stuck is part of life. Sometimes we get stuck in traffic, you get stuck on a project, you get stuck on a level of a video game, you get stuck on a bad team at school. What to do? You have a choice. You can decide to get stressed out about it, or you can choose to pray, leave it in God's hands, and not worry about it. Yes, worrying is a choice. I don't recommend it!

Going Nowhere Fast

"Look, he is coming with the clouds,"
and "every eye will see him,
even those who pierced him";
and all peoples on earth "will mourn because of him."
So shall it be! Amen.
REVELATION 1:7, NIV

Several years ago my wife and I accumulated enough frequent flier miles to take our family to South America. We had already visited Chile, Peru, and Argentina, so we both agreed that the first place to visit was Brazil. We also decided that on this trip we'd visit a few new parts of Argentina and Chile. We arranged vacation time and booked our tickets to Rio de Janeiro, Brazil, as our first stop. Our trip wouldn't happen for six more months, so we had plenty of time to plan.

When the date came, we packed up our things and drove to the airport in Chicago. As we walked up to the counter, we assumed everything was going as planned, but we had a big surprise in store for us. When we arrived at the counter, we gave the woman our tickets and passports. Then she asked us, "Where is your visa?" My wife and I looked at each other. *Visa?* A visa is a document that gives you permission to enter a country. I soon discovered that sometime between the time I had booked the ticket and the travel day, Brazil had started a new requirement that U.S. visitors had to have a visa to enter. When they told us what was required to get a visa, we knew it would take us at least a week to get it. You can imagine how disappointed we were. Fortunately, the airline was able to reroute our tickets, and we went straight to Argentina.

Have you ever heard of the Great Disappointment? One of our church's founding fathers, William Miller, calculated that the Second Coming would be on October 22, 1844. Many people accepted his calculations and were extremely disappointed when Jesus did not come. We need to be prepared every day, because Jesus will come soon!

Passage to West Berlin

Yes, there is a time and a way for everything, though man's trouble lies heavy upon him; for how can he avoid what he doesn't know is going to happen?
ECCLESIASTES 8:6, 7, TLB

It was 1989, and one of the first places we wanted to visit was West Berlin, West Germany. Where did the "west" come from? Today, the city is simply called Berlin, but in 1989, Berlin was actually two different cities, East Berlin and West Berlin. In 1961, political changes caused the city to be divided, and the Berlin Wall was built around the "free" side of Berlin. The wall was still there when I visited in 1989, and we decided we wanted to go see it during that trip. Getting to West Berlin was a little complicated, though, since it was completely surrounded by East Germany, where tourists weren't allowed. We decided that the best option was to try to hitchhike in. We took the train as close as we could get to the border, then we walked to the onramp that took cars to the highway to West Berlin. The four of us stood at the edge of the road and put our thumbs out. To our disappointment, no one stopped. We arrived at that spot at 7:00 P.M. and by 4:00 A.M., we were still there—cold, hungry, and frustrated. By 5:00 A.M. we had decided to come up with a different plan—we'd split up. Two guys would hitchhike from a different spot, while the other two would stay there. Since our original plan was to stay in the basement of the Adventist church in West Berlin, we agreed to meet up at the church in twelve hours. We split up, and within an hour we were picked up; we were finally headed to West Berlin! Fortunately, our two friends were also able to get a ride pretty quick, and by that afternoon we had reunited at the church in West Berlin.

We tend to conclude that our timing and plan is the perfect timing and plan. The reality is that God's timing is always right. That means when we have to patiently sit and wait for God, it's really a test of faith. God knows the big picture; trust in God's timing!

A Part of History

Remember that you were at that time separate from Christ, excluded from the commonwealth of Israel, and strangers to the covenants of promise, having no hope and without God in the world.
EPHESIANS 2:12, NASB

Just as we met up with our friends at the Adventist church, we were told something was happening at the Berlin Wall. There was talk that after so many years, the wall was finally going to open up. When we got there, thousands of people were gathered at the Brandenburg Gate, one of the most famous spots along the Berlin Wall that surrounded West Berlin. We pushed as close to the wall as we could and got to within one hundred feet of it. Off to the right there was a park with some trees, so we went over to the trees. Four or five other people had climbed the trees to get a better view, so I did the same. From up in the tree I could easily see over the wall to an area called the Death Strip, where people weren't allowed to cross or they risked getting shot by snipers. After being up there for quite some time, I heard some announcements in German over a loud speaker, and then shortly after that I saw something that shocked me. From the other side of the Death Strip I saw a guy running through the Death Strip toward the wall on our side! I was terrified for him because he could get shot for crossing! Moments later, he jumped up on the wall with his arms in the air, and the crowd cheered. Over the next few minutes it was chaotic as people from both sides started climbing the wall. The wall was as wide as a sidewalk in that spot, so there was plenty of room for lots of people to climb up and stand there. We were in awe as we watched this whole historic event unfold.

It's sad that East and West Berlin were separated for so many years. It's also sad that we have been separated from our Creator even longer. When Jesus died on the cross for us, He tore down the wall that separated us. Now we can live knowing that we will be reunited with Him!

The Ultimate Celebration

And God will wipe away every tear from their eyes; there shall be no more death, nor sorrow, nor crying. There shall be no more pain, for the former things have passed away.
REVELATION 21:4, NKJV

I have shared with you the story of being at the Berlin Wall, and how I perched up in a tree to watch as people from both sides of the wall climbed onto the wall and celebrated the end of the separation between East and West Germany. After twenty-eight years, Germany was reunited. I climbed down from the tree, and we decided to see if we could also climb up on this historic wall. Before we knew it, we were giving each other a boost so we could get up on the wall. I was the last one after making sure everyone else got up, but now there was no one to give me a boost. Suddenly, a total stranger grabbed me by my legs and lifted me up high enough for my friends on the wall the reach me. They pulled me up, and we joined the celebration on the wall. People were singing, hugging, and crying because the two Germanys were finally together again. People could now reunite after decades apart. The feeling up on that wall was that of a giant family reunion.

I have been to events where people are happy and joyful: family reunions, NFL games where the home team scores the winning touchdown, deafening international soccer matches. But the joy and celebration on the wall was much more intense. It was a celebration and reunion that had been on hold for twenty-eight years, and even though most of the people on the wall didn't know each other, they were overwhelmed with joy. I remember everyone breaking out into song, but I didn't know the song. I was so overwhelmed by the moment, I started singing anyway.

Being united after being separated is a powerful experience. Someday soon we will be reunited with God. There will be no more separation, no more tears, no more pain, no more death. It will be much greater than our celebration on the wall, and the reunion will last forever!

The Crossing

Cease from anger, and forsake wrath;
Do not fret—it only causes harm.
PSALM 37:8, NKJV

As we celebrated that day on the Berlin Wall we watched something we thought we'd never see—people were freely moving back and forth over the wall between the east and the west sides of the city. All of a sudden it hit us that if we climbed off the wall on the east side of the wall, we would officially be in East Berlin. We never dreamed this would be possible! We convinced ourselves to climb down, and for an hour or so we walked around East Berlin. We didn't want to stay too long, so we headed back to the wall so that we could safely get back to "our" side of the wall. When we got there we were a bit surprised to find that a large part of the crowd had already been cleared out by the police. Off to the side we were excited to see that someone had taken a barricade and stood it up against the wall like a ladder. This provided an easy method for us to get back over the wall. I was the last one to go over, but as I started to climb a man suddenly ran up to the wall a few feet away from me, took out a metal stick, and started hitting the wall with it. I figured he was venting his anger at the wall, but a minute later, a few pieces of the wall fell to the ground. He dropped his stick, picked up the pieces, and ran off. It hit me—he wasn't angry; he was collecting pieces of the east side of the Berlin Wall. Immediately, without thinking, I jumped down and did the same thing.

Anger clouds our minds. The man at the wall who I thought was angry was actually thinking very clearly. It turns out that the souvenir pieces of rocks we both got that day from the rare east side of the wall were very valuable. Do you have a short temper? Do you get angry easily? Our verse today is a reminder that we must resist anger; it only causes harm.

An Incredible Destination

So overflowing is his kindness toward us that he took away all
our sins through the blood of his Son, by whom we are saved.
EPHESIANS 1:7, TLB

In yesterday's devotion, I told you about our long and challenging trek to reach a unique place in China. We managed to hail several taxis but couldn't tell them where we wanted to go. I did not speak their language, and they did not speak mine. Since I speak a few languages, I tried all of them to see if one driver could understand any of them, but none worked. I finally had an idea. I pulled out my travel journal and began to draw a picture of where we wanted to go. I'm not an artist, but he was able to understand my sketch, and soon we were finally on our way out of the city. In the distance I could see our final destination!

Soon we were dropped off at the edge of the Li River, and we boarded a low, flat boat and headed upriver. To our joy and delight, we had finally made it to our destination! We were now surrounded by the mysterious limestone mountain formations of the Li River valley! The entire journey from the airport in Hong Kong to the Li River boat had been done all in the same day! It was an amazing journey with many steps and challenges along the way. That day we rode on trains, cars, boats, buses, trams, and airplanes in order to reach our destination.

God has invited each one of us to an amazing destination—heaven. But since we have fallen in sin, there is a penalty to pay. The good news is that Jesus took away our sins with His blood; it's as though He paid the price for our ticket to heaven. We don't have to buy any tickets or draw pictures of our destination. Everything has been paid for, and all we have to do is accept this free ticket. Will you accept this free ticket today?

A Difficult Path

"Enter by the narrow gate; for wide is the gate and broad is the way that leads to destruction, and there are many who go in by it. Because narrow is the gate and difficult is the way which leads to life, and there are few who find it."
MATTHEW 7:13, 14, NKJV

A few years ago I stood at the base of Mount St. Helens, getting ready to hike. The sun was about to rise, and we had a full day ahead of us in order to make it to the rim of the crater. The violent eruption had caused a massive landslide that now left a mile-wide crater at the top of the mountain. Our goal was to climb to the rim of the volcano, about eight thousand three hundred feet above sea level. The first part of the climb was mostly flat, easy, and wooded. Soon there were no more trees, and we entered the next type of terrain—big, jagged boulders. Next, we were faced with powdery pumice, which was hard to walk through. We continued to climb, hour after hour, until we finally reached a large, snowy section of the mountain. The snow was a welcome sight because it was much easier to hike on the snow than on the large boulders or pumice.

The new challenge was that we now had reached a very steep part of the climb. With the slippery snow, we had to be extra careful. We had to slam our boots hard into the snowpack in order to get enough of a grip to take the next step. One missed step would cause us to lose traction and slide down the steep mountainside. Soon we even encountered crevasses—huge cracks in the snow pack that we did not want to fall into.

Though this seemed dangerous, was there any better way to proceed? The Bible tells us that there is a path in the world that leads to destruction, and many people follow that trail. On the other hand, it says there's also a narrow path that leads to life. This is the more difficult path. I'm pretty sure you follow what the Bible is saying. Following God will not always be the easiest path, but you can be sure that it's the path that will lead to happiness, joy, love, and life.

Journey to the Crater

*All Scripture is given by inspiration of God, and is profitable for doctrine,
for reproof, for correction, for instruction in righteousness.*
2 TIMOTHY 3:16, NKJV

After passing the steep portion of our climb of Mount St. Helens, we were able to put our snowshoes on and continue climbing in the snow. The snowshoes helped a lot because they spread our weight out on the snow and prevented us from sinking deep in the snow. Our snowshoes also had large claws under the toes, which gave us extra traction. Although the location and the adventure were exciting, the actual activity was reduced to hours of putting one foot in front of the other, tens of thousands of times.

It was early evening when we finally reached the summit and stared out over the enormous crater before us. In the middle, a huge lava dome was continually forming as clouds of sulfuric gases rose from the crater. There were no words to describe the incredible view from the rim of the crater. It had taken us the majority of the day to get there, and we had not brought camping gear, so we now needed to get off the mountain in a hurry. Our guide introduced us to a very simple way down called glissading. We climbed back down to the steep snowpack and simply sat down on the snow and slid most of the way back down the mountain on our bottoms. The important part was to make sure we kept our eyes open for rocks or boulders hidden in the snow. In about an hour we slid most of the way down a mountain that had taken us all day to climb!

Snowshoes weren't the only gear we used that day. We had special boots, walking poles, pants, jackets, gloves, packs, and other things that helped us make the journey. God has also provided us the perfect gear for our journey through life—the Holy Bible. It has inspiration and promises; it teaches truth, corrects us, showing us how to improve and how to do what's right. I don't climb a mountain without gear, just as I wouldn't dare go through life without the Bible.

Back in Time

"When a foreigner resides among you in your land, do not mistreat them. The foreigner residing among you must be treated as your native-born. Love them as yourself, for you were foreigners in Egypt. I am the LORD your God."
LEVITICUS 19:33, 34, NIV

A while back, my wife and I decided that we wanted to plan a visit up north to Mackinac Island in Lake Huron. Mackinac Island is right between the Upper and Lower Peninsula of Michigan, and it's listed as a National Historic Landmark. When the weekend for our trip to Mackinac Island arrived, we packed the car and drove the six hours north to Mackinaw City, on the coast of Lake Huron. We bought our tickets and boarded the ferry. This ferry held lots of bikes but no cars. When we arrived we also noticed that there were no motorized vehicles to be found anywhere. We soon learned that motorized vehicles have been prohibited on the island for more than one hundred years! The only vehicles allowed were emergency and service vehicles and, in the winter, snowmobiles.

There is only one small town on the island, and we saw that all travel was either by foot, bicycle, or horse-drawn carriage. There was an eight-mile road around the entire island, M-185, which happens to be the only state highway in the United States that doesn't allow motorized vehicles! As we walked through the quaint little town we quickly realized another thing this island was famous for—fudge! Of course, we had to try some. One of the other main features on the island is the Grand Hotel. It's a huge, historic, Victorian-era hotel that overlooks the lake, which to this day continues to fill up rooms since it was built in 1887.

Everywhere we went, the people were super nice and friendly. Someday, strangers may come visit your community. The Bible says we are to treat foreigners kindly. It even says we are to love them as we love ourselves. Satan has worked hard to put a "fear of foreigners" in people's hearts. Instead, God encourages us to choose love when a stranger is among you.

A Mammoth Adventure

"Be strong and of good courage, do not fear nor be afraid of them; for the LORD your God, He is the One who goes with you. He will not leave you nor forsake you."
DEUTERONOMY 31:6, NKJV

Have you ever been to Mammoth Cave National Park in Kentucky? During my visit we signed up for an exciting wild cave tour. No nicely paved trail, no nicely lit passages, and almost no smooth walking surfaces for the next six or seven hours; it would definitely be an exciting adventure! I put on my heavy lug sole boots and geared up with headlamps, kneepads, elbow pads, and heavy gloves. The group had about a dozen people, and our two guides would lead us to some of the most exciting and hard-to-reach areas of this enormous cave system. They estimate that there are more than one thousand miles of caves there, most of which have never been mapped or explored. This was no ordinary tour, and we had plenty of questions about what was going to happen during the tour.

We knew that we were in for some interesting moments because, before we left, the guides measured our chests to make sure we would fit through some small openings we would encounter. One of the men was a little larger and he barely qualified to be on the tour. We wondered how this tour would go for him, since he insisted on coming even though his size was right on the edge. Since we were going to spend so many hours down there, we even had to bring a small lunch and a water bottle. We also wondered if the batteries on our headlamps were going to last long enough. The idea of getting stuck down there in darkness was creepy.

We often have lots of questions and concerns when we are facing things that are unknown. That is a natural human reaction, especially when we feel as though we are facing the unknown alone. The good news is that we're never alone. God promises that He is always with us. What a relief!

Small, Scary Spaces

He restores my soul;
He leads me in the paths of righteousness
For His name's sake.
PSALM 23:3, NKJV

When we began our wild cave tour at Mammoth Cave National Park in Kentucky, one of the first challenges we encountered was a long crawl on our bellies that ended with an extremely tight push through an opening that was barely big enough to fit our bodies through. We learned that this was basically a "gut check" for the tour, and it was the reason they had measured our chests before coming down. As the larger man in our group reached the far end of that crawl, he became stuck. The guides immediately went to help him. We could hear him pushing, grunting, and wheezing as he tried to get through the opening. We were about three hundred feet below the surface, so there was no one else around to help this man, plus battery power on our headlamps was limited. After about ten minutes, two women on the tour started to panic.

By the time the man finally made it through, the two women were so freaked out they needed to be evacuated. One of the two guides was forced to backtrack with them to the surface while we continued forward though the cave system, except now we only had one guide in the very front. I was asked to bring up the rear of our expedition. During another crawl later that day, we came across another space that was so tight that the only way though was to turn our helmet to a certain angle in order to get through the opening that was only about nine inches wide. Since I was the last person on the tour, I could have gone off on my own to explore, but do you think that would have been a good idea? No way.

Why would we try to go down our own path in life? Satan would love it if you followed him down the wrong path. But the God who created you has offered to lead you, and you can be sure that He will never lead you down the wrong path.

The Twenty-Four-Hour Visa

"Do not lay up for yourselves treasures on earth, where moth and rust destroy and where thieves break in and steal; but lay up for yourselves treasures in heaven, where neither moth nor rust destroys and where thieves do not break in and steal."
MATTHEW 6:19, 20, NKJV

While studying in France, we were given two weeks off to explore Europe, so I joined up with four other buddies and we rented a car to tour Eastern Europe. At that time, communists ruled in several eastern European countries, and opportunities to visit those places were very rare. We thought it would be educational to visit a place living under the communist rule, so we decided to visit Czechoslovakia. Today, this country doesn't exist, because after communism fell, it divided into two countries, Slovakia and the Czech Republic. During our expedition, it was still one communist country. Part of the requirements to enter was to convert a minimum of ten U.S. dollars into their money to spend there.

After fulfilling all the requirements, we excitedly received a visa to visit the country—for twenty-four hours. We drove to the capital, Prague—a beautiful city. There was no commercialism there like in North America. There was nothing to buy or sell. No one could have their own business. When it came time to spend our ten dollars, we discovered there was nothing to buy! The only thing we found was an ice-cream stand that charged five cents per cone. I think we each ate four or five cones, but we still had to leave with most of our Czech money because there was nothing to buy. Once we left, we never found anyone to trade our Czech money back into U.S. dollars.

Even though it's been more than twenty-five years, I still have my Czech money. Of course, the money is worthless since that country doesn't exist anymore. As a matter of fact, everything on this earth will someday have no value. Earthly treasures are temporary. I suggest we instead focus on heavenly treasures!

Picture Trouble

*And be kind to one another, tenderhearted, forgiving
one another, even as God in Christ forgave you.*
EPHESIANS 4:32, NKJV

The day after visiting Czechoslovakia, we got a special visa so we could visit the Eastern European country called Hungary. Things in communist countries were different, so we were fascinated with many of the things we saw. After arriving in Budapest, I pulled up to a stoplight, and to our left we noticed the Turkish Embassy. At the front there was a huge gate with several heavily armed soldiers standing guard. It was an interesting sight to see so many weapons, so my friend in the backseat decided to pull out his camera and take a picture of the soldiers. Just then I pulled away from the light. A minute later I was pulled over by the Turkish soldiers. I was the driver, so I had to answer to the guard. The problem was that I didn't speak Turkish and he didn't speak English. We were stuck! I knew it was a long shot, but I asked him if he knew Spanish. Nope. My French was pretty rough, but he didn't know any French at all. I turned to the other four guys in the car and asked if anyone else knew any other languages. One of them spoke Korean. That didn't work. My Jamaican friend spoke Patois, but that didn't help at all.

Finally, one of the guys spoke a little German, and we were relieved that the guard also spoke a little German—enough to sort out the problem. We were not supposed to take photos of the soldiers as they guarded the embassy because it was a security breach. We apologized, and we were released.

Everyone makes mistakes—some big, some small. When we make a mistake, it's important to own our mistake and ask for forgiveness. If others make mistakes, we are to forgive them too, even if they don't ask for forgiveness. I know that's hard, but when love and kindness rule, that's what you do. It's what Jesus did as He hung on the cross.

Stuck in Hungary

My little children, these things I write to you, so that you may not sin. And if anyone sins, we have an Advocate with the Father, Jesus Christ the righteous.
1 John 2:1, NKJV

In yesterday's devotion, I shared about our little run-in with the Turkish soldiers. Something else happened that same day in Hungary. We were very excited that we were visiting Hungary, but the problem would be in leaving Hungary. You see, that same day, one of the guys traveling in our group had lost his little traveling belt pack. Inside was his U.S. passport, his visa to enter and exit Hungary, all his money, and his camera. This was not good. Being in a communist country without any documentation was a very bad situation to be in. He would not be allowed to leave the country without an exit visa, and you had to have a passport to have an exit visa. He had neither. What would we do?

We went directly to the U.S. Embassy in Budapest and talked to someone who helped us. It turns out that they had a process where our friend could get a new passport in one day. Once we had that, we spent the following day getting a new exit visa from Hungary so that we could leave. During this time, our friend completely depended on the other four of us traveling with him. Without us he had nothing. No money, no documentation, nothing. Of course, we all pitched in and covered his costs for the rest of the trip. We even shared our pictures with him.

It felt good to know that we had an advocate at the embassy when we got into trouble. The employee worked to get us out of the mess we were in. An advocate is someone who stands up and defends us and pleads on our behalf. My friend was also grateful we were there to be his advocates too. When we sinned, Jesus stepped up as our Advocate. Not only did He fight to defend us, He also died to save us. Jesus is the ultimate Advocate. Thank Him today!

It's a Small World

Two are better than one,
Because they have a good reward for their labor.
For if they fall, one will lift up his companion.
But woe to him who is alone when he falls,
For he has no one to help him up.
ECCLESIASTES 4:9, 10, NKJV

During the year I lived in France, one of the easiest ways of getting around was by hitchhiking. I know that may sound kind of creepy and dangerous, but at that time and place, hitchhiking was as common as taking a bus, and probably more reliable. One day I was trying to catch a ride from the outskirts of Geneva, Switzerland to the city center. I was picked up fairly quickly by an older woman who was also on her way to Geneva's city center—usually a ten- to fifteen-minute ride. She asked where I was from; I told her I was an American student studying language nearby in France. Somehow the topic came up that I also spoke Spanish. Next, she asked how it was that I also spoke Spanish since I lived in the United States. I told her that my parents were of Hispanic descent. She asked which country they were from, and I told her that my mother was Cuban and my father was Chilean. Next, she told me that her son had lived in Chile for a short time and that he liked it there. I asked her which city he had lived in and she replied, Chillán. I was quite shocked, because that was the same city my father had grown up in. Over the next few minutes we discovered that her son had really enjoyed his experience in Chile because this one family had gone out of their way to make his time there pleasant. When she said the names of the people, I was completely shocked—they were my aunt and uncle!

You are going to meet lots of people in your life and make lots of friends. Friendships are a blessing from God, but don't take them for granted. Friendships are a two-way street. You must be loyal and never break trust in order to expect the same thing in return.

The Troubled Hiker

"But whoever drinks the water I give them will never thirst. Indeed, the water I give them will become in them a spring of water welling up to eternal life."
JOHN 4:14, NIV

Before hiking down the Grand Canyon, one of the most important factors of our hike was to make sure we had plenty of water. There were many signs around each trailhead warning hikers to make sure they took enough water. By late afternoon we were on our way back up the canyon after finishing our filming. As we hiked up, we took breaks every once in a while in a shady spot. We were still about an hour from the rim when all of a sudden a young woman came around the corner on her way up the canyon by herself. She was about seventeen years old, and I sensed something was wrong. As she passed by, I stopped her and asked, "Excuse me, are you OK?" That's when I noticed she was in tears and something was clearly wrong. She cried even more as she told me that her family had decided they would hike down into the canyon but didn't think they would need to bring any water since they'd only be gone a couple of hours. This was clearly a huge mistake her family had made. People had died of dehydration on this trail before. She finally decided to leave her family behind and turn around and head back to the rim to find water. She looked dangerously dehydrated, and her lips were cracked. I told her, "It's still another hour to the rim; you better drink some of my water." At that moment a look of shock came over her face, and she started to cry even more. "Are you serious? You're willing to share your water with me?" I responded, "Of course. You really need to get some water in you so you can make it to the rim." She eagerly gulped the water, and then out of nowhere she hugged me. "Thank you so much, sir!" she said, still crying. And before she left she also said, "May God bless you!"

When we are a blessing to others, God has promised to bless us too. Go out today and be a blessing to others!

Egyptian Bus Stop

"Behold, I stand at the door and knock. If anyone hears My voice and opens the door, I will come in to him and dine with him, and he with Me."
REVELATION 3:20, NKJV

Our first day in Egypt, my three friends and I found ourselves in the middle of Cairo with a plan to go visit the pyramids of Giza. But we couldn't find the bus that would take us there. As you know, many countries have a different language but still use the same number symbols we do in North America. But Egypt doesn't. Their numbers are totally different, so it took us awhile to find the correct bus stop. After fifteen minutes, we saw a bus approaching in the distance with the number symbol we were looking for. This was our bus!

As we looked to the right where our bus was approaching, all the other people waiting at our bus stop suddenly started to run to the left, away from the oncoming bus! *What was going on?* The bus never stopped; it only slowed down. A moment later it passed us and caught up to the people who were now running alongside the bus at about the same speed. In a flash, the people running alongside the bus jumped onto the bus, and the bus sped off. It all happened so quickly, and we realized we had just missed our bus. We missed it because we didn't know the system. Twenty minutes later, another bus came, and this time we boarded it successfully and made it to the pyramids!

Getting to heaven doesn't require us to be aware of any special systems, characters, or languages. God doesn't want us to "miss the bus," so He's made it very simple for us to get to heaven. Jesus knocks on the door of your heart every day. Every day you must answer the door and decide if you will accept Jesus into your heart by asking Him to be part of everything you do that day. What will you decide for today?

Five Guys and a Movie

For I am not ashamed of the gospel of Christ, for it is the power of God to salvation for everyone who believes, for the Jew first and also for the Greek
ROMANS 1:16, NKJV

One of my favorite European cities is Salzburg, Austria. Yes, it sits in one of the most picturesque settings in Europe. Yes, it is a city that is rich in history, art, and music. Yes, it is a city famous because Mozart lived and worked there. Yes, it's famous for its towering fortress perched up on a rock overlooking every part of the city.

Even though these are all wonderful reasons to love Salzburg, I must confess that I enjoyed Salzburg because of another reason. Before I tell you the reason, let me tell you a little about my childhood. Like other kids growing up in the 1970s, I didn't have the option of renting DVDs or streaming movies on the Internet. We didn't even have remote controls. Once in a while, my mom and my sister would get excited because one of their favorite movies would be broadcast on TV—*The Sound of Music*. Naturally, I joined my mom and sister to watch the movie, and it became a tradition to watch it whenever it was broadcast. Fast-forward fifteen years. I was studying in France and touring Europe with four friends. As we neared Salzburg, we started talking about the different things to see there. We were pleasantly surprised to learn that all five of us had grown up watching *The Sound of Music* on TV, and we were all a little embarrassed to admit that we were secretly hoping to visit some of the locations seen in the movie. When we arrived in Salzburg, we spent the entire time looking for the places where the movie had been filmed.

Sometimes people feel embarrassed and ashamed about being a Christian, but we shouldn't. Satan is trying to make you feel ashamed, because he doesn't want you telling others about the joy that is in your heart. Don't fall for his tricks. Proudly live the gospel of Christ everywhere you go!

The Sea of Ice

And do not be conformed to this world, but be transformed by the renewing of your mind, that you may prove what is that good and acceptable and perfect will of God.
ROMANS 12:2, NKJV

I recently visited France with my family, and we went to visit the Mer de Glace, or the Sea of Ice. It's a fitting name because it is the largest glacier in the western Alps. The glacier is located deep in the French Alps, so we had to drive to a town called Chamonix, which lies in a valley surrounded by tall mountain peaks. The glacier was on the other side of a mountain from Chamonix. Chamonix is a charming town that has hosted the winter Olympics twice. When we arrived in Chamonix, we then had to find a small train depot at the edge of the town that had a unique little old train that would take visitors up and over the mountains.

We bought our ticket and waited for the old wooden train to arrive. Soon we were on our way climbing up the steep mountainside. The train went through tunnels, forests, and along sharp cliffs as it climbed more than two thousand eight hundred feet toward the glacier. The train finally pulled into a little station on the other side of the mountain. As we exited the station, the sidewalk led us right to the edge of an incredible overlook. In front of us was the glacier, extending four miles down the mountain in an impressive, yes, sea of ice. The glacier is constantly moving downhill from the pressure of its own weight and gravity. Some parts of the glacier are up to six hundred feet deep, so imagine how heavy that much ice would be as it slowly slides downhill. As it slides downhill, huge cracks, called crevasses, form. From the lookout there was more to explore, including a chairlift that goes right down to the ice field! From there, we could visit a cave that is cut out of the ice each year!

Pressure from gravity pushes a glacier down a mountain, but destructive peer pressure from your friends and from this world can really mess up your life. Don't get tricked into following this world; follow God instead!

My Olympic Experience

And whatever you do in word or deed, do all in the name of the
Lord Jesus, giving thanks to God the Father through Him.
COLOSSIANS 3:17, NKJV

In 1996 the Summer Olympics took place in the United States, near the city of Atlanta, Georgia, where my wife's parents were living at the time. With the Olympics so near my in-laws, we decided to plan an Olympic adventure. About six months before the Olympics, I bought tickets to five Olympic sporting events.

Our Olympic adventures started by driving from Michigan to Maryland. The plan was to meet my brother and his wife and together attend an Olympic soccer doubleheader—that's when two matches are played back to back. First, we saw a women's match, then a men's match. The next day, we drove from Maryland to Georgia. In the morning we took the MARTA—the public transportation system that goes from the suburbs to the city center, where the events were mostly taking place. The first day, we went to a baseball game to watch the Cuban national baseball team. It was a lot of fun because we also got tickets for my in-laws and two other relatives, who are Cuban. The second and third days we went to a basketball and volleyball game. On the fourth day in Atlanta we went to our final Olympic event, tennis. This event took place north of Atlanta near a place called Stone Mountain. This was an exciting final day, because we got to see several professional tennis players compete. The tennis tickets were good for all events that day, so we were able to enjoy watching several well-known tennis players in action all in one place.

Athletes at the Olympics represent the best athletes in the entire world. These people commit to doing their best in their sport. I'm sure you've been told many times to always do your best, but today I want to challenge you not only to do your best but to do it in a way that honors God.

An Explosive Day

*Then God blessed the seventh day and sanctified it, because in
it He rested from all His work which God had created and made.*
GENESIS 2:3, NKJV

After attending the five Olympic events, we were sad our time there was coming to a close. As a celebration of our time there, that final Friday we decided to spend the day in downtown Atlanta at the Centennial Olympic Park, a twenty-one-acre park developed for the Olympics. One of the unique features in the park is the Fountain of Rings, an interactive fountain that is computer controlled to create a synchronized show of squirting water and music. On hot days, kids can play in the middle of the jetting fountains.

After visiting the park for several hours, we looked at the time and saw that the sun would be setting soon, so we headed home since we wanted to observe the Sabbath hours. The following morning we heard about some very shocking news that rattled the entire Olympic Games. A man had gone to the center of the Centennial Olympic Park, where he planted and detonated a bomb, killing several people and injuring more than a hundred others. We later discovered that only a few hours before the bomb was detonated, we had been hanging around that exact same spot where the bomb had gone off. The fact that my wife and I had insisted on honoring the Sabbath day, and leaving the Olympic village before sunset, may have saved our lives.

How do you keep the Sabbath? It's a question we each have to answer. The Sabbath is a special and specific day God has asked us to keep separate and special from the other six. It was given to us as a gift, a special day when we can show God our love, obedience, and respect. The Sabbath is a specific day of the week—it's the seventh day, also called Saturday. Some people think it's OK to keep any day of the week holy, but God was very specific about which day to keep. In my case, honoring that commandment may have saved my life.

Ancient Mysteries

*For you yourselves know perfectly that the day
of the Lord so comes as a thief in the night.*
1 THESSALONIANS 5:2, NKJV

If you've ever been to England, one of the first things you may have noticed is that they drive on the opposite side of the road than we do in North America—and the driver's side is on the right side of the car. The first time I visited England I went by train, but the second time I decided to rent a car. I knew this would be a bit of an adventure, but I concluded that I could adjust to the driving. Within the first ten minutes, I had my first minor problem. While driving down a very narrow street in London, I got a little too close to the cars on the left side, and my left side-view mirror clipped the side-view mirror of a parked car.

Our first stop on that trip was to a place called Stonehenge. Maybe you've heard of it. Stonehenge is an ancient monument a few hours outside of London made up of a collection of large stones. Historians think they are more than four thousand years old, but the most intriguing thing about the site is the fact that no one really knows what the meaning or purpose for this monument was. The culture responsible for the construction of Stonehenge didn't leave any kind of written record, so there are many myths surrounding the stones. When we arrived, we parked the car at the visitor's center and walked a short way to the monument. Tourists are only allowed to walk around the perimeter of the stone, but it's still very exciting being around something that is so old. There are many mysteries about this site that will never be known this side of heaven.

One of the greatest mysteries is the question about when Jesus will return. People have tried to calculate and guess, but the Bible clearly says that only God knows. Our job is to be ready every day by living each day completely for God.

The Tea Story

*Put on the whole armor of God, that you may be
able to stand against the wiles of the devil.*
EPHESIANS 6:11, NKJV

We landed in Cusco, Peru, high in the Andean mountains, more than eleven thousand feet above sea level. Cusco is a beautiful, historic city where you are greeted with very thin air because of the high elevation. Some people get sick under these conditions, but it didn't affect me. I found it interesting that after getting off the airplane, you are immediately greeted with a person who offers you a free cup of tea. You are encouraged to drink it because they have discovered that this particular type of tea has positive effects in dealing with altitude sickness. As soon as we arrived at the hotel and walked into the lobby, we were again served this same tea, free. On the street, vendors were selling the tea, and that evening at our restaurant we sat down and, without asking, the server automatically brought us a cup of tea to start with. Clearly the people there in Cusco wanted to do everything possible to keep us from getting altitude sickness.

I've been to higher altitudes in the past and never gotten sick, but I was still grateful to the people, and I went along with the "tea medicine" while I was there. The surprise came later when I decided to ask what kind of tea I was drinking. They nonchalantly said the tea was made from coca leaves— which are used to make the dangerous drug called cocaine. The leaves have to go through a rigorous chemical process in order to make the drug, but I was still quite alarmed when I found out about this.

All that time I thought I was putting something good in my body, but was I? Satan works like that; he's always sneaking and deceiving. He's always trying to hide the truth. If you want to stand up to Satan's tricks, put on the armor of God today. His armor is things like truth, righteousness, peace, faith, the Word of God, and prayer.

The Journey to Machu Picchu

Therefore, my beloved brethren, be steadfast, immovable, always abounding in the work of the Lord, knowing that your labor is not in vain in the Lord.
1 CORINTHIANS 15:58, NKJV

My family and I were on our way to visit the ancient ruins of Machu Picchu, high in the Andes Mountains of Peru. From Lima we flew to Cusco, and the following morning we planned to take a train to another city called Oyantaytambo, but we soon discovered that the train going to this city had derailed the day before and was going nowhere. Immediately, we scrambled and went to plan B, discovering that we could get to Oyantaytambo by bus too. But would it get there in time for us to catch the next train? It was worth a try! We got on the bus and headed out. About a mile from Oyantaytambo, the bus stopped. We looked out the window, and about one hundred feet in front of us, an army vehicle had just stopped and army soldiers were unloading. It turns out there were some riots in the city, and the army had been called in to control the situation. We were told the bus would go no farther. Great.

The bus driver knew where we were trying to go, so he told us to get off the bus, walk back a couple hundred yards to the railroad tracks, and walk along, hoping to catch our train. We followed his advice, found the tracks, and started walking. We were very happy to discover that the train had not left yet. We boarded, and it took us to a tiny village called Aguas Calientes. From there, we boarded another bus that would take us the final leg up to the ruins. The narrow dirt road looked very dangerous and contained dozens of switchbacks to get us up this mountain. The road didn't even have rails. After hours of travel, we finally made it to Machu Picchu.

Achieving certain things in life requires persistence. Working for God can be hard at times. Satan will try to discourage you, but stay strong and immovable, and know that nothing you do for God is a waste of time.

The Remote Mountain

For we are God's fellow workers; you are God's field, you are God's building.
1 CORINTHIANS 3:9, NKJV

We had traveled for days before arriving at Machu Picchu, ancient ruins that were built by the Incan people in the 1400s. It was occupied for about one hundred years and then suddenly it was abandoned. Little by little, memory of the city was lost, and the city became overgrown by the jungle for almost four hundred years till it was rediscovered in 1911. Since then, tourism to this unique site has steadily grown. Even after arriving, in order to visit the ruins you have to be able to walk long distances and climb lots of treacherous steps and paths. But, once you get there, it is truly an amazing place. Because of its historical importance, there is even a no-fly zone in effect there that means no airplanes can fly overhead.

After the couple of days it's taken you to get there, you begin to appreciate just how remote and isolated this place is. It's easy to see how incredibly complicated it must have been to build this city in such a hard-to-get-to place. It's also easy to appreciate the precision of the stonecutters who worked there. The buildings were not made from mud bricks. They were hand-carved by stonecutters. In most other ancient ruins it's easy to see how the ancient builders accurately cut rectangular rocks to build their buildings, but the structures at Machu Picchu are different. I remember seeing many huge rocks that had more than ten sides, and each stone perfectly fit in with the one next to it. Every rock was cut completely different, but each did an important job there.

When I think about how difficult it was to build places like Machu Picchu or the pyramids of Egypt, it makes me grateful knowing that God is the ultimate planner and designer. His plans are always perfect!

Life-Changing Roadblock

And we know that all things work together for good to those who
love God, to those who are the called according to His purpose.
ROMANS 8:28, NKJV

As a young man, my father enlisted in the Chilean navy and served during World War II as a communications officer on land and aboard a navy destroyer. During his sixth year of military service he became a Christian, resigned, and decided to travel to the United States to get an education at a Christian university. He made it as far as Havana, Cuba, where he decided to stay. Nine years later he had graduated, gotten a job, gotten married, and become a father when my older brother was born. Since my father was considered a missionary, he was given a three-month furlough—a period of time given to missionaries to return home and be with family. After spending three months in South America, it was time to return to their home in Cuba.

It turned out that while they were traveling, a famous historical event was unfolding: the invasion at the Bay of Pigs, Cuba, in April 1961. The relationship between the United States and Cuba was already strained, but this event quickly made things worse. Diplomatic relations were broken off, and the church administrators told my father he would not be able to enter Cuba yet. He was told to wait to see how this situation developed—and six months later it was determined that he would not be able to return. He was reassigned to work in the Dominican Republic and later Puerto Rico. He left his home, his car, his clothes, his bank account, and everything else in Cuba. To this day, more than half a century later, my parents have never returned. At the time, my father simply didn't understand God's plan for him, but he decided to trust God anyway.

Looking back, my parents quickly admit that the entire episode turned out to be a huge blessing. Will you trust God today? Even if you don't understand why certain things happen? God has a plan.

A Family Reunion

*After these things I looked, and behold, a great multitude which
no one could number, of all nations, tribes, peoples, and tongues,
standing before the throne and before the Lamb, clothed with
white robes, with palm branches in their hands.*
REVELATION 7:9, NKJV

A few years back I found myself traveling to Chile to attend a family reunion. I was going to meet relatives whom I had seen once or twice in my life and many others I had never met before. I had never been to a family reunion before, so I was excited. Growing up as a pastor's kid, I never lived near relatives. On both sides of my family, we were scattered all over the world. I have relatives from Norway to Cuba, from Chile to the Philippines and Australia. I represent a small part of our extended family that ended up in the United States.

We landed in Santiago, Chile and traveled by bus north to the city of La Serena, about an eight-hour bus ride. We were met at the bus station by a group of relatives. My uncle who lived in that city owned a hotel, so during those few days, our families took over all the rooms, and we spent a few days reuniting and getting to know new relatives. That first evening, we all walked to the city plaza, a bustling park where the locals come in the evenings to walk around, sit on park benches, listen to music, and participate in the local folk dances. At one point during the reunion we put a very long table in the middle of the hotel, and every person in the family sat at this table. It must have been thirty feet long with more than fifty seated at the table! During those days we shared photos, played games, and walked around the city. One afternoon my wife and I took all the young cousins walking to the center of town to buy them ice cream.

The time we spent there is time I will cherish and remember for the rest of my life. I've never been to a family reunion like that since, but there's another family reunion I'm already looking forward to—the big reunion in heaven!

Nine o'Clock in Havana

"At that time they will see the Son of Man coming in a cloud with power and great glory."
Luke 21:27, NIV

For many years my mother lived in Havana, Cuba. When I was a kid I remember her telling me about something that happened every night in the city, called *El Cañonazo de las Nueve,* which translates to "the nine o'clock cannon blast." For years I remember hearing her say that, but I never really understood what that meant till I finally visited Cuba myself. My first visit occurred in 1999, and for a few days we stayed in Havana. Each night at precisely nine o'clock, I heard a big boom.

Before I left, my Cuban relatives decided to take us to see what the "boom" was. We traveled to the fortress in the old part of the city. We crossed through the fortifications and into the protected part of the fortress. A little before 9:00 P.M., a door opened and a large group of soldiers dressed in colonial soldier outfits marched out. A small group of tourists had assembled there, and we slowly followed the troops as they marched in formation toward the edge of the city wall and up to a spot that overlooked the entire city. The captain would shout out orders as the men marched around and followed their instructions as they approached a large iron cannon that was positioned on the wall. Some soldiers were commanded to prepare the cannon with gun powder as 9:00 P.M. approached. Soon they were ready, and a few seconds before nine, a drum roll began as people waited. The cannon would be fired at exactly nine o'clock. When it went off, it was loud! *Ka-boom!* I remember being startled by how loud it was!

When Jesus returns someday, the Bible says everyone will know He has come. The Bible says His arrival will be with power and great glory! Unlike the cannon boom at nine o'clock in Havana, everyone on the planet will know about Jesus return!

Interesting Accommodations

So he came to a certain place and stayed there all night, because the sun had set. And he took one of the stones of that place and put it at his head, and he lay down in that place to sleep.
Genesis 28:11, NKJV

The first day we arrived in Cairo was a bumpy one. As students we were poor, and we couldn't afford fancy lodging or food. We took the public bus from the airport to the center of Cairo, where it dropped us off. It was about 10:00 P.M., and we knew it was not a great time to arrive in a strange city. A guy pointed us in the direction of where we might be able to find lodging nearby. We walked a few blocks and finally found a sign that said "Hotel–5th floor." We decided to go up—we were ready to rest. On the fifth floor we found the hotel.

To our surprise, they had a room available. To our bigger surprise, the cost was only one dollar for the room. Naturally, this immediately made us concerned and suspicious, but we were so tired we figured we could stay anywhere for just one night. The owner led us down the hall to our room, where we soon found out we had overpaid for our room. The room had no door. The beds were ancient metal beds with a piece of foam on top. There was no operable bathroom or running water anywhere on the floor, and the window was just an opening in the wall looking to the courtyard. No matter what country you are traveling in, each country has its nice high-end accommodations as well as its low-end accommodations. We're pretty sure we found the low end in Egypt, but we were so exhausted, we stayed there anyway.

One night when Jacob was traveling, the Bible says, he used a rock as a pillow. I can sort of relate to that, but the important thing to remember is that whether you are sleeping in a comfy bed or your pillow is a rock, may the last thing you do each day be to pray that God blesses you as you rest.

The Big Mistake

Therefore, whether you eat or drink, or
whether you do, do all to the glory of God.
1 CORINTHIANS 10:31, NKJV

As we walked down the street in Cairo, we came upon a tiny hole-in-the-wall restaurant. The owner was right at street level, making food in a giant pot right by the doorway. The man called the food "kushari," and upon closer inspection, it seemed to be made of rice, lentils, pasta, and onions. The food looked very delicious, and we decided to eat there. It turns out that this little restaurant only served one food, kushari, and only in one size, so ordering turned out to be quite easy. The man took us upstairs to a little dining area and sat us down. The four of us sat at the table and immediately noticed that the table had one cup and one jug of water. Apparently the cup sat there all day, on that table, for every customer who sat there. We decided we would not touch the cup or the water because we'd run the risk of getting sick. The most basic rule of thumb for travelers is to always stick to bottled water.

Since there was only one food choice, he simply brought each one of us a bowl of kushari. He also brought a small bowl with Parmesan cheese. We generously sprinkled cheese on our dish and started to eat. Moments later we quickly discovered that it wasn't Parmesan cheese; it was some kind of spicy sea salt! At first we all choked, but soon we had an intense burning sensation that quickly became unbearable. The cup and jug of water suddenly looked very good, and we each took turns gulping down cupfuls of water in order to cool off our burning mouths. As you can imagine, for the next twenty-four hours all four of us got a stomach sickness from drinking the water.

You already know that it's important to control what you put in your mouth. I also think you already know the difference between things that are good for you and things that will harm you. So how do you decide when you're not sure? Read today's verse.

Don't Jump

A wise man fears and departs from evil,
But a fool rages and is self-confident.
PROVERBS 14:16, NKJV

My wife and I were in Cairns, Australia on vacation. Our plan was to drive our rental car to the middle of the country to a place called Uluru, also known as Ayers Rock. Uluru is famous for being the largest single rock in the world, but since it's located in the middle of the continent, it's not easy to get to. I had a good map, and the trip was expected to take two days of driving. We soon realized that during these two days of driving we would pass through one of the most isolated parts of the country. Although we realized the place was isolated, we were not alone. We encountered all kinds of wildlife during our drive through the red center of Australia. In particular I want to tell you about our frequent encounters with kangaroos. As we drove, we would see them running around in the bush very often.

Many times kangaroos startled us by standing on the side of the road as we drove by. The reason this was a little scary is that when you drive through isolated stretches of desert for hours, there is no posted speed limit. In order to cross such a long desert in the shortest amount of time, everyone tends to drive as fast as they are willing to drive. The fastest I dared to drive was about ninety miles per hour, while other cars would sometimes pass me going even faster. When you are driving ninety miles per hour and see a kangaroo standing on the side of the road only a couple of feet away from your car, only one thing comes to mind: "Kangaroo, don't jump!"

Sometimes we position ourselves near danger, thinking we're strong enough to resist temptation. We convince ourselves that we can get close to a fire without getting burned. Our verse today clearly tells us that only a fool tries to see how close he can get to danger. A wise man gets as far away as possible. Which will you be today? I pray you choose to be wise.

A Dark Day in History

If we confess our sins, he is faithful and just and will forgive us our sins and purify us from all unrighteousness.
1 JOHN 1:9, NIV

On this day in 1963, a very sad thing happened in Dallas, Texas, while U.S. President John Kennedy and his wife were riding around in a convertible limousine. Hundreds of people lined the streets to get an opportunity to wave hello to the president as he passed by. As the presidential motorcade of cars entered Dealey Plaza, shots rang out and the president was hit. His limo sped off to the hospital, but it was too late. It was a dark day in American history.

A few years ago, I was in Dallas with my family, and I decided to take my family to Dealey Plaza. We drove downtown and parked around the corner and walked to the plaza. People and traffic carried on like nothing had happened, but for us, there was a raw reminder of a terrible thing that had happened decades before. As we stood on the sidewalk we noticed an X-shaped mark on the pavement in front of us on the road. The X marked the exact spot where the president was when he was shot. The government investigation says the shooter was in the Texas School Book Depository building behind the president, but other witnesses say the shooter was in front of the president. Regardless, it's sad to think of the many horrible things that people do. Because of sin, there are many terrible things that happen every day all over the world.

Sin is a sickness that has affected every person on this planet. Sin started in the Garden of Eden when Satan tempted and lied to Adam and Eve, leading them to disobey God. The good thing is that there is a cure for this sickness. The cure is God. In order for Him to remove our sins, we must confess our sins to Him and ask Him for forgiveness. He has the power to change us, but first we must allow God to work in our hearts. Will you invite Him into your heart today?

Miracle in the Red Center

For by grace you have been saved through faith, and that not of yourselves; it is the gift of God, not of works, lest anyone should boast.
EPHESIANS 2:8, 9, NKJV

The drive between Cairns and the Red Center of Australia took us two full days. During the first part of our long drive, we discovered that there were almost no towns along that stretch. We drove hundreds and hundreds of miles without seeing anything, except an occasional roadhouse. Roadhouses were the only place to stop during this long voyage. A roadhouse is like a rest area with a gas station, a restaurant, and a hotel with a few rooms.

During one stretch of highway, we made the mistake of not stopping to fill up at the last roadhouse, and we were beginning to run out of gasoline. The next stop was a very long way ahead, and we were getting nervous that we wouldn't make it. We prayed that day that we could make it to the next roadhouse. Being stranded in the middle of the desert didn't sound very fun. We were completely isolated, and this was not a good place to run out of gas. The needle neared empty, and we kept on going; we had no choice. We soon discovered that there was a roadhouse ahead, but it was still sixty miles away. At this point, the gas light had already turned on, and we were becoming very concerned about our situation. Again we prayed for God to perform a miracle with our car. My wife and I knew that once the light came on, there's usually around twenty to twenty-five more miles it will go. Soon the needle hit empty, but the car kept going for those sixty miles!

I know that God still performs miracles to this day, and our verse today reminds us that He does it to remind us that that there's no point bragging about the things we can do. God proves to us repeatedly that we worship an all-powerful God.

The Incredible Echo

"Sing to Him, sing psalms to Him;
Talk of all His wondrous works!"
1 CHRONICLES 16:9, NKJV

When I was a student in France, I joined the school choir that practiced in the evenings several times a week. After a couple of months of practicing, the director determined that we were ready to perform in public. He first arranged for us to sing on campus during Sabbath worship service. Soon after, he arranged for us to travel to a church in Switzerland to sing on Sabbath morning. Later we did a short tour, singing at several churches around Paris. Eventually we learned that in April we would have our largest tour—to Italy.

The director worked to book concerts for us all through Italy for about a week. Our concerts took place in the evening, which meant during the day we would travel from one city to the next and do a little sightseeing. Most of the time we sang at smaller churches and schools, but during one of our stops we were going to sing in a city called Milan in northern Italy. As part of our daytime sightseeing, we went to the Milan Cathedral—an incredible work of architecture. The ceiling is super tall, and there are incredible details carved into the stone and wood all around. Cathedrals also have great acoustics—making music sound extra nice. As we toured through the cathedral, some-one suddenly suggested that we sing one of our songs. Right there in the middle of the cathedral, about twenty-five of us started to sing one of our worship pieces. It sounded incredible. As we sang, a small crowd formed around us as we elevated our voices to heaven in song. At the end of our last note, everyone stopped and held their breath to hear how long the echo would carry. It went on for several seconds as we stood there in silence.

Singing praises to God is one of the most popular ways of worshiping and praising Him. All heaven rejoices when we sing praises to God!

The Lowest Place on Earth

Let your speech always be with grace, seasoned with salt,
that you may know how you ought to answer each one.
COLOSSIANS 4:6, NKJV

During the summer I spent in Jordan, I was able to take several side trips on the weekends. One weekend, I and three other guys borrowed the staff car and decided to drive down the Dead Sea between Jordan and Israel. I say "down" because the Dead Sea is the lowest place on earth at 1,407 feet below sea level. The area is very desert-like and very hot. We had all heard stories of the Dead Sea from the Bible, and it was exciting to be there in person. It's called the Dead Sea because there is absolutely nothing living in this body of water. No fish, no plants, nothing. The reason is that it is extremely salty. It's so salty that if you put your hand a couple of inches under water, you can't see it anymore. Because the water is so salty, it makes everything very buoyant. That means things float in the water very easily. We had heard that one of the popular things to do at the Dead Sea was to get in and just lie down in the water and float. We came prepared with our swimsuits, so we changed and got in the water. Sure enough, we floated on the surface. If you wanted to, you could just sit there and read a book while you were floating! As we played around for a while, water would occasionally splash up on our faces. A couple times I got some in my eyes and mouth, and it was shocking just how salty that water was compared to regular ocean water. It stung!

Salt is mentioned many times in the Bible. Our verse today says a Christian's speech should be graceful and "seasoned with salt." This means we are to be careful how we speak to people. Are you confrontational? When you speak, do people get offended? When you speak, the words you choose and the way you say them should reflect that you are a follower of Christ. Make a conscious choice today about how you speak to others.

Parisian Meeting Place

Be joyful in hope, patient in affliction, faithful in prayer.
ROMANS 12:12, NIV

After my year studying in France, my family decided to come over from the United States and we would spend the last two weeks traveling around Europe. My parents and my sister flew in from California, and my brother and his wife flew in from Florida. The plan was to meet up in Paris and go from there together. Now, in 1990, communication was very different than today—there were no cell phones, no texting, there wasn't even e-mail! You could either call on a wired telephone or write a letter. The challenging part of this whole plan was that my brother and his wife were going to be in Europe traveling on their own for a week before meeting up with us in Paris. My parents and sister planned to fly in a couple of days before to Geneva, Switzerland, hang out with me for a couple of days, and then we would take the train together up to Paris to meet my brother. Our plan was to meet on Monday morning in Paris, France, right in front of the Notre Dame Cathedral at 10:00 A.M. The tricky detail was that if anything went wrong with our plans to meet, there would be no other way to communicate with each other in order to arrange a new meeting time or place, and we'd miss traveling together. It was important that our plan work.

Monday came, and as I was traveling to Paris with my parents and sister, we encountered a delay! There was no way we would be in front of Notre Dame by 10:00 A.M. We were going to be about an hour or two late. We decided to go anyway. Would my brother and sister-in-law be there waiting for us still? Fortunately, they had decided to be patient and wait the extra time.

It's hard to be patient sometimes. We get used to having what we want when we want it. If we don't get it, we often get impatient. Pray today that God helps you to be a patient person. This is a quality that will make you a better person.

The Big Little Country

Bear one another's burdens, and so fulfill the law of Christ.
GALATIANS *6:2, NKJV*

I once drove around Europe with five guys in a rented car for two weeks. Since we were poor students, we rented the smallest car we could find and smashed ourselves into it. We had heard about a tiny little country in Europe between Switzerland and Austria called Liechtenstein. The country is only about four miles wide and about fifteen miles long, and the capital is called Vaduz. When we arrived, it appeared that the majority of the country was on the side of a mountain. We first went straight to the capital, Vaduz. We heard stamps were collectable items here, so we went to the post office and bought some.

We also heard there was a castle up on the mountainside. There were lots of winding switchbacks as we climbed higher. Eventually we made it to the castle, but then we kept driving higher in order to get a view of the castle from above. After a few minutes of driving downhill, we all started to smell something. Minutes later we realized that the smell was our brakes! We pulled over immediately and checked them out. With our small car, our extra weight, and the steep downhill ride, the brakes were overheating! None of us were mechanics, so we decided to let them cool off. The sun was starting to set, so we decided that we would just camp the night up there—it was a cold night! The next morning we woke to a couple of inches of snow!

All this happened because we were too heavy for our car. Every day we each have burdens that weigh us down. Wouldn't they be easier to carry if someone helped us? The Bible encourages us to help carry each other's burdens. Sometimes you help others with troubles, other times they help you with yours. Go today and be ready to help someone in need; someday it will be you in need.

The Undiscovered Country

Those who trust in the L<small>ORD</small> are like Mount Zion,
which cannot be shaken but endures forever.
P<small>SALM</small> 125:1, NIV

Recently I traveled through Italy with my wife and two sons. We had just finished visiting Rome, and we were now driving toward Venice. During my trip planning back home, I had decided that it would be worth taking a little detour during this part of our drive to visit the tiny country of San Marino—which is bordered on all sides by Italy, between Rome and Venice. The drive to Venice would take several hours, and I calculated that a quick detour to visit San Marino would add less than one extra hour of driving. That seemed like a good idea considering we could be able to claim one more country to our list of countries we'd visited. As we left Rome, I programmed the GPS to go to Venice, and then I added a "via-point" to San Marino along the way. All I had to do now was follow the GPS directions to San Marino and eventually Venice. The hours went by as we drove through the Italian countryside, enjoying the views, the different towns and terrain. Every step of the way I obeyed the GPS. Eventually I saw a sign that said we were only about an hour away from Venice. That's when it suddenly hit me, "What about San Marino?" I started pressing buttons on the GPS to see what had happened. I finally announced to my family, "Uh, family, I have a strange announcement to make. About an hour ago we drove through San Marino!" For some reason I never realized we had arrived at our via-point. We had driven right through San Marino without realizing it!

There are lots of things that happen in our lives we don't know about. That is why I find so much peace in just trusting God with my life. He understands everything that is happening. Sometimes I pray to God asking for something, but because He knows the big picture, I don't worry when I don't get my way. I try to just continue trusting that God is the ultimate GPS!

A Family Tradition

Be sober, be vigilant; because your adversary the devil
walks about like a roaring lion, seeking whom he may devour.
1 Peter 5:8, NKJV

Back in 1969 my father traveled to Europe to attend meetings in Amsterdam, Netherlands. After the meetings he toured Europe. Growing up, I always remember looking at the pictures he took during that trip, but there was one that always stuck out in my memory. It was taken at the Roman Colosseum in Rome, Italy. History and legend teach that during the glory days, Romans would hold events that included lions roaming around the center arena. In one of the pictures, my dad had climbed up on one of the side rails at the Colosseum. He would show us the picture and then he would ask us, "Do you know why I climbed up on that railing?" Even though we already knew the answer, we always asked why. "In case there were still any lions left roaming around!" As little kids, we loved that story and that picture.

When I was in college and spent a year in Europe, I was excited to finally visit the Colosseum myself. When I got there, can you guess what was the first thing I did? Yep, I looked for a similar-looking rail, and I climbed up and asked my friend to take a picture. My friend thought that was strange, but I soon explained why. About five years later I returned to Rome, this time, with my wife. Once again, we found a similar spot in the Colosseum. Together we climbed the rail and took the picture again. Just recently, I returned to Rome again, this time with my wife and my two sons. You guessed it. I had been telling them the original story of my dad since they were little, so this time it was our turn to take the traditional picture in Rome. This time, all four of us were up on the rail, in case any lions were still running around.

Although that was a humorous story, the Bible reminds us that Satan is like a lion, prowling around. Fortunately, we don't have to worry as long as every day we hang on to God, our perfect railing, where we can be safe!

A Day in Morocco

For you formed my inward parts;
you knitted me together in my mother's womb.
I praise you, for I am fearfully and wonderfully made.
Wonderful are your works;
my soul knows it very well.
PSALM 139:13, 14, ESV

We once crossed the Strait of Gibraltar between Europe and Africa on a ferry on a day trip from Spain to Morocco—we'd be back in Spain by night. First thing we did was to visit some of the typical historic places, forts, and ancient buildings. There was never a shortage of locals trying to earn a few coins from us. At one of the places there was a snake charmer. If you thought that was only in the cartoons, think again. A man sat on the ground, cross-legged, with a basket in front of him. Soon the man started playing his flute, and a cobra rose up out of the basket. It seemed to be mesmerized by the music. At the end, the man gladly received coins for his performance.

Soon it was time for lunch, and we went to eat at a typical Moroccan restaurant. We sat on the floor on top of big fluffy pillows while servers brought delicious new foods to try. Our next stop was a store that bottled spices and herbs. We got to smell and taste a bunch of exotic flavors. Our final stop of the day was a carpet store. In North America, we use machines to make rugs and carpets, but in this Moroccan store, they made each one by hand. In the end, we bought a small carpet. If I ever have the privilege of having you as a guest in my home, I will show you the carpet, which is right by my front door.

If you think about it, you were handmade and designed by God. He knows everything about you. You were created with a purpose, and each one is special and unique. You are the only "you" God made on the whole planet, which is why you are so valuable to God!

Pointy Mountains

The soul of a lazy man desires, and has nothing;
But the soul of the diligent shall be made rich.
PROVERBS 13:4, NKJV

My favorite mountain range is the Alps in Europe. I find them amazingly beautiful because they are so rocky and pointy. During the year I studied in France, I never got tired of visiting the Alps. In the fall of that school year I asked the school administrators if the school had a ski club. They said there wasn't, but if I wanted to organize one, they would help and support our plans. Immediately I went to work talking to the other students to see how many people were interested. I also went to work researching which of the ski places was best to visit and close enough to do as a Sunday day trip, and I figured out how to transport all the people there and back, purchase lift tickets, and pay for rentals and meals.

I was so excited about the thought of skiing in the Alps that I was very happy to do all the work to organize these details. When the first day came we were ready—a bunch of people signed up, I had a bus, I had costs figured out for the group, and I had found a place to ski. We left early that Sunday morning and spent the entire day skiing and exploring the mountain. I had never skied at such a large ski area before. I knew right away that I would never get to ski every trail or part of the mountain because it was so big. It was a perfect day, and I will never forget the incredible view I had from every spot on the mountain. No matter which direction I looked, it looked like an endless range of beautiful, pointy mountains. My favorite!

It took a lot of work to organize this outing, and I was happy many people were able to benefit from it, but if I had chosen to be lazy, it's likely nothing would have happened. God loves when we are diligent, hardworking, and organized. We are challenged to be this way in everything we do.

A Challenging Adventure

"Behold, I am the LORD, the God of all flesh. Is there anything too hard for Me?"
JEREMIAH 32:27, NKJV

A few years back I went on a mission trip to Venezuela to build a cafeteria on the campus of a small school in a remote part of the country. The day we arrived into Caracas was Election Day; a new president had just been elected, President Hugo Chavez. We had flight delays as well as challenges in bringing in hundreds of Bibles we had brought with us to give away. I spoke with the customs officers at the airport and told them why we were bringing hundreds of Bibles into the country—hoping to convince them not to charge us a customs fee. We were thankful to God when they finally allowed us in without charging us.

Next, we took another flight to a city called Ciudad Bolivar, deep in the tropical jungle. The city lies at the edge of an enormous river called the Rio Orinoco, where the river narrows to "only" one mile wide. During the rainy season it can swell up to fourteen miles wide! The location we'd work in was very rustic. There was no electricity or running water. Once a day in the evening for an hour or so, the locals would turn on a generator to give everyone a chance to do a few "electric" things. If you didn't want to bathe in the river, during this hour you could run a water pump and get a cold shower. I chose the cold shower since I had been told there were piranhas in the river.

Getting there was not easy, and being there was not easy, but we were so happy to be there working for these kind people, who were excited that we were there to help them.

While we each struggle with challenges, I am comforted knowing that there is nothing God can't do. Nothing is impossible for Him! If we align ourselves with God, it won't matter where you are or what you're doing; God will give you the strength to do amazing things if you let Him.

The Gift of Interpretation

To another the working of miracles, to another prophecy, to another discerning of spirits, to another different kinds of tongues, to another the interpretation of tongues.
1 CORINTHIANS 12:10, NKJV

Yesterday I started to tell you about a mission trip I went on to Venezuela. Our plan was to prepare the land, dig the foundation trenches, pour the foundation, and lay the foundation blocks. Since we were in such a remote part of the country, all this work had to be done by hand. Our team of workers consisted of a mix of local workers and our group from North America. Our combined team worked all day long for almost two weeks to achieve these goals. If any of you have ever been on a mission trip, you know that it's one thing to get there and work, but it's another to meet the local people and make new friends.

I've been on several mission trips, but this one was unique because I was the only person in the group who spoke both English and Spanish. Although I went to work building, I found myself spending a lot of time serving as the interpreter between our team of volunteers and the local team of workers. That was not my intention for the trip, but that ended up being a productive way for God to use me. During some of the other evenings we went into the nearby Ciudad Bolivar to talk to people and give away Bibles. Again, a lot of the weight fell on me as we interacted with the people of this town. It was a fascinating experience, and these were things I had never done before.

At first it took me way out of my comfort zone, but soon I adapted. What impressed me the most was how God used my gift of speaking different languages to advance His work in Venezuela. Do you speak more than one language? If you have the opportunity to learn more than one at home, don't squander it. God may need you to develop that gift so that you can use it someday. You are responsible to use the gifts God has given you.

In the Middle of the Jungle

Blessed is the man who remains steadfast under trial,
for when he has stood the test he will receive the crown
of life, which God has promised to those who love him.
JAMES 1:12, ESV

On the last day of our mission trip to Venezuela we were given the day off to do whatever we wanted. I got together with a couple of friends and we made a plan. We went to the local airport and chartered a small plane and pilot to take us to Canaima National Park. Since the place where we were working was already on the edge of the jungle, it was not too far away. This is no ordinary park—it's the sixth largest national park in the world—as big as the entire state of Maryland! The curious thing is that we had to charter an airplane to get there because there aren't any roads that go into the park because of its remote location.

We flew in a single-engine Cessna, staying low, which was a great way to appreciate the vastness of this park. We passed miles and miles of untouched jungle below us. There were no clearings or open areas, just endless trees. Suddenly, up ahead, we saw a huge river, and farther ahead a clearing in the jungle. In the clearing was a small airstrip. The pilot landed, and we got out and walked to the only building in sight, noticing that we were the only tourists in the area. Over the next half a day, we hiked through the jungle, then took a rustic canoe across a lake and walked through a portion of the savannah. Finally, we arrived at a magnificent waterfall called Canaima Falls. We first hiked to the base of the falls and climbed behind the falls. Then we swam in the water at the base of the falls, and later we found a trail that led us up to the top of the falls. It took some effort to get to this place, but the reward was worth it.

There will be difficult trials when we serve God, but the Bible tells us to continue doing our best to follow Him. The good thing is the reward in the end will be well worth it!

Magnificent Falling Water

*"Behold, I will stand before you there on the rock
in Horeb; and you shall strike the rock, and water
will come out of it, that the people may drink."
And Moses did so in the sight of the elders of Israel.*
EXODUS 17:6, NKJV

Yesterday I shared with you how we spent time exploring Canaima Falls in Venezuela. Soon it was time to continue the rest of our day trip. We got back on the small plane and took off, heading deeper into the jungle, where table-top mountains called "mesas" began to pop up on the horizon. The elevation of the mesas was very high, and below, an endless jungle.

We were on our way to visit Angel Falls, the tallest waterfall in the world. Our pilot navigated between the mesas till we finally approached one in particular, and right before our eyes was the magnificent Angel Falls. The water falls from the top of one of the rocky mesas down to the jungle floor. The falls are more than thirty-two hundred feet high. We knew this was an incredibly unique site because there are only two ways to view Angel Falls. You either have to charter a small airplane, like we did, one that was small enough to fly low and get close to the mesa and waterfalls, or you had to hike on foot, which we were told was a long expedition down rivers and through the jungle. Our time observing the falls was short since we were flying, but I will never forget those few minutes we had marveling at the highest waterfall in the world.

During the Exodus, the Israelites were thirsty, and God told Moses to strike the rock and water flowed out, just like a waterfall. You may remember that the second time this happened, Moses was supposed to just speak to the rock, but he disobeyed God and tried to take matters into his own hands. When God gives us specific instructions, we need to trust that He has a reason why we need to fully trust and obey Him. Will you trust God completely today?

One Amazing Fishing Spot

Then He said to them, "Follow Me, and I will make you fishers of men."
MATTHEW 4:19, NKJV

Chile is a couple of hundred miles wide at the most, but it is more than two thousand six hundred miles long! Because it is oriented vertically, the country has almost every imaginable type of landscape. In the north, there are some of the hottest and driest deserts in the world. In the middle, there are lush agricultural areas. In the south, there are thousands of islands, lakes, and fjords, and in the very southern tip—Tierra del Fuego—the closest landmass to Antarctica. The west coast has thousands of miles of coast, while the eastern border has thousands of miles of mountains.

During one of my trips to Chile, I decided to spend a few days with my uncle in a city called La Serena. It's a beach town with miles and miles of untouched beaches. When a country has thousands of miles of beaches, it's easy to find beaches that are rarely visited. My uncle knew where to find some of these, so we jumped in his four-wheel-drive vehicle and cruised for miles on the sand down the totally empty beaches. Eventually we stopped because we had arrived at one of his favorite fishing spots. He kept his fishing gear in his trunk, ready to go, and even a spare in case someone came with him. I had never fished directly from the sandy beach into the ocean, so he had to give me a few pointers. Over the next hour or so, we caught a handful of fish and enjoyed standing around and talking about life on such a beautiful beach. It was one of the most memorable and relaxing moments of my visit to Chile.

The Bible talks about fishermen, except that in today's verse Jesus is calling fishermen to be fishers of men. Followers of Christ have been given the job of being fishers of men, of women, and of children. Jesus has asked us to go out and invite the world to follow Him. Will you share Jesus with someone today?

A Watery Grave

"My God is my rock, in whom I take refuge,
my shield and the horn of my salvation.
He is my stronghold, my refuge and my savior—
from violent people you save me.
I called to the LORD, who is worthy of praise,
and have been saved from my enemies."
2 SAMUEL 22:3, 4, NIV

While traveling in Hawaii, we decided to visit the U.S. naval base at Pearl Harbor on the island of Oahu. Pearl Harbor is the headquarters of the United States Pacific Fleet. On December 7, 1941, the Empire of Japan attacked the base, immediately bringing the United States into World War II. During the attack, several warships were destroyed, and a bunch more were damaged; in addition, many aircrafts were destroyed and about twenty-three hundred servicemen died. About half of the people who died were onboard the *USS Arizona*, a battleship that was bombed from the sky, exploding while it sat in the harbor. As a way to remember this dark day, it was decided that the sunken *USS Arizona* would remain submerged and a memorial would be built above it.

When we arrived, we boarded a small boat that took us out to the memorial. Everyone on the boat was silent as we passed over the waters where 1,177 crewmen from the *Arizona* died during the attack. Once at the memorial, we saw the names of the crewmen, and just under the surface of the water, we could see the wreck of the *USS Arizona*. Part of one of the gun turrets was still above water. Even though it's been resting there for about seventy-five years, the memorial stands as a reminder of the crewmen who were willing to give their lives in the name of freedom.

Freedom is wonderful, but sometimes we forget that it's not free. Thank God today for the servicemen and women who are willing to put themselves in harm's way in order to protect your freedom today. And if you know one personally, thank them too!

The Largest Concentration of Life

"... (for the LORD your God is a merciful God), He will not forsake you nor destroy you, nor forget the covenant of your fathers which He swore to them."
DEUTERONOMY 4:31, NKJV

During a trip to Australia, we knew we had to visit one of the most famous places on the continent—the Great Barrier Reef. It's well-known for being the largest reef in the world and the largest concentration of life in one place. We flew into the city of Cairns in Queensland, in the northeast part of the country. At the airport, we got our rental car then found a place to stay. We also found a tour company that would take us out to the reef on a boat. If you've ever gone to a reef in the Caribbean, it's often accessible right from the beach. The Great Barrier Reef is not like that. You have to take a boat a couple of hours out into the ocean. We booked a tour and made plans to be there bright and early the next morning. Traveling to Australia from North America often involves jet lag, so we went to sleep early to make sure we were well rested for the next day.

The next morning, we geared up and went to the dock and boarded the boat. Soon we were on our way to the reef. It took us about two hours to get to the location where this company took its tourists, a shallow reef right against a wall that dropped down a hundred feet or so. There were nice shallow areas for those of us who wanted to snorkel. For those wanting to dive, there were deep areas as well. I am not certified to dive, so my plan was to snorkel, and for the next hour I marveled at the incredibly diverse marine life I was able to observe. We were out there for hours, and it was unforgettable.

Why are there some things in life we forget and others that we'll never forget? The good news is that God is not a forgetful God. He has made hundreds of promises of love and protection in the Bible. I love knowing that He will never forget a single promise.

Encounters of the Deep

Yea, though I walk through the valley of the shadow of death,
I will fear no evil;
For You are with me;
Your rod and Your staff, they comfort me.
PSALM 23:4, NKJV

I had been snorkeling in the Great Barrier Reef in Australia for hours, enjoying the amazing diversity of life in the water. During one of the breaks on the boat, the dive master asked me if I wanted to try a quick dive. As long as he accompanied me, I didn't have to have a certification—this sounded exciting! Over the next fifteen minutes, the dive master prepared me for the dive. We talked about the oxygen tank and how to use the regulator for breathing. We also talked about some basic sign-language signals we could use to communicate under water. In the event any water seeped into my mask while diving deep under the surface, he also showed me how to blow water out of my mask without having to surface. I wasn't certified, but at least I knew the safety basics. We jumped in the water, and I tried my best to quickly adjust to breathing through a regulator. After a few moments, the instructor motioned me to follow him.

I was immediately impressed with the weight of the water. The lower I went, the heavier the water pressed against my body. Water is heavy! We spent about ten minutes checking out the deeper parts of the reef. At one moment, the instructor pointed something out to me about twenty-five feet below us—it was a shark! I estimated that it was about five feet long. During the ride out on the boat we had actually spent some time learning about sharks, so I was able to quickly identify it as a nurse shark. Fortunately, nurse sharks do not bother humans and are not considered a threat. For a moment, though, I was a little startled!

Because of sin, fear is a normal part of life. Everyone has fears. The good news is that God promises to comfort us when we're scared. It's so comforting to know that we can go through life being fearless because God is with us.

The Tower of Steps

*But when He saw the multitudes, He was moved with compassion for them,
because they were weary and scattered, like sheep having no shepherd.*
MATTHEW 9:36, NKJV

The Eiffel Tower is one of the most iconic landmarks in the world and a very unique architectural feat. When we arrived in Paris, the first item of business was to find a parking spot and walk to the tower. Soon we came to a clearing where we had a fantastic view of the tower. Naturally, we had to stop and take pictures. We finally made it to the base of the tower and looked up. It was enormous! Turns out it's the equivalent of an eighty-story building! Since I spoke some French, I went over and asked for information about going up. Turns out we had a few options. The Eiffel Tower has three levels, and you can pick how high you want to go. When I inquired at the booth about costs, I was quite shocked at how expensive it was to take the elevator up. I had visited twenty-five years before and had gone up, but it was a lot cheaper back then!

We were happy to learn there was another option—taking the stairs—lots of stairs! For a much reduced price, we could take the stairs up to the second level. I asked my family what they thought, and I got a very predictable answer from my boys: they loved that idea even more than riding the elevator. We got our tickets and started climbing. Seven hundred steps later, we arrived at the middle level, about halfway up the tower. It was quite a workout getting there, but my wife and I were amazed at how our two boys practically ran up the steps without losing their breath. During our climb, I noticed a couple struggling to make it up. I wanted to help them, but there was nothing I could do. It's not like I could pick them up and carry them. I mention this because my heart felt compassion for those poor, exhausted people.

Jesus asked us to have compassion for the people around us. Look around today; God might put someone in your path today who needs your compassion.

The Presidential Encounter

Better is the poor who walks in his integrity
Than one who is perverse in his lips, and is a fool.
PROVERBS 19:1, NKJV

It was a few days before Christmas in the year 2000, and we had traveled to Maryland to visit my brother's family for the holidays. During our time there we decided to do a little bit of sightseeing around the Washington, DC, area. We checked out one of the Smithsonian museums. We visited the Vietnam War memorial, and walked around the White House, where then-president Bill Clinton lived and worked. That evening, my brother took us to Union Station, a historic train station and shopping mall. We noticed a small crowd had developed in front of one of the stores. I couldn't resist walking in that direction to see if I could see what people were trying to see. I looked around and didn't see anything. My curiosity finally got to me, and I asked a man standing near me why we were all standing here. He turned to me and said, "President Clinton is Christmas shopping in this store, and he's about to come out." Sure enough, moments later, President Bill Clinton came out of the store accompanied by his Secret Service agents. Since the crowd that had gathered was small, he came over to greet us. I reached out my hand, and he shook it. I remember exactly what I said. I said, "Hey, Mr. President." Yes, I probably could have come up with something a little classier to say, but that's what came out.

Politicians are involved as leaders all over the world. Sadly, politicians often get themselves in trouble by lying or making promises they can't keep. Sometimes they'll say things only to get people to vote for them. The problem is, it's not just politicians. As sinners there are times that we all tell lies. The Bible warns about people who aren't truthful. It says it's better to be poor and honest, because people who lie are fools. Don't be a fool today. Choose to use words that show honor and integrity.

DECEMBER 12

The Unusual Ski Trip

Jesus said, "I am. And you will see the Son of Man sitting at the right hand of the Power, and coming with the clouds of heaven."
MARK 14:62, NKJV

A couple of summers ago I was filming a video series, and our production travel had brought us to Mount Hood, Oregon. Mount Hood has some great skiing, and we knew this would be a great place to get wonderful footage for the video we were producing. The reason I'm sharing this story is that it was the middle of July! That morning when we left Portland, it was eighty degrees! Now we were on our way to shoot snowboarding scenes. Mount Hood is the only place in the lower forty-eight states that offers year-round skiing. Mount Hood has twelve glaciers near the top that provide year-round snow. The ski area has a special chairlift that is mainly open in the summer when the lower slopes are closed. This chair is called the "magic mile" because it takes skiers one extra mile higher up the mountain during the summer, allowing visitors to reach the glacier to ski.

We took the chairlifts to the highest point possible. The view was incredible. The sky was super blue because we were thousands of feet above the clouds. All we could see was an endless sea of clouds. In order to get off the mountain we would have to ride down into the clouds. It was definitely a unique experience!

Clouds are mentioned in the Bible several times. My favorite mention is when the Bible reveals to us that one day Jesus will return to earth in the clouds. What a wonderful day that will be! If you have clouds in the sky today, think about that joyous day when Jesus will return to take us to our new home in heaven!

The Water Bottle Walk

So then, my beloved brethren, let every man be
swift to hear, slow to speak, slow to wrath.
JAMES 1:19, NKJV

When I traveled in Egypt, we ended up getting sick on the first day from drinking the water. For the rest of our time there, we made a point of making sure we always drank bottled water. Egypt is not like North America, where there is a convenience store or gas station on practically every corner. It was a lot harder to find stores with something as simple as bottled water. We decided it would be best to ask for directions to see where we could find a nearby place to buy some bottled water. We spotted a local man and approached him. We didn't speak any Arabic, and he didn't speak very much English, although he did speak enough to tell us that he knew where we needed to go. He motioned for us to follow him, and soon we were on our way to find bottled water. We were very excited because we were very thirsty, but we started to get concerned when, ten minutes later, we were still walking. We were also concerned because the streets we were walking on were getting narrower and quieter. We thought it was unusual that we would have to go to such lengths to find bottled water. After a forty-five-minute walk, our guide finally announced that we had arrived. We went into a little old storefront, and the man introduced us to the owner. That's when we discovered just how much we had been misunderstood. Even though we had asked for "water bottle," he had somehow understood "water bong." A water bong is a type of water-pipe apparatus used in Egypt to smoke!

Misunderstandings between people are common. Sometimes they lead to arguing and fighting. What should you do when there is a possible misunderstanding between you and someone else? The answer is in today's verse!

The Unusual Hotel

And one cried to another and said:
"Holy, holy, holy is the LORD of hosts;
The whole earth is full of His glory!"
ISAIAH 6:3, NKJV

From Athens, Greece, my wife and I boarded a boat that would stop at several Greek islands in the Aegean Sea. There was one in particular we were planning to visit called Santorini. The island is made up of half an enormous volcanic crater, and the dock was on the inside of the flooded crater. From the dock, a bus took us up a bunch of very steep switchbacks to the rim, where all the towns were located. In town, we rented a car so that we could explore this unique island. Many of the towns there were perched on the edge of the crater on a cliff hundreds of feet above the sea. The villages were very beautiful, since most of the buildings were painted bright white. Our next task was to find a place to stay.

In North America we're used to familiar names when it comes to hotels, but in Santorini it seemed that every place was a small, family-owned hotel. The place we found was quite interesting. The main office was up high on the cliff, but in order to get to our room, we had to climb down the cliff face through a series of steps and paths that resembled a maze. When we made it to our door, we discovered that our room was actually a nicely finished cave with a door on it. Just inside the front door was a little seating area, then farther in was the bathroom, and all the way to the back of the cave was a little bedroom. The room was built directly from nature.

The God who created our world is the most creative being in the universe. The evidence is everywhere. Look at the nature around you today, and you will see evidence of His creativity and glory. You are also part of His creation; may your life today give Him glory.

Parking in Paris

You are my hiding place;
You shall preserve me from trouble;
You shall surround me with songs of deliverance.
PSALM 32:7, NKJV

Recently, I was in the middle of Paris trying to park a car. From the street level, I could not recognize the parking garage because it looked like a regular building. Looking at the building from the street, I noticed that the windows had curtains and plants in the windows where people lived. I finally noticed a square blue sign with the letter "P" on it—the only clue to the entrance. We drove through a small opening in the building just wide enough for a car. Next, there was a gate where we took a ticket, and then the gate opened and allowed us through. To my surprise the ramp did not lead me upward; it led me down. I followed the ramp down to a previously unseen parking garage in the basement of this building. When I got there, there was a sign blocking entry into the parking area because that parking level was full. To my surprise, the ramp actually led down to another level below that one! It was like a second basement below the first basement! I followed it deeper under the ground. When I got to the next level, negative two, I discovered that one was reserved for people who worked and/or lived in the building. To my surprise, it went down another level! I was now three floors under the street level. Next, I went to a fourth, then to a fifth, then to a sixth! I finally found a parking spot six stories under the ground! You would have never known from the street.

Just as I could not see where the cars were being kept safe, Jesus has angels that we don't see that are surrounding and protecting us right now. If you ever feel as though you're in trouble, go to God and ask Him to be your hiding place.

The Lookout Volcano

"Therefore take heed to yourselves and to all the flock, among which the Holy Spirit has made you overseers, to shepherd the church of God which He purchased with His own blood."
ACTS 20:28, NKJV

The Canary Islands are located about sixty-two miles off the northwestern coast of Africa. Not long ago I visited one of the islands called Tenerife. My mother's family originally came from the Canary Islands, and she would tell me stories about these islands. I would find them on the map and think to myself, "Wow, they're in such a remote part of the world!"

You'll never guess what is right in the middle of Tenerife—a giant volcano, Mt. Teide. A road led up to the crater, so we rented a car and drove to the crater. After a while we got above the tree line, and eventually all that was left were endless lava flows. Miles and miles of terrain, where all you see is lava and more lava. Soon, even the clouds were down below us. We finally made it to the rim of the crater. At this point, we were miles from the nearest tree or any type of vegetation. It looked as though we were on the moon or some alien rock. To our surprise, the volcano still went up another several thousand feet! And we discovered that there was a cable car that could take visitors to the summit of the volcano! This was an exciting opportunity, so we went up and saw that the view was spectacular indeed. Tenerife is a good-size island, but from up there we could see the entire island and even a few of the neighboring islands.

As we live out our lives here on earth, God has asked each one of us to be guardians and overseers of God's church. Just as I could see the entire island from the top of that volcano, God has asked us to be aware of the needs of the people in our church and community. They may be hard to see sometimes, but ask God today to reveal the needs of others around you.

A Waterfall Shower

"I will sprinkle clean water on you, and you shall be clean from all your uncleannesses, and from all your idols I will cleanse you."
EZEKIEL 36:25, ESV

While in South America, I was able to travel to one of the most amazing waterfalls in the world—Iguaçu Falls. The falls are located on the border between Brazil and Argentina. Once you get there, there are several different hiking trails, each offering a great view of the waterfalls. There are even some boardwalks that take you right out to the edge of where the water is falling. If you really want to get a close-up look at the falls, you can take a jet boat to the place where the falls are crashing down at the bottom. After getting our tickets for the boat, we were handed a package and soon discovered it was a rain poncho. Apparently we were going to get wet!

Soon, the jet boat took off and sped toward the base of the waterfalls. As we neared the falls, we noticed an increase of mist in the air. As we got closer, it became more like a solid sprinkling. Moments later it felt like a heavy rain. The boat pushed even closer to the base of the falls, and the rain became more like a storm with raindrops pelting us *hard*. Finally, the boat reached as far as it could go, only feet away from where the waterfalls were crashing into the pool below. We were only there for a few intense moments, but we experienced hurricane-type conditions. We were getting pounded, and even though we wore ponchos, by the time we reached land again we discovered that all our clothes were completely soaked anyway. One thing is for sure though, we felt clean afterward!

Everyone uses water to get clean, but God uses water in the Bible as an example of how He can clean us from impurities. We are born sinners to this world, but God offers us a way to be cleaned when we repent and ask God for forgiveness. Ask God to give you a clean heart today.

Close the Door!

Or do you not know that your body is the temple of the Holy Spirit who is in you, whom you have from God, and you are not your own? For you were bought at a price; therefore glorify God in your body and in your spirit, which are God's.
1 CORINTHIANS 6:19, 20, NKJV

When my wife and I decided to explore Africa, our doctor suggested we take a few precautions. He told us there was a slight possibility of contracting diseases, especially malaria, so as part of our preparation for the trip we had to take some medicine every day for a month before going, during the trip, and for a month after the trip. He also warned about some of the possible side effects, such as hallucinations—seeing something that's not really there.

During our time in Africa we mostly stayed at nature reserve parks, which have been set aside for animals to roam around freely. As we drove up to the lodge the first day, a huge herd of zebras and wildebeest stood around the parking area. Also, behind the lodge there was a watering hole where many other wild animals were drinking water. It sure left an impression in our minds. When we got into our room, the first thing we noticed was a big sign in the room that said, "Do not leave room door or windows open; monkeys may get into your room."

Of course, we took care to make sure our room was secure, but we kept thinking and talking about that lodge till we went to bed. That night my wife woke up, screaming, "Wake up! There's an impala in our room!" The medicine she was taking was causing her to hallucinate! Of course, I woke up and calmed her down and helped her realize there was not an impala in our room.

Even though we were taking these special drugs to help keep us safe from malaria, there are other drugs out there that can harm your body and mind. The Bible refers to our bodies as temples of the Holy Spirit. Make good decisions today and every day about what you put in your body. Glorify God with how you treat your body.

The Strangest Hotel

*The LORD shall preserve your going out and your coming in
From this time forth, and even forevermore.*
PSALM 121:8, NKJV

During the year I studied in France, a few times I bought a rail pass that allowed me to use the trains all I wanted for two weeks. Some trains in Europe are not like the trains in North America. Instead of endless rows of seats on either side of a middle aisle, each rail car contains a bunch of individual compartments that hold two bench seats that face each other. The neat thing is that the facing seats can actually fold down to create one giant flat bed at night. It wasn't the most glamorous accommodation, but I saw this as an acceptable solution for sleeping at night, and of course, very affordable.

If you have ever traveled in Europe, you know that it can be expensive, especially for students like we were. During this trip, the three friends and I decided to try an experiment. The idea was to use the train as our hotel every night. All we had to do was go to the train station each night and find a train that was going somewhere that would take at least eight or ten hours to reach. During the night we'd find empty compartments, fold down the seats, and sleep until we reached the next city. For almost two weeks we did this every night. We'd jump on the train one evening in Copenhagen, and wake up in Paris. The next night we'd jump on the train and sleep till we reached Venice. You get the idea. For two weeks we crisscrossed Europe each night in order to save money on lodging. It was a strange way to lodge, but it actually worked for us.

Throughout my life, I was taught to pray before going anywhere. Even today, before I travel anywhere, I pray, asking God for travel protection and that His will be done in my journey. Ask God today and every day to be part of your journey.

Amazing Undersea Discovery

I will meditate on the glorious splendor of Your majesty,
And on Your wondrous works.
PSALM 145:5, NKJV

Every chance I get I love to go snorkeling; it's one of my favorite activities to do in nature. Since I live in Michigan, I don't get a chance to go snorkeling as much as I would like, so every time I am traveling somewhere warm and tropical, I check to see if there are any reefs nearby to explore. One summer when I was in Jordan for an archeological dig, our group went on a weekend tour to the south of the country, which touches the Red Sea. Yes, the same Red Sea you've read about in the Bible story about Moses and the Israelites. It was neat being there at the Red Sea, but it was also exciting to learn there was a reef in the waters there. Three of us arranged for a side trip that would take us to a spot down the coast that was supposedly one of the best spots to snorkel. We arrived and the people there equipped us with fins, masks, and snorkels. Moments later we dipped into the water to snorkel, right off the shore.

I have been snorkeling in many spots all over the world—from the Great Barrier Reef in Australia to the Caribbean and Hawaii—and I generally try not to compare them, but from my personal experience, this was the most amazing snorkeling spot. The reef wall was full of all kinds of marine creatures of every size, shape, and color. I had never seen so much diversity of coral in one place. The water was clear, and the variety of fish was incredible. We snorkeled for hours, and it was not long enough. I wanted to stay and see more, but it was time to return.

I left that day amazed by an incredible display of God's creation. It reminded me that everywhere on earth there is evidence of God's power and love as seen in His creation. No matter where you go today, look around and see God's nature and be inspired by His wondrous works!

The Creepy Old Forest

"The wolf and the lamb shall feed together,
The lion shall eat straw like the ox,
And dust shall be the serpent's food.
They shall not hurt nor destroy in all My holy mountain,"
Says the LORD.
ISAIAH 65:25, NKJV

A few years ago I traveled far off the beaten path through Patagonia, in the south of Argentina. It was an area surrounded by very old trees. This really looked like a place that hadn't been touched in the past few hundred years. The air was cool and crisp. I had read about old-growth forests in Patagonia, so I thought it would be good to pull over and check it out. I figured I'd just take a quick hike into the forest to see what I could see. Within a few steps it looked as though I was swallowed up by the forest.

The ground was dense with soft peat, and the tree canopy above me was thick, making the forest floor dark. That's when I looked down and noticed something on the soft forest floor. It was a footprint. This was no ordinary footprint though, it was huge—the same size as the palm of my hand. I'm not great at identifying animal tracks, but I could easily tell this was the print of a very large animal. Upon further inspection, I noticed the print was quite fresh. I also noticed a few feet away a pile of dung, and steam was rising from it! In other words, it was *very* recent, and the creature that did this was not far away. At this point I was a little nervous, so I slowly stood up and carefully backed out of that spot and quickly made my way back to the car.

In heaven we won't have to worry about scary animals. The Bible says the wolf and the lamb will play together, and the lion will be a vegetarian again. I can't wait to see how God will recreate His creations to His original plan before sin—and that includes you and me. Are you looking forward to going to heaven? I am!

Long-Distance Listening

*"He who is of God hears God's words; therefore
you do not hear, because you are not of God."*
JOHN 8:47, NKJV

During a recent filming trip, we were in northern California looking for a huge telescope array I had read about. Our plan was to film a few scenes there. I had never seen a telescope array, so I was eager to find this one. A telescope array is a place where there are a bunch of telescopes in an open area, pointing to space. The telescopes look like giant silver bowls on stands, and they're usually pointing in the same direction. There are a couple of types of telescopes out there. There are the kinds that look into space and the kinds that listen into space. The array we were going to visit was radio telescopes, the kind that listen into space. Telescope arrays are always located very far away from anything, avoiding lights and sounds.

Sure enough, this telescope array was way out in an isolated part of the state. When we arrived, we met up with the people who worked there, and soon after, we began filming our scenes. It was a fascinating place. There were forty-two of these huge radio antennas, and once in a while all the telescopes would start moving in exactly the same direction and speed. It looked like an army of dishes, and they appeared to be very obedient, moving together exactly as they were programed to move. They were all working together to listen deep into space.

The funny thing is that the most important thing in space we should be listening to is God! Our verse today says that those who listen for God will hear Him. If you are not listening for God, you won't hear Him. Millions of dollars' worth of telescopes will never hear God because they are not trying to listen to Him, but when we aim the telescopes of our heart to hear God's will in our lives, we will hear and we will know. Open your heart and your ears to God speaking to you today!

Unseen Treasures

"Ask, and it will be given to you; seek, and you will find; knock, and it will be opened to you."
MATTHEW 7:7, NKJV

On a recent trip through Arkansas with my family, we stopped by the Crater of Diamonds State Park—a place you can go and pay a few dollars and they let you enter a big area where diamonds are commonly found. Whatever you can find is yours! Wow, that sounded pretty fun! I plugged it into the GPS, and we were on our way. We arrived and paid a small fee and rented a few simple tools to help us dig. It was exciting to know we were digging for treasure! During every moment we were there digging, we felt like at any moment we could find a giant diamond!

We were there for a couple of hours, digging in the dirt and searching around for those small, elusive, and precious rocks. It was fun digging around, and my boys had fun knowing somewhere nearby, the next big diamond was waiting to be discovered! Unfortunately, we ran out of time, and we needed to keep going on our journey. We did not find any diamonds, but we found several other cool-looking rocks. A staff geologist working there identified what we had found. Several of the rocks were nice looking, but they were all pretty common rocks such as quartz. Even though we didn't find any "treasure," we had a great time looking. A week later, in the national news, we heard about a boy who found a diamond in that exact same place we had been digging! The reports said it was valued around fifteen thousand dollars! We had been so close!

God loves us so much that He has many wonderful treasures in store for us, but how do we find them? He tells us plainly in the Bible that we are to keep asking, to keep seeking, and to keep knocking. In other words, pray for all things big and small! God is listening to you today. What will you ask Him?

Life Is Full of Surprises

Trust in the LORD with all your heart,
And lean not on your own understanding.
PROVERBS 3:5, NKJV

The school I studied at in France was just across the border from Geneva, Switzerland and the magnificent Lake Geneva. One weekend I decided to go hitchhiking along the northern edge of the lake to a beautiful town called Montreux. When hitchhiking, it's rare to get picked up by someone going all the way to the same destination you are going to. Usually you get there by getting a ride with several people along the way. During one of my car rides to Montreux, something unexpected happened—the person driving the car got into a small "fender bender" accident. I felt bad for the driver, but then I felt worse when I discovered who he had gotten into an accident with. It was with the police! Not good.

It took awhile for him to sort out the mess, and even though I really felt like getting out of the car and continuing on my journey, I stayed there in the passenger seat as if to support him during this situation. Eventually I made it to Montreux and back. The following weekend I decided to go out for another hitchhiking tour; this time my goal was to get to a town about an hour away that was just over the Italian border. Eventually I made it to Italy, but you'll never guess what happened in Italy. The driver I was riding with got into a "fender bender" with the police! I couldn't believe it! What are the chances of that? Two weekends hitchhiking. Two accidents. Both times with the police! It's pretty rare to be in an accident, and it's even rarer to be in an accident with the police. It's even *more* rare to do that two weekends in a row!

Life can be full of surprises. Sometimes things happen and we do not understand why, but God is all-powerful and all-knowing and the Bible says we should trust Him with all our hearts. Will you trust your life to God today?

The Copycat Kid

Be imitators of me, as I am of Christ. Now I commend you because you remember me in everything and maintain the traditions even as I delivered them to you.
1 CORINTHIANS 11:1, 2, ESV

When I was about ten I found a small piece of leftover red fabric in my mom's sewing kit. Having watched my mom sew, I secretly took some thread and a needle and somehow managed to hand-sew a very simple Santa hat. In my closet I found red pants and a burgundy coat, and I attempted to assemble a Santa outfit. On Christmas morning I snuck down to the living room before anyone else and put all the gifts we had under the tree in my pillowcase. After breakfast, I snuck off to my room and dressed up as Santa, stuffing my pillow under my shirt to look chubby, and I came out with gifts over my shoulder, saying, "Ho, ho, ho" to my family. They were quite surprised! We all moved to the living room, where I proceeded to give each one of them their gifts. They loved this new tradition, and for several years I did the same thing.

Many years later, when I and my siblings were grown up, with families of our own, we did something very different for Christmas. We decided to rent a cabin in the mountains near Gatlinburg, Tennessee. During our gift exchange, I surprised everyone by sneaking off and imitating Santa to give all the young nieces and nephews their gifts.

Every family celebrates Christmas differently, with their own traditions, and there's nothing wrong with having fun as long as we don't forget the real reason for the season. Remember, Satan is working hard to remove Jesus from Christmas by substituting Him with many other distractions, but we must make sure Jesus is at the center of everything we do. After exchanging gifts, we always finish with a worship that celebrates the birth of Christ and reminds us of the real reason we celebrate Christmas and how we are to spend our life imitating Jesus.

The Express Tour

For You formed my inward parts;
You covered me in my mother's womb.
PSALM 139:13, NKJV

One of the world's largest museums is in Paris, France, called The Louvre. Every time I've visited it, I've been overwhelmed at its size—it is *enormous!* It goes on and on for blocks. There are around three hundred fifty thousand objects exhibited and room upon room of endless works of art to see. Experts say you could spend weeks in there looking at everything. I'm a fan of art, but the last couple of times I went, I decided to try a different approach to visiting the museum. The problem is that when I go, I only have a day or two to see a bunch of things in Paris, so I typically do a little research and spend one hour at the museum. I know that doesn't sound like much, and it's not— especially for such a fantastic museum as The Louvre.

Nevertheless, the last time I was there, I went online and did some research and found out about three or four awesome pieces of art and sculpture I wanted to see. I went to the museum, bought my ticket, and with a museum map in hand, I went directly to the various parts of the museum to the see the works of art I had selected. They were well-known pieces you may have heard of: the Mona Lisa, by Leonardo Da Vinci; Venus De Milo; and Winged Victory. When I left, I thought I would be a little disappointed that I was in such an amazing museum and had only seen a few things, but I discovered that by doing the tour that way, I appreciated those few pieces even more. Now those pieces of art have an extra special place in my heart because I spent the time enjoying each one individually.

The same God loves each one of us individually. We simply can't imagine how God could individually love billions of people, but He can and He does. He knows us inside and out!

The Longest Ten-Hour Train Ride

For He shall give His angels charge over you,
To keep you in all your ways.
PSALM 91:11, NKJV

During one of my breaks while studying in France, we decided to take a ten-hour train ride to Athens, Greece. The problem was that we would have to cross through the country of Yugoslavia, which was at war. I know this doesn't sound like a great idea, but at the time I had asked around, and I was told it shouldn't be a problem. The only thing was that I would only be permitted to go through if I had a transit visa—a special permission that would allow me to cross through the country without exiting the train at any time. I was traveling with some friends, and we decided to go for it and quickly ride through Yugoslavia on our way to Greece. As we approached the border of Yugoslavia, the train slowed down and came to a stop. A bunch of police and soldiers came aboard and thoroughly checked every inch of the train and also checked our paperwork. We had the necessary paperwork, so we weren't too worried. Finally, the train continued forward again, but an hour later it stopped again, this time in the middle of a field. Again, a bunch of soldiers came on board and did another thorough check of the train and inspected everyone's paperwork. Soon we were on our way again, but about an hour later we were stopped again. Each time we stopped, we would sit for a few hours while the soldiers checked everything. We finally made it to Athens, but what should have taken us ten hours ended up taking us fifty-two hours. That's more than two full days!

We were a little nervous crossing through Yugoslavia, but we knew God's angels were watching over us. Let me tell you, there is no army or kingdom in the world that has power against God or His people. Ask God today to watch over everything you do and everywhere you go.

Are You a Good Neighbor?

*"So which of these three do you think was neighbor to him
who fell among the thieves?" And he said, "He who showed
mercy on him." Then Jesus said to him, "Go and do likewise."*
Luke 10:36, 37, NKJV

The summer after I graduated from college was spent in Jordan on an archeological dig. Each afternoon we rested and met up with the archeologists to clean and study the objects we had unearthed. In the evenings we could do whatever we wanted. On Sabbath we also had the day off. On this dig there was a staff car available in case anyone needed to go somewhere. One particular Sabbath afternoon, a couple of friends and I decided to borrow the staff car and drive to the nearby ancient Roman city ruins of Jerash. It really was amazing to walk around the ancient ruins of a city that was once filled with people and shops and life. After walking around for a few hours, my friends and I were tired and hungry, but we had brought nothing with us to eat. It would take some time to get back to where we were staying too.

Then something unexpected happened. Nearby, a Jordanian family was sitting under a tree, eating. There were about twelve of them: adults, elderly people, and kids. A man stood up and came over to where we were standing. He spoke very little English, but he insisted that we join his family to eat. We thanked him and joined his family. For the next hour, we spent time with this generous family under a tree, talking and laughing and sharing the best we could.

This experience reminded me of a question asked in the Bible, "Who is my neighbor?" Jesus answered with the parable about the man who was attacked by thieves and how the Good Samaritan showed mercy and kindness to someone even though he could not repay the kindness.

Who is your neighbor? Will you go out today and show kindness to everyone? That is what Jesus said we should do.

The Longest Shot

*For what credit is it if, when you are beaten for your faults, you
take it patiently? But when you do good and suffer, if you take
it patiently, this is commendable before God.*
1 PETER 2:20, NKJV

In the center of Havana, Cuba there is an area where the main government
buildings are mostly congregated, and, as you can imagine, this place is
very well guarded and protected. During our trip, we noticed that one of
the buildings had a very large artistic drawing on the wall of one of their
past leaders, Ernesto "Che" Guevara. We had seen it several times during the
day, but this time when my wife's cousin was driving us through at night, we
noticed they used beautiful, dramatic lighting at dark. I asked the cousin if
we could pull over so I could take a picture. We pulled over, and I jumped
out of the car with my camera and tripod. In order to get a good picture,
I would have to set my camera on the tripod and set the camera to leave
the shutter open and patiently wait about a minute to let enough light in
to get a good picture. I carefully set up my tripod and arranged the camera
settings, properly aimed and focused, and then I pressed the shutter. Just as
the shutter opened, a police car screeched up to where we were parked. He
got out and ordered us to leave.

We hadn't seen any signs or anything saying we couldn't take any pictures,
but we knew it was important to obey the authority of the police. We tried
to explain that I just needed about one minute to get the shot and that the
camera was already in the middle of taking the shot. He still insisted we had
to leave. I had no choice but to get my camera. Just as I was about to grab
the camera, the shutter closed. The shot was successfully taken, and it was a
beauty!

Sometimes it's hard to be patient, especially when you haven't done anything wrong. Have you ever been accused of something you didn't do? What
should you do? The Bible says even when we suffer, we will honor God by
being patient.

A Crowd in the Wilderness

*Therefore receive one another, just as
Christ also received us, to the glory of God.*
ROMANS 15:7, NKJV

Over the years I have spent a lot of time traveling to do presentations around the world to people of all ages. Since I also speak Spanish, I was once invited to speak at a Pathfinder camporee in Venezuela. Getting there was a challenge because I first had to fly to Caracas, the capital of Venezuela, then I had to stay in a hotel overnight. The next morning I was to take a flight to one of the smaller cities, where I was picked up by the organizers. From there we drove another few hours into the country to the location where the camporee was taking place. I thought I was being taken to one of the most remote wildernesses in Venezuela, but when I got there I discovered that almost ten thousand Pathfinders, TLTs, and Master Guides had assembled there!

The organizers put up a giant stage and a giant screen in a field where the meetings would take place. The location was made up of orchards, fields, and hills, and many of the clubs had to squeeze in and find a place to set up their camp for their clubs. During the week I spent there, I got to spend a lot of time at the camps of different clubs. Each mealtime I would be taken to a different club, where they would share their food and we could share time talking to each other. Everyone I encountered was incredibly generous, kind, and friendly. At every moment I felt as though I were with family. My own family wasn't able to come with me, so naturally I was missing them, but God blessed me with a church that helped me feel less lonely. The kind people there made a special effort to accept me and make me feel at home.

When you realize how Jesus accepts you just as you are, it is an example for us to see other people as Jesus did and accept them with kindness and love.

An Amazing Factory

Create in me a clean heart, O God,
And renew a steadfast spirit within me.
PSALM 51:10, NKJV

Nestlé is a European company that makes chocolate—and I have to admit they do a very good job! Naturally, since there are some people who really love and appreciate chocolate, Nestlé decided to offer tours of their chocolate factory in Switzerland, and I went as part of a class trip. The guide was great, and the tour was fascinating. We got to see how chocolate is made from the first step all the way to the packaging. When the tour finished, we were brought to a room where Nestlé was displaying many of the different types of chocolates they made. What an amazing display of chocolate! They were neatly piled up on beautiful plates so you could see the various kinds and sizes of chocolates they made. The shock came when the tour guide announced that the tour was now over but that we were welcome to try as much of their chocolate as we wanted! Yes, you read correctly. We were put in a room with hundreds of beautiful chocolates and told that we could eat as much as we wanted. Of course, I tried quite a few pieces.

At first I thought I would be able to clean out the place, but after a few minutes I discovered I had eaten more than enough and I didn't want anymore. I remember thinking at first, "I'm going to eat fifty pieces of chocolate!" but I ended up eating about twelve pieces. Why? The first ones were pretty good, the next few were OK, but the last five were sickening.

It's definitely possible to fill your stomach with the wrong stuff, but what about your heart? If we are not careful with what we allow into our hearts, we may end up filling it with bad things that will separate us from God. Today, ask God to clean your heart, then choose to fill your heart with things that will bring you closer to God.

PRAYER REQUESTS

PRAYER REQUESTS

PRAYER REQUESTS

PRAYER REQUESTS

NOTES

NOTES

NOTES

NOTES